Track and Field Techniques
for Girls and Women

Track and Field Techniques for Girls and Women

Second Edition

Ken Foreman
Seattle Pacific College

Virginia Husted
University of Washington

WM. C. BROWN COMPANY PUBLISHERS
Dubuque, Iowa

CONSULTING EDITORS

Physical Education

AILEENE LOCKHART
University of Southern California

Parks and Recreation

DAVID GRAY
California State College, Long Beach

Health

ROBERT KAPLAN
Ohio State University

Printed in the United States of America

Contents

Part III

JUMPING EVENTS

Part IV

THROWING EVENTS

Preface to the Second Edition

When the first edition of this book was written, track and field was just beginning to catch on with girls and women in the United States. During the five years which have since passed, track and field has become one of the most popular areas of activity in which the female sports enthusiast participates. Support for this contention is to be found in the number of colleges and universities that now offer technical courses in track and field for prospective teachers. It is to be noted in the greatly expanded competitive program of track and field in the public schools as well as in the increased popularity in Junior Olympic and A.A.U. programs in towns and cities all over America. It is also evident in the growing interest manifested by professional physical educators; in the number of articles on track and field appearing in the literature; in the number of new and authoritative textbooks now available; and in the fact that the recent Fifth National Institute on Girls' Sports again highlighted track and field as an area of major concern.

As might be expected, the growing interest in track and field has resulted in vastly improved performance at each level of competition. For every knowledgeable female teacher at the beginning of this decade, there likely are now ten or more such individuals. Watching a track and field meet reveals just how far girls and women really have come. No longer does one see a characterization of technique, but rather one sees the grace and beauty of the highly skilled performer. Indeed, many female athletes have become so proficient in their event that they rival the best male performers for technical excellence. The motivating force behind the writing of this second edition has been this new interest, this greater knowledge, this improvement in performance skill.

Perusal of the second edition will reveal to the reader that major changes have been made in nearly every chapter. Not only are the most recent research findings generalized into practical hints for competitor and coach, but two entirely new chapters have been added to the text. These chapters represent the first authoritative discussion of long-distance running for girls and women. The special qualifications of the senior author—team leader for the 1967 Women's National A.A.U. team, interim high-elevation running coach for the 1968 Olympic team, coach of several international and world-class distance runners— afford him a unique position from which to discuss this subject.

Extensive revision is to be noted also in the chapters dealing with the field events. New photographs of "Champions in Action" have been added. The chapter on conditioning has been markedly extended by a woman who personally has tested each concept and principle as an athlete and a coach. Surely no other track and field book for women can boast two authors so well qualified for an undertaking of this kind.

The authors again wish to give credit for many of the ideas expressed in this book to the coaches and athletes with whom they have been privileged to associate during the past two decades. No work of this kind is entirely original, though we accept full responsibility for all of the statements which are made. We express our special appreciation to Mrs. Sarah Furtado and Mr. Cal Fanders whose assistance has contributed greatly to the completion of the book.

Preface to the First Edition

For many years track and field has been considered a controversial activity for the American girl. Perhaps one of the most obvious reasons why this point of view has prevailed is that few women in physical education have had the training or experience to teach girls the finer techniques of running, jumping, and throwing. Thus track and field programs have been forced outside the controlling environment of the public schools and, in most instances, have been fostered by interested, though nonprofessional, people.

Times are changing, however, and we are entering an era of growing interest in track and field for girls and women. Old prejudices are giving way to new understanding about the nature of the female and her role in our contemporary society. Where criticism once prevailed there now is a spirit of acceptance and cooperation. Indeed, the recent National Institute on Girls' Sports was an unprecedented example of how interested individuals, expert and layman alike, could work harmoniously together for a common cause.

The two authors of this book, both professional physical educators, are well prepared for an undertaking of this kind. One has had extensive experience in track and field, having taught and coached young men and young women for more than fifteen years. He has worked with individuals at every level of proficiency and in two instances has guided a competitor from her first day of instruction into competition at the national and international levels. His present coaching responsibility with the Falcon Track and Field Club offers daily contact with unskilled beginners as well as with young women who are highly skilled Olympic material.

The other author teaches track and field to girls in a large metropolitan high school. She is a nationally ranked javelin thrower and the Canadian women's open champion in this event, with a best mark well over 160 feet. Her versatility in track and field is perhaps best evidenced by her consistently high scores in the women's pentathlon.

During the past several years both authors have become keenly aware that little authoritative information about track and field for women is available. They have discovered that many girls enjoy running, throwing, and jumping when they are given the opportunity. Moreover, experience has shown that a majority of the girls who excel in these activities desire to be ladies and are different from their peer group only in that they have disciplined their time and energy in a particular manner.

This volume has grown out of the satisfying experiences of the writers and has been prepared with a sincere desire to provide a practical source book for the teacher and competitor alike. It is written in language which is understandable, with no attempt to present extensive documentation. The selection and presentation of only one technique for performing each track and field event has been deliberate, for the authors believe that consideration of several alternative techniques frequently leads to confusion rather than enlightenment. While it is freely acknowledged that many of the ideas in this book have been gained from other teachers and coaches, the writers take full responsibility for all of the material which they have presented.

Special features of this book are the two chapters which deal with the principles of teaching and learning and the mechanics of movement as they relate to track and field participation. The chapter on conditioning exercises has special relevance to the beginner. The chapter on running represents several years of practical experimentation and presents ideas which are nowhere else in print. The photographs of highly skilled girls and the action sketches provide an accurate guide for analysis of movement in each of the chapters on performance technique.

The authors express their appreciation to Colleen Lynch for reading the entire manuscript and commenting on its content and organization. They also express their thanks to Kay Steddom, Anita Yoder, Caroline Stratton, Marilyn Danskin, and Dorothy Foreman for their assistance in the preparation of the manuscript.

Introduction

Teaching is a high and worthy calling. Perhaps no other vocation or profession offers a comparable opportunity to share so constructively in the lives of others. The physical education teacher has an especially unique opportunity to effect desirable changes in students through purposefully planned contacts in the relaxed atmosphere of the gymnasium, the open field, and the dance studio. Most students enjoy activity, appreciate personal attention, and respond to constructive guidance and encouragement. Because of its individual nature, its never-ending challenge, and its exciting element of competition, track and field provides an environment in which the highest goals of both the teacher and the learner can be realized.

It seems to be a characteristic of the human being, however, only to say and think these high-sounding ideals and in the saying and thinking to satisfy the need for committing one's time and energies toward their realization. For this reason, any real benefit stemming from the reading of this or any other book is the result of the careful application of that which is read and understood. The teacher must recognize that she is an educational planner and that it is her responsibility to visualize, to formalize, and to put into practice all that she knows. She also must be keenly aware that real change in students stems not alone from doing but more so from knowing. Her attempts to teach, therefore, involve organization and instruction which give answers to the question *why* as well as emphasis to a consideration of the question *how*.

WHY TEACH TRACK AND FIELD TO GIRLS?

This is a question which obviously has no simple answer, for such a question involves purposes and values and cannot be adequately dealt with in a book of this kind. On the other hand, it seems as though some attempt should be made to justify track and field as a worthy activity for girls. Justification in this instance is intimately related to purposes—and purposes are absolutely essential to a program.

In our profession, as in others, the simple questions sometimes become the most difficult to answer. To ask a teacher why she teaches seems almost ludicrous, and yet the implications of such a question are far more profound than they first appear. Why do we teach—not just track and field, but why do we teach anything?

It is the strongly held belief of the authors that we teach because we must. Man is a complex organism with virtually unlimited potential for growth and development. Moreover, man is a totally integrated being and that which affects part of him affects all of him. Thus each experience we face, each decision we make, each demand we impose upon ourselves, each attitude and each insight has an effect on what we are and what we will become. In the broader sense, therefore, we teach track and field because it offers a situation in which students can have new experiences, make decisions, impose demands upon themselves, and in so doing catch insights into their nature and potential for improvement. Like other educational experiences, the unit on track and field becomes a medium of exchange between students and between students and instructor, possessing the essential elements for the "quickening of the human life."

The Specific Objectives of Track and Field

Track and field activities are natural; they involve such basic movement patterns as running, jumping, throwing, and thrusting. Though high-level competition may impose questionable demands on a girl, participation in the activity class will not. On the contrary, the track and field activity class very likely would improve the symmetry of a girl's body and contribute to her poise and grace of movement. Certainly greater strength and improved circulatory-respiratory response are worthwhile and realizable objectives for all girls to seek.

Track and field offers an opportunity for all girls to participate. There is a place for the tall, the short, the heavy, the fast, the slow, the strong, and the weak. Every girl without physical limitations should be able to adapt satisfactorily to some running, throwing, or jumping event.

The track and field unit is inexpensive; it can be modified for indoor as well as outdoor participation.

There is great diversity in track and field, permitting the teacher to divide the class into small instructional units, assign them to several different work stations, and supervise them with a minimum of effort.

DEVELOPING THE TEACHING UNIT

Since the discussion of teaching units, class organization, and the like, is not the primary purpose of this book, the section which follows contains little detailed information. It is expected that the reader will consider the two models in light of her personal teaching situation, extracting from the body of the text those particulars which give life and meaning to the day-by-day interaction with students.

The first model represents a progressive curricular pattern which includes grades seven through twelve. The teaching unit in this situation should be a minimum of four weeks, or twenty days, in length.

Grades 7-8   Teach running skills, including the sprint start, sprinting, and sprint relays.

Teach the high jump—scissors and straddle roll.

Teach the long jump and the softball throw for distance.

Give emphasis to special conditioning activities for track and field.

Grades 9-10   Introduce hurdling, progressing from the modified hurdle to the regulation low hurdle event.

Introduce cross-country and distance running.

Teach the basketball throw and shot-put, adding medley races to the relay events.

Grades 11-12   Teach the discus and javelin.

Develop skills in the high hurdles.

Give attention to the strategy of track and field as well as the techniques of officiating.

The second approach assumes a cyclic schedule in which the teaching units are longer and repeated once (perhaps two times) during the junior-senior high school physical education program. In this instance, the unit should be a minimum of eight weeks in length. Such a unit would include all of the activities related to track and field, with an emphasis on the development of intermediate skills when the unit is repeated at a higher level.

Grades 7-9 Teach running, including the sprint start, sprinting, relay work, and distance running.

Develop throwing skills, including the softball and basketball throws and the shot-put.

Introduce hurdling, progressing from modified hurdles to the low hurdle event.

Teach the long jump and high jump events, including the stride in air and the straddle roll technique.

Give special emphasis to conditioning activities for track and field.

Grades 10-12 Build on previous track and field unit with emphasis on skill improvement. Add the discus and javelin (which were excluded from the lower grades for safety reasons).

Give greater emphasis to strategy and officiating techniques.

NOTE: A college service course in track and field would be longer and more comprehensive than the high school course, including skill development, strategy, and officiating techniques.

A track and field unit would follow the traditional pattern, with an introductory period during which time such things as films and demonstrations are provided for instructional and motivational purposes. This phase of the unit would likely involve one or two class sessions. The second phase of the unit would include additional explanation and demonstration, though primary attention would be given to supervised participation. This is the body of the unit and would encompass approximately ninety percent of the available class time. The third phase of the unit would involve some kind of evaluation, perhaps an interclass track meet, a postal meet, or an all-school pentathlon.

Class Organization

When the members of a class have learned several different skills, it is relatively simple to divide the class into small working groups and send each group to a different activity station. The problem is different, however, for the class which has little knowledge about the activity to be learned. In the latter instance the students do not know what to do, how it should be done, or what precautions they should take to protect themselves from injury. If the class is large, the teacher has a particularly difficult job of organizing the learning situation so that the energies of all individuals are expended as effectively as they ought to be.

One way to approach this situation is to present to the entire group one new skill each day. The teacher explains the skill briefly, demonstrates it accurately three or four times, and then divides the class for squad practice. She attempts to locate each squad so that she can keep all of the students in view while giving special attention to each group or person individually. When using this organizational pattern, the teacher moves about until she has contacted each squad separately. She then very likely will call all of the girls together for a second time to reemphasize certain points or to introduce new information about the skill. This procedure would be repeated daily until three or four new skills have been explored by the class. The squads would subsequently be assigned to a teaching station for extended practice on a specific skill. The teacher supervises each station carefully to make certain that the skills are performed correctly and that each individual participates to the full extent of her ability.

(Hints for teaching each specific track and field event are given in the chapters that follow.)

Inasmuch as learning stems from purposeful practice, it is important that squads be small enough to insure a maximum of activity for all of the students. Perhaps six is an optimum number of squad members. For large classes there should be more squads rather than larger squads. If a class were working on the high jump, the long jump, middle-distance running, and the hurdles, and only two jumping areas were available, six or even eight squads could be adequately handled as follows:

SQUAD	ACTIVITY	AREA
A	Long-jump approach (determining check marks)	Grass area west side of track
B	Long jumping (pop-up jumps)	Jumping pit
C	Middle-distance running (work on pace)	South 110-yard straightaway

(Continued)

SQUAD	ACTIVITY	AREA
D	Middle-distance running (work on curve running)	East end of track
E	High jumping (review the scissors)	Jumping pit
F	High jumping (fundamentals of the straddle roll)	Grass area east side of track. Practice on the *tour jeté* (see chapter on high jump)
G	Hurdles (trail-leg drill)	North straightaway
H	Hurdle form	North straightaway (work over six-inch barriers to avoid injury or inhibition)

GETTING READY FOR COMPETITION

Competitive running, jumping, and throwing are natural, though not necessarily inevitable, outcomes of the track and field activity program. The reader should be aware that while not every girl who explores a track and field event will one day be a championship performer, it is very certain that every championship performer was one day a beginner. For this reason, it is natural to consider the teaching of beginners and the training of highly skilled performers in a single volume of this kind. The real difference is only relative: It depends upon the intent of the learner, the nature of her motivation, her capacity for development, and the quality of the instruction she receives. Perhaps if every teacher would deal with each student as if she had a potential champion in her care, if she would take a personal interest in her and guide her carefully, she would find that most individuals are closer to being champions than one might think.

Part I

Principles, Learning, and Performances

Chapter 1

Mechanical Principles

The human body might appropriately be described as an intricate mechanism capable of unlimited movement combinations within the dimensions of time and space. Like other mechanisms, the human body is subject to the laws of nature. The effects of these laws in operation may be positive or negative, depending upon man's adaptability. An understanding of the laws of motion and the means of coping with them is therefore essential to effective teaching and performance.

Movement is basic to participation in sports. In track and field the performer runs, jumps, throws, starts, stops, and changes direction in a variety of movement patterns. Each pattern is determined by the purpose to be accomplished, the forces encountered in attaining the purpose, and the movement capability of the performer. The skilled person is one who can make appropriate mechanical adaptations and exert her energies in the most economical and effective manner.

NEWTON'S LAWS

It will be recalled from courses in physics and kinesiology that force is a predictable phenomenon. Newton noted this consistency in his experimentation and was led to formulate certain laws of motion. These include the laws of inertia, momentum, and interaction.

Simply stated, the law of inertia tells us that a body at rest remains at rest or a body in motion tends to continue in motion with constant

Figure 1.1. The runner is completely relaxed; her weight is distributed between the knee of the near leg, the feet, and the hands. The head hangs naturally to minimize tension in the neck and shoulders.

Figure 1.2. In the "set" position, the center of the body mass is shifted upward and forward. The hips are slightly higher than the shoulders; the shoulders have moved beyond a line perpendicular to the hands. This shifting of the body mass, coupled with the explosive action of the leg extensors, provides the essential force for overcoming inertia.

speed in a straight line unless acted upon by some outside force. This law has significance for the track and field participant. She must overcome inertia when starting a race, when beginning her drive for the shot-put or her spin for the discus throw. She also must combat inertia when throwing the javelin, when changing her direction in the high jump, or when maintaining her speed around a curve.

To overcome the inertia of the body, force must be applied. This force may be gravity, it may be the contractile force of muscular tissue, or it may be a smoothly coordinated linking of the two. For optimum performance, this force must be applied at the right time, in the appropriate direction, and with proper intensity.

The force needed to overcome inertia depends upon the weight of the body and its rate of motion. More force is required to overcome the inertia of the heavier performer than of one who is smaller and lighter.

This principle applies to starting and stopping, to changing direction, or to controlling such implements as the shot, the discus, and the javelin. The greater mass of the body or object or greater speed compounds the effects of inertia.

The correct techniques for performing each track and field event make it possible for the participant to utilize or control inertia to her best advantage. Two examples are the sprint start and the shot-put shift and lift. The sprinter starts from a crouch. In the set position she moves her center of gravity over her hands so that the action of her legs drives her forward out of the blocks. In this instance, both gravity and muscle power are used to overcome inertia. When putting the shot, the participant assumes a preliminary standing posture at the back of the circle; she dips and then drives forward across the ring. Gravity initiates the first action while muscles of the legs and hips keep the body moving forward.

Inertia also has an effect on running form and energy expenditure. Once the participant has overcome the resting inertia of the body and has begun to move, the energy expenditure for continued movement is less than the initial cost of getting under way. A constant rate of speed is therefore less fatiguing than a pace which is variable. On the ends of the track the runner tends to fall away from the curve (centripetal force) and must compensate for this tendency by leaning and swinging her arms to the inside of the track (centrifugal force). Efficient running form thus involves a relaxed, steady pace and compensatory postural adjustments when running on the curve.

A second phenomenon was noted by Newton, namely, when a body is acted upon by a force, that body is changed in the direction of the force and in proportion to the amount or duration of the force. This is called the law of momentum, a law which describes force quantitatively as the product of mass or weight and velocity.

Momentum has an effect on all track and field events but it is particularly significant in the shot-put, discus, and javelin throws. Momentum, like inertia, may affect performance positively or nega-

Figure 1.3. The preliminary stance for putting the shot. Lynette Matthews demonstrates the focus of attention immediately outside the shot-put circle. Flexion of the right hip and leg, followed by a forceful driving extension of the hip and leg, permits the performer to overcome the inertia of the body.

Figure 1.4. Mrs. Doris Brown running the turn. This is an excellent example of the body lean which a runner must assume to compensate for the force of inertia on the turn. Mrs. Brown, former American record holder in the 880-yard run, fixed her angle of lean as she came into the turn. She maintains this lean by swinging her right arm across the chest toward the curb until she moves back into the straightaway.

tively. Other things being equal, the performer having the fastest approach has the greatest potential for achieving maximum throwing distance. Too much speed, on the other hand, increases the performer's momentum to a point where it cannot be adequately controlled.

To overcome inertia and acquire the desired momentum, movement is started along lines of low resistance. In the throwing events, especially the shot and discus, preliminary postures cause the largest and strongest muscles to act as prime movers. Subsequent action is aimed at producing greater speed and a balanced position for applying force. Proper technique places the working muscles on stretch and permits them to contract explosively through their most effective working range.

Figure 1.5. The sudden breaking of forward progress and transfer of momentum are essential to championship performance in the javelin. Virginia Husted, former ranking American javelin thrower, is shown lifting upward into her throw. In this position all of the forces of momentum and muscular power are being expended into the javelin.

The third law of motion involves interaction. This law states that for every force in nature there must be two bodies, one to exert the force and the other to receive it. Or, stated in other terms, the law says that for every action there is an equal and opposite reaction.

Figure 1.6. Gail Davis in an attempt of 5′ 6″. In this excellent example of the bent-leg straddle jump, Miss Davis demonstrates the principle of equal and opposite forces. The high kick of the forward knee, coupled with the completely extended takeoff leg, indicates that the jumper has expended her force explosively against the firm takeoff surface.

In track and field, interaction affects performance in numerous ways. The sprinter drives from the blocks, alternately thrusting her arms forward and backward in opposition to the movement of her legs. The high jumper plants and drives up over her takeoff foot in a kicking-lifting maneuver. The shot-putter plants and drives up and out through the shot. Thus each performer in her own way drives against a firm surface to attain the maximum result from her expended energies. (The drive and the firm surface are essential.)

ROTARY MOTION

Rotary or angular motion is a very special problem in all athletic activities. In track and field this is particularly true as the performer seeks to produce great torquing force for an event such as the discus throw or to skillfully control this force in the jumping events and the hurdles.

The laws which applied to linear motion also apply to angular motion, with certain modifications. Perhaps the most important modification is to be noted in the application of Newton's second law dealing with acceleration. In linear motion, acceleration—or the change of speed of an object—is proportional to the force imparted to the object and inversely proportional to its mass. Accordingly, when great force is applied to a light object, it accelerates markedly, though the same force might have little effect on a much heavier object.

In angular motion, acceleration is determined by the force applied and the relationship of the mass to the rotational axis of the object in question. Thus an object turns more rapidly when acted upon by a force if the mass is near to the axis of rotation than when the mass is distributed at a distance from the axis of rotation. This is easily demonstrated on a free-spinning turntable where merely raising the arms sideward reduces the turning speed by nearly 300 percent.

Figure 1.7. During the early part of the turn, body parts are held close to the axis of rotation. This minimizes rotational inertia, permitting the performer to attain maximum torquing speed which is essential to success in the discus event.

The significance of this principle is obvious. The discus thrower who needs to increase her turning speed must keep all body parts as close to the central axis as possible during the spin across the circle, whereas the long jumper who chooses to control rotary motion lengthens her body in flight to reduce forward or rearward turning speed.

The sprinter faces a somewhat different, though important, problem concerning rotation. As she runs, each arm and each leg establishes its own center of rotation. These individual rotational forces may complement each other or they may seriously limit the stride length and subsequent speed of the runner. Flexing the free leg during the forward swing permits rapid recovery, and when accompanied by vigorous arm action, it tends to increase stride length and running speed.

Since rotary motion is so important in track and field, it behooves the teacher to understand how this motion can be produced. *First,* it can be produced by checking a linear motion. An example would be the final stride in the javelin approach wherein the forward leg acts as a break and fulcrum. (In kinesiology this is referred to as the "hinged principle" and is applicable to those activities in which the sudden fixing of one end of a lever system contributes to the turning speed of the other end.)

A *second* means of producing rotary motion is the transference of angular momentum from a part of the body to the entire body. Perhaps the most important illustration of transference in track and field occurs in the high jump. Following a short, controlled approach, the performer in this event lengthens her final stride to prepare a base from which a lifting-turning force can be imparted. The latter is initiated when the kicking leg is swung upward toward the crossbar. This kicking force is thus transferred to (added to) other forces produced at takeoff, helping to drive the body mass to its maximum height.

A *third* means of producing rotation is by application of what some choose to call "eccentric thrust." Closely associated with the principles of checking and transference, this principle is nevertheless an important one to comprehend. If a coiled spring were depressed so that all downward forces were perpendicular to the supporting surface, theoretically it would spring straight upward when released. If, on the other hand, the forces depressing the spring were at a tangent to the supporting surface, the energy within the spring would be expended back through a similar tangent upon release. In like manner, the jumper who leans into the bar at takeoff expends part of her force horizontally. If the lean is greater than is necessary to produce rotation around the crossbar, force is dissipated inefficiently.

ACTION-REACTION

Implications of the third law of motion already have been discussed with respect to the impulse effect when initiating movements from a firm surface. The results were the *actions* of running, jumping, and throwing which were consequences of *reaction* to the firm surface. Movements occurring in space are unique, however, for the body, rather than the performance surface, absorbs the forces imposed and tends to *react* in different ways. At times the reaction is positive; at times it is negative.

Indeed, the finer points of performance technique often concern themselves with the maximum utilization or control of the force effect on airborne bodies. While these are discussed in detail in later chapters, comments pertinent to the hurdle event are made here to emphasize the importance of the principle in question.

There are three instances in the hurdle event when performance is seriously affected by the action-reaction phenomena. The first involves the "takeoff," a point when the hurdler is still in contact with the ground. To utilize the action-reaction principle positively, she "bucks" or pikes forward to facilitate lead-leg lift and negate any tendency to rotate rearward away from the hurdle.

Figure 1.8. The bucking action at takeoff facilitates lead-leg lift

The second instance of action-reaction occurs during the step down of the lead foot beyond the hurdle barrier. The tendency here is for the head and chest to rotate up and rearward (reaction) toward the heel of the lead foot which is driving downward and rearward (action). This negative force opens, or extends, the body, producing a breaking rather than a driving action, thus reducing the length of the important first stride after the hurdle step.

Figure 1.9. Continuance of the bucking motion during hurdle clearance minimizes the straightening reaction which stems from the step down (action) beyond the hurdle.

In the case of both examples thus far noted, the rotational effect is forward or rearward around the transverse axis of the body. In this third example of action-reaction, rotation occurs around the longitudinal axis of the body. The trail leg initiates this force as the knee is "punched" forward and upward in preparation for the next stride. The knee punch thus is the action with inward rotation or displacement of the opposite shoulder constituting the reaction. If not compensated for, this force produces a rotation away from the desired line of progress, shortening the stride and negating forward speed.

Figure 1.10. Karen Frisch coming off the hurdle in perfect balance. Note the high trail leg with the right toe rotated upward from the barrier. The wide swing of the left arm was a characteristic which Karen manifested to counterbalance her trail leg. (Taken from 16 mm. movie film.)

The technical components of hurdling described in chapter six, namely, the buck, the delayed layout over the hurdle, and the reach toward the lead foot, all constitute means of utilizing or compensating for the action-reaction phenomenon.

SUMMATION OF FORCES

Motor skills represent a complex pattern of interrelated movements. In skilled performance, parts or segments of the total pattern are discernible only to the trained observer. Skilled performance seems to flow from beginning to end. The pattern of events is a model of perfect timing, a summation of all related forces.

Each track and field technique is a unique combination of movements. To appropriately apply each technique for its intended use the teacher must sense the relationship of the parts to the whole. She then must help the performer to integrate her movements efficiently, adding force to force at the proper instant in order to attain the maximum expenditure of energy. Only by attaining a perfectly coordinated summation of forces will the performer realize her highest potential.

It is for this reason that the javelin thrower approaches the throw from 80 to 100 feet. She gradually increases her speed, turns into the throwing position, and releases her javelin in a beautifully coordinated act. The running speed is transferred to the body an instant before delivery; the leg drives against the ground, ankles, knees, and hips extending. The trunk is flexed, the arm is pulled upward and forward, and a final whiplike motion combines all of the potential energy to send the javelin on its way. Each successful track and field technique must be performed in the same manner. All available forces are applied, one to another, in a perfectly coordinated summation.

CENTER OF GRAVITY AND BALANCE

Gravity is a constant force acting on the body. A body is said to be balanced when the force of gravity falls within the base of support. When the force, or center of gravity, falls outside the base of support, the body is said to be off-balance, and a new base of support must be established in order to regain stability. These and other important properties of gravity and balance have numerous implications to the skillful performance of track and field events.

When starting, a girl utilizes gravity by leaning forward over her supporting arms. When she changes direction, she shifts her center of gravity toward her intended line of progress. When she stops, she lowers her center of gravity and shifts it rearward to avoid falling. This latter point is especially important to the javelin thrower, the discus thrower, and the shot-putter, for these performers must learn to explode into their implements with abandon and then control their momentum in an instant of time. They do this with a follow-through which broadens their base and lowers their center of gravity.

In hurdle races, control of the center of gravity is extremely important. It is costly in terms of both time and energy when the body mass is moved up and down during the course of a race. The skilled performer thus bucks into the hurdle at the instant of takeoff, keeping her center of gravity at a constant height.

The high jumper has a unique problem involving gravity and balance, for she must drive her body mass to its greatest height and then maneuver it economically around a crossbar. To do this she stamps, kicks, and thrusts her body upward. At the peak of her jump, she turns sharply to the side, assumes a layout position, and rolls over into the landing pit. If she is skillful, she is able to gain the last bit of elevation by counterbalancing one part of her body against the other. The head in this instance is dropped downward, and the hips and legs are lifted upward over the fixed center of gravity.

The long jumper also must reckon with the force of gravity, for she is in a sense a missile and is subject to the laws of nature. Her pathway from takeoff to landing is a parabola, the pattern of which is determined by the speed and the angle with which she leaves the

Figure 1.11. The expert hurdler maintains her balance through bilateral action of arms and legs during hurdle clearance. Her head is erect, and her eyes are focused on the next hurdle barrier several yards away.

ground. Unlike a true missile, however, the long jumper possesses some control over her center of gravity. She can elevate her legs at takeoff and extend them during her landing to attain maximum distance from her flight, or she can drop her legs, lower her center of gravity, and fall prematurely into the landing pit.

Stimuli which control balance arise from the field of vision, mechanisms in the inner ear, and special nervous tissues located in the muscles and tendons. The latter are especially prolific in the muscles of the neck. Whenever possible, the track and field performer should keep her head erect, her eyes focused on some stable object, and her hands and feet free from cumbersome restrictions. For example, the high jumper should fix her attention above the crossbar, the long jumper should look upward and forward, the hurdler should shift her attention from hurdle to hurdle, and the shot-putter should keep her eye on a spot outside and behind the shot-put circle. By following these principles she can best cope with the force of gravity and attain the poise and balance which are essential to efficient performance.

TRAJECTORY

All airborne bodies, within certain limits, adhere to the physical laws governing trajectory. According to these laws, the center of gravity of every missile follows a symmetrical path (a parabola) from the point of release to the point of landing—when these two points are equal in height. These laws thus govern the flight of all objects thrown by track and field performers as well as the flight of those who jump for either height or distance.

It is easy to calculate how far a given body will travel when its velocity and angles of release are known and when either its resistance to movement or its tendency to "fly" can be determined. In the case of the shot, there is little tendency to fly and minimal loss of velocity due to friction. The distance a shot will travel is thus a straightforward matter of imparting maximum velocity to the implement whose angle of release is between the optimum point of forty to fifty degrees. Since velocity is more important than trajectory, modifications in technique which are compensatory to individual differences should, if possible, affect the release angle rather than release speed.

While the discus and javelin also are projectiles, these implements possess special aerodynamic properties which necessitate some marked modification of the angle of release. Modern javelins have been constructed to sail. When released at too steep an angle, they tend to rise abruptly, then die and eventually fall far short of the distance they might go with an appropriate expenditure of energy. Indeed, recent research has shown that an aerodynamically sound (distance-rated) javelin attains its greatest distance when the release angle is between thirty and thirty-five degrees and the "attack" angle (difference between tip and center of gravity) is from three to five degrees.

The discus also tends to sail and, like the javelin, is vulnerable to the direction and force of the wind. When thrown into the wind the release angle should be from twenty-five to thirty degrees, with an attack angle of one to two degrees. When thrown with the wind, the angle of release should be several degrees greater so the implement may ride the air currents as far as possible. Within limits, both the javelin and the discus tend to travel farther into the wind than when thrown with a following wind.

MECHANICAL PRINCIPLES WHICH MAY INFLUENCE TRACK AND FIELD PERFORMANCE

The reader should be aware that human differences make it impossible to apply these mechanical principles to all individuals and all events without some reservation. Anatomical and physiological variations in individuals do not permit exact prediction. Individuals differ in temperament, body type, strength, and other factors which influence performance. Then, too, the skill and the ability to use force effectively are often matters of disciplined attention to the task at hand. The best teacher is one who recognizes that individuals are different, who understands that physical laws do not exactly fit human performance, but who applies whatever principles she can, as best she can, with each girl with whom she works.

1. When overcoming the inertia of a resting body, force should be applied by the most powerful muscles in the direction of the intended line of flight. This principle applies to the sprint start and to those events which involve throwing and jumping as well.
2. To counteract centrifugal force the runner should lean into the curve, swinging the arms vigorously across the body.
3. In the throwing events the lighter performer can compensate for her weight disadvantage by learning to move with greater speed (Momentum = Mass × Velocity).
4. The force effect is greatest when applied through the longest possible range of motion—and when it is applied in the shortest possible time. (When throwing and jumping, the performer should learn to apply force explosively.)

5. The acceleration (rate of speed increase) of a body is proportional to the force causing it. For this reason, strength is an important factor in successful track and field performance.

6. The effect of interacting forces is greatest when applied to a firm surface. The shot-putter and the discus and javelin thrower should release their implements while in contact with the ground.

7. All moving bodies are influenced by the effects of rotation. To cope with these effects a counterforce must be applied. The long jumper runs in the air. The sprinter shortens the radius of the legs for greater leg speed, coordinates the arm swing with the stride pattern, and thus utilizes the rotary effect in a positive manner.

8. The successful performance of a complex skill will be determined in part by an effective summation of forces. All available forces should be utilized, each new force being added to the peak of the previous one, with the final force expended explosively. (When two forces are applied simultaneously, the weaker force prevails.)

9. Whenever possible, gravity should be used to overcome the force of inertia. This would involve leaning forward at the start of a race when either starting blocks or a standing start is being used.

10. To effectively control momentum in the javelin, shot-put, or discus, the performer follows through by widening her base of support and lowering her center of gravity.

Chapter 2

Motor Learning
and Motor Performance

Gross motor performance can be defined as performance in which the major segments of the body are involved. All track and field events fall within this definition. This chapter has been written so that the reader can better understand the nature of gross motor performance and apply this understanding to the teaching and learning of track and field activities.

CONDITIONS ESSENTIAL TO LEARNING

Authorities in the area of educational psychology agree that certain conditions are essential to learning. Kingsley has stated, "Learning takes place through activity. . . . The result is a new kind of performance or change in activity.[1] Other writers agree, though they hasten to add that if change is to take place, the learner must be purposefully motivated. Just being active is not enough; the learner must be active toward some predetermined, personally meaningful goal.

A part of the process of learning is the recognition that former behavior or performance is unsatisfactory. When an individual wants to improve and is given adequate guidance, appropriate materials with which to work, and meaningful practice, new levels of skill can be

1. Howard L. Kingsley, *The Nature and Conditions of Learning* (Englewood Cliffs, N.J.: Prentice-Hall, Inc., 1946), p. 12.

achieved. Other factors which seem to have a positive effect on learning are satisfaction and the challenge of progressively more difficult tasks.

STEPS IN THE LEARNING PROCESS

Nearly all educational psychologists have identified certain steps which they believe to be essential to the learning process. Though these have been stated in various ways, it seems certain that explanation, demonstration, exploration-participation, and evaluation constitute a very acceptable procedure for the teacher to follow.

Explanation

A clear and meaningful description of a gross motor task is virtually impossible. Words do not carry the same meanings as do patterns of movement. For this reason, verbalization should be brief. This is especially true with beginners, though the advanced performer can make some modifications in her style or technique as a result of verbal direction.

The teacher should recognize that initial explanation should be aimed at setting the task. She should give the learner the big picture, a broad generalization of the skill to be practiced. She should tell her students what to look for, that is, what cues they ought to see when observing a demonstration.

Demonstration

It is generally concluded that a clear, accurate demonstration produces the best results with beginners. The teacher should set the stage with brief verbal cues and then demonstrate to the best of her ability the skill to be learned. According to current research findings, three demonstrations give the learner nearly all of the information that she can comprehend.

It is noteworthy that the ability to perceive varies with individuals. All students do not see the same things when they watch a motor skill demonstration. Some students lack experience and do not sense what is taking place. Other students perceive more readily or, having had a wider motor experience, catch even the details when a skill is demonstrated. Teachers must recognize this difference in perceptual ability and give demonstrations which have meaning for all of the students with whom they work.

Exploration-Participation

Teachers explain and demonstrate so that students can participate and learn. The wise teacher recognizes that when a student is ready to act, it is pleasurable to act and not pleasurable not to act (Thorndike's Law of Readiness). She encourages her students to touch, to feel, and to explore. She motivates them as best she can, gives them something to do, and gets them started before they lose their keen edge of anticipation.

Since much learning is a trial-and-error process, the first attempts of the learner tend to be random. The effective teacher recognizes this and moves from learner to learner, making specific, brief comments. She directs her attention to individuals, helping each girl make the adjustments which are necessary for her improvement. The teacher should not overcoach, but she should make every attempt to shorten the period of trial and error.

Evaluation

In track and field the goal is both proper form and successful performance. In most instances, the results of one's practice are readily discernible. Opportunities should be given to run, to jump, and to throw. Competition offers an incentive to work hard and affords the teacher and learner a chance to evaluate the changes which have taken place.

CRITICAL ISSUES IN MOTOR LEARNING

Research has provided some answers for many of the perplexing issues concerning learning. It is the intent of this section to identify several of these issues and to note what research tells about each of them. The material which is presented represents the best evidence available at this time. The reader should be aware that information about learning will change as more research is completed and should be prepared to modify her point of view as it is reported.

Speed versus Accuracy

Speed and accuracy seem to be different factors. The improvement of one does not necessarily affect the other. When a skill involving speed and accuracy is to be learned, both factors should receive approximately equal attention. When speed is more important than accuracy, speed should receive primary attention; when accuracy is more important than speed, accuracy should receive primary attention.

Teachers should recognize that speeds tend to be specific factors. Running speed is not the same as quickness in changing direction. Speed training or practice should therefore be very specific, for skills learned at one rate of speed are different from skills learned at another rate of speed. Practice thus should be at the rate of speed at which the skill will be performed.

Whole versus Part Learning

This issue is closely related to a definition of the terms *whole* and *part*. Obviously every part represents a whole if presented as such; therefore, it is perhaps more meaningful to distinguish wholes and parts in terms of skills or parts of skills.

What the teacher should know is that the unit of activity to be learned must be meaningful to the learner, for the learner must perceive what she is trying to do before she can use her time and energy effectively.

In general, the *whole* method is superior for individual activities, namely, jumping, throwing, starting, and the like. Thus each track and field event should be explained and demonstrated in its entirety, explored this way for a time, and then broken down into smaller units for further practice.

The *part* method is best for complex activities involving several skill components. When the part method is used, the activity or event to be learned is broken down into meaningful units, each of which is practiced separately. When the smaller units or components have been mastered, they are properly oriented and the whole skill receives the learner's full attention.

Whether practicing on parts or wholes, it should be remembered that the final bottleneck to skillful performance will be the weakest part of the whole.

Frequency and Duration of Practice Periods

There is some evidence that optimum learning depends upon a minimum of three practice sessions each week. This is particularly true in those activities in which endurance plays a major role. Although the attention span of younger children is short, the writers have successfully worked with girls of high school age for periods as long as one and one-half hours.

It is likely that the competitive athlete should train five days each week. Skill and endurance are developed over extended periods of time, thus distributed practice is more effective than massed practice. Some recent experimentation has shown that certain women athletes respond best to alternate periods of work and rest rather than the "typical" five-two schedule which has predominated for years. These women have attained outstanding success by alternating two days of practice with a day of rest. They have discovered that the 2-1, 2-1, 2-1 schedule seems to eliminate much residual fatigue and soreness, permitting them to work harder during their training sessions than they could when training every day.

Knowledge of Results

Most authorities seem to agree that knowledge of results is essential to learning. When a student knows her scores, she tends to show improvement during subsequent performance. The feedback information may be verbal, visual, or tactual. It may be purposefully given to the learner or it may stem from the performance experience itself. At least one study has shown that graphic information provides an excellent incentive for the learner.[2]

It is likely that the track and field performer is never without some knowledge of her level of achievement. Performance is recorded in understandable units of measurement. When times and distances are not available, there usually is some relative place or rank to be considered. The more interested and experienced competitors almost always have some knowledge of their performance. As a general rule, teachers should help beginners to set frequent attainable goals for themselves; she should test them and then show them how well they performed.

There are some noteworthy exceptions to this general rule. Although most individuals rise to a challenge, some do not. Mismatching may destroy a loser's incentive. The constant pressure to improve or the awareness that a watch is ticking away may defeat the very purpose for which it is being used. For these reasons, individual differences must be considered and the pressure to excel kept at a level that is compatible with relaxed performance.

2. Franklin M. Henry, "Force—Time Characteristics of the Sprint Starts," *The Research Quarterly* 23, no. 3 (October, 1952), p. 301-318.

Mental Practice

A former coach and leader of men at the University of California used to tell his athletes to "throw their hearts" into the contest. He wanted his athletes to think about success, believing that victories were won in the mind before they are won on the field of contest. In his book *Psycho-Cybernetics*, Maltz discusses the effect of thinking and believing on learning and performance.[3] He has noted that what we think and believe about ourselves tends to determine what we can do and what we will become.

Research evidence has long indicated that mental practice can improve learning and performance. By re-creating a skill in the mind, by thinking it through serially again and again, the learner can effect a change in her performance. Mental practice helps her to get a feel for performance. She can improve her perceptual ability, cues become more meaningful, and timing is quickened.

While mental practice and the process of thinking and believing have their limitations, it is quite likely that tracing, sketching, reading, and looking at pictures may have a positive effect on learning and performing. Whereas prolonged introspection may inhibit the learner, intelligent and purposeful mental review can contribute to her success.

Effect of Warming Up

Though long considered essential, there is now some question about warming up prior to performance. Studies have shown that warm-up did not improve performance nor did the lack of warm-up increase the incidence of injury to the participating students. On the other hand, selected research has shown definite improvement in jumping, in some events involving accuracy, and in events involving strength when these were preceded by warm-up.

What does seem apparent is that there are many kinds of warm-up. In some instances a general program of running and calisthenic activities has proved of little value, whereas prior warm-up with like elements has seemed to improve performance. In light of this conflicting evidence, it seems advisable that the performer in both track and field events should warm up by gradually increasing the intensity of her activity. Stretching apparently is important, but prolonged running may do little more than produce fatigue and thereby limit the learner's span of attention or level of efficiency.

3. Maxwell Maltz, *Psycho-Cybernetics* (Englewood Cliffs, N. J.: Prentice-Hall, Inc., 1960), pp. 1-13.

A recommended warm-up might include one or two laps of walking and jogging, ten minutes of stretching, and several minutes of formal activity in the event to be performed. These activities may help the performer to get set mentally for her event and thereby contribute to her poise and confidence. A relaxed and positive mental attitude is essential to effective learning and performance.

Working with the Slow Learner

There is little relationship between mental and motor ability, though some girls may have inherent limitations so far as their ability to learn motor skills is concerned. On the other hand, the slow learner probably was reared in an environment barren of motor experiences. The slow learner tends to be weak, tense, and frustrated. She lacks experience and does not "catch on" because her frame of reference is definitely limited. These girls have not performed and cannot perform motor skills well; they often lack motivation and are disinterested in an activity-oriented program.

The teacher must recognize these limiting factors. She must manifest sincere concern for the slow learner, giving her special time and attention. The environment in which these girls practice must be relaxed. The element of competition should be minimized and equated to the girl's level of ability. They should be encouraged to loosen up, to think positively, and to develop a higher level of strength and endurance. Explanation and demonstration must be simple and meaningful.

Since few girls have had experience in track and field, it is likely that teachers in this area will be confronted by many beginners who manifest the characteristics of a slow learner. These girls will profit from an explanation of mechanical principles. They need to recognize that their bodies are machines which are capable of producing force; that the effect of this force is modified by the duration of its application and the point at which it is applied. They need to know that speed of movement can compensate for greater size. They must practice and practice until they get the "feel" of leaning into the run, of driving up through the body, of turning in the air. Track and field is fun. It can be fun for more girls if they are guided properly, given a sense of security, and challenged at their own level of ability.

Perhaps this analogy from the fascinating frontier of automation would be a fitting ending for this chapter. This is a story about learning machines, feedback, and the effect of teaching, or input, on performance.

Several contemporary writers have noted that man, like some machines, possesses the capability of a servomechanism; that is to say, man's performance tomorrow will be determined in part by what is experienced today. A chess-playing machine has been developed which tends to prove this point. The machine operates electronically, scanning the chessboard and countering each move that its human opponent makes. Every move is recorded and stored on tape inside the machine. Subsequent moves and games are therefore played in light of prior experience. Like the human being, this machine will always reflect its prior experience. If its experience has been good, the quality of the chess game it plays will be good. If the machine "learned" to play chess from a poor player, it tends thereafter to play an erratic game.

What a potent reminder to the teacher that her skill and ability make a permanent impact on the learner! What the teacher says and does, what the learner hears and sees, the explanation, the demonstration, the exploration, participation and supervision—all affect the learning process. That which is recorded is part of the permanent record.

Part II

Running Events

Chapter 3

Running—A Lost Art

Man has run throughout his long history. Some of the earliest art records show men running for joy, for food, and for their very lives. Perhaps this is why so little attention is given to how he runs; it is assumed that running is part of our natural heritage. But is this true?

Just watch a group of youngsters at play and see how they run. Watch them in a game of baseball and observe the way they run the bases, chase fly balls, and charge the grounder. Watch two girls' teams playing soccer or field hockey. Watch a man or woman who has nearly missed a bus. These experiences will likely provide convincing evidence that few individuals really know how to run. The majority of people one sees running struggle with sagging knees, tight hips, and wildly flailing arms, giving the impression of frustrated effort and an inefficient use of force and energy.

Certainly running is one of the most neglected of all gross motor skills. We teach youngsters how to throw and catch, to shoot a basketball, to spike a volleyball, and to move rhythmically to music. Seldom, if ever, however, do we take time to teach them how to run. Perhaps we need to remember that running is a basic skill, that it is an essential part of nearly every active game, and that proper running form can be learned.

PRINCIPLES OF RUNNING FORM

Walking, jogging, and running are part of the same continuum. The differences in gait stem from alterations in such factors as body form, the application of force, rhythm, and amplitude. Each alteration is self-imposed, either voluntarily or involuntarily, to accommodate the forces of inertia, momentum, and interaction. The graceful, flowing motion of the skillful runner represents months of practice in an effective and economical transition along the walking-running continuum. The skillful runner has learned how to control her body in this beautiful way.

Analysis of efficient running form reveals several important modifications of walking gait. The most obvious are an increase in speed, a greater stride length, and periods of nonsupport. These and other essential modifications are discussed in detail in this chapter and again in those chapters where they have specific relevance. Comments about how to teach girls to run more effectively also are included at the end of this chapter.

MORE EFFECTIVE RUNNING

1. The running stride is longer than the walking stride. To increase her speed a girl must exert greater force against the ground. This added force drives the body upward and forward through alternate periods of single-foot support and nonsupport. As the speed increases, the strides become longer and the rhythm is faster. Tall girls will have a longer stride and somewhat slower rhythm than short girls. Short girls will have a shorter stride and somewhat faster rhythm than tall girls. Fast girls will have a faster rhythm than slow girls regardless of the length of their strides.

Overstriding and understriding both constitute inefficient forms of movement. Every girl has an optimum stride length for every race. While this optimum is not readily identifiable, it is safe to say that in nearly every instance a girl's half-stride (R to L or L to R) should fall somewhere between six and eight feet in length. When other corrections have been made, it is probable that a runner's optimum stride length will accrue from hours of purposeful practice.

2. High knee action is essential to running speed. Knee lift permits the runner to reach ahead and thus extend her stride. Low knees, on the other hand, restrict forward movement and cause the runner to stumble in her attempts to attain greater speed. This is particularly true in starting where a new base of support must be quickly es-

tablished out ahead of the runner. When the knees are low, the foot contacts the running surface prematurely, forcing the runner into an upright position. Balance and momentum are destroyed, and the runner's speed is seriously curtailed.

3. It is a fundamental law of mechanics that the short radius or lever turns more rapidly than the long radius. Since the legs swing through an axis of rotation, they operate within the context of this mechanical law. The skillful runner, therefore, lifts the heel of the back foot near to the buttock, shortens the radius, and speeds up the forward swing of her leg. If the radius is not shortened, the performer must exert great force with each stride; she becomes fatigued more readily and is unable to attain maximum speed.

4. If running speed is to be increased, there must be a compensatory forward inclination of the body. The distance runner tends to run in an up and down motion, while the sprinter must lean forward to utilize the force of her driving legs effectively. There also is less wind resistance against the forward leaning body, a factor which can appreciably reduce running speed.

5. Arm action is an extremely important part of proper running form. The arms are carried at a fixed (not rigid) angle of about ninety degrees. They swing from the shoulder like porcelain arms on an old rag doll. The movement plane is rearward and forward, the hands passing back to the buttock and up to the level of the eyes. Except when running around a curve, there is no action across the body, as all available forces are expended straight ahead.

Because the human machine operates in a bilateral manner, efficient movement often demands a synchronous counterbalancing of opposing forces. The forward extension of one leg must be counteropposed by the forward swing of the opposite arm. Rapid movement of the legs demands an equally rapid movement of the arms. Heavy legs must be counteropposed by vigorous action of the arms, or the leg swing will upset the balance of the entire body. When the arms and the legs are coordinated, the expenditure of energy moves the body straight ahead. An unequal distribution of force causes the body to rotate toward the lesser force, restricting the stride length and reducing the forward speed.

6. Foot placement should be directly forward when running. The weight of the body is caught, carried, and transferred primarily by the toes (except in the case of the distance runner, who lets the weight shift briefly to the heel in a rocker motion involving the toes, the heel, and the toes).

Research has revealed that half the body weight should be borne by the great toe and half by the four remaining toes at the instant of push-off. If a girl toes in or out, she must learn to shift body weight through the foot with the final thrust being applied at a point between the two largest toes.

7. Strength and flexibility are essential to graceful, rhythmic running form. Relaxation permits the runner to lift her knees, to swing her arms, to roll her hips. The strong, loose runner virtually bounces over the track. She is explosive in her actions—ankle, knee, and hip muscles contracting powerfully in their extension against the running surface.

8. Every experienced runner has a rhythm. It is essential that the beginner develop her own rhythm and maintain it throughout a race. The skillful and experienced runner never falls into the running pattern of her opponent. To do so would be to expend her energy ineffectively and would likely lead to her defeat.

Applying all of these principles is no simple task, but when they are applied, results are obvious. The highly skilled runner is relaxed. Her arms swing freely, fingers and thumb pressed together to dissipate tension in the shoulders and neck. She utilizes her energy efficiently; there is little extraneous movement since the resultant of all force is forward along the intended line of progress.

The skilled runner tends to lean forward, holding the head in a natural position. The eyes are focused down the track, her legs move smoothly and rhythmically, the knees are lifted to hip height on the front swing, and the heels are carried up and into the buttock on the back swing. There is little or no sideward movement. The driving force is provided by a powerful extension of ankle, leg, and hip muscles against the running surface. The entire motion is flowing and graceful, with the center of gravity maintaining an even path from the beginning of the race to the end.

TEACHING GIRLS TO RUN

Beginners are inclined to manifest similar characteristics when learning a new motor skill. They are tense and uncoordinated. First attempts at learning tend to be random. If the skill is complicated, the learner frequently becomes discouraged and thus requires constant encouragement. Running is not a complicated skill, but since it involves both form and speed, it does pose a problem for the learner.

One effective way to teach girls to run is to have them practice in groups over a premarked pattern course (fig. 3.1a). This course has several sectors in which fixed lines have been placed on the running surface. Each sector varies in its pattern; some have short intervals, some medium, and some long (ranging between six and eight feet). The purpose of this course is explained to the students. They are instructed to run through each sector at about half speed, keeping in mind the importance of leaning forward, lifting the knees, and swinging the arms. Proper form is demonstrated, and the learners are permitted to explore the course for themselves.

There are several advantages to the pattern course:

1. The course permits the teacher to observe small groups of students. She is in a position to make pertinent comments to individuals while they are trying to change or improve their running form.
2. The fixed stride sector forces the learner to develop a rhythm. Girls discover that stride length and running form are under their voluntary control; they can make changes if they want to.
3. The pattern course permits an exploration of running styles, giving each girl an opportunity to discover that her stride pattern will vary with speed. Moreover, girls tend to develop a feel for the

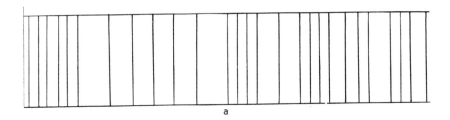

a

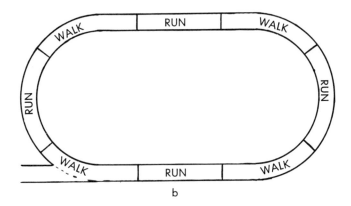

b

Figure 3.1. Pattern course showing run-walk sectors

stride plan which seems best fitted to their height, weight, and leg length.

4. The pattern course introduces an element of fun into the practice sessions. Students tend to lose their inhibitions and run with relaxed freedom.

5. By alternating running and walking, students develop higher levels of strength and endurance. These contribute to improved form, increased speed, and greater satisfaction on the part of the learner.

When practicing, students are encouraged to "let go all over." There should be little pressure on the performer, but rather such cues as "let your ears flop" and "let your jaw drop" will depict a proper sense of looseness. The beginner is encouraged to run over the track as if it were a patch of prickly nettles, not pounding but bouncing lightly like a rubber ball. There is no substitute for work, but even work can be fun when the conditions are right. The pattern course has proved to be effective in this respect. It is fun and it is satisfying when properly used.

The Pattern Course

A pattern course can be prepared in the gym or on the track. When space is available, four pattern sectors of twenty-five or thirty yards in length seem to be most effective. Under these conditions, eight groups of girls can practice at a given time, four groups striding and four walking to the next sector. The teacher is free to observe from a distance or to give individual attention at any point she chooses (fig. 3.1b).

The placement of written cues on the track just ahead of each work sector tends to set the conditions for practice. These cues can be changed from time to time, though the single words *lean, knees, arms,* and *relax* give the runners four important factors to think about.

Chapter 4

Sprinting

Professionalism in athletics has tended to occur after an activity has produced a high degree of popular appeal. The opposite seems to have happened in track and field, however, where women were once forced to compete for money or prizes if they were to compete at all. Thus it was that in Great Britain, following World War I, several outstanding female sprinters competed year after year in specially organized events.

Women were first permitted to participate in the Olympic Games at Amsterdam in 1928. An American performer, Elizabeth Robinson, won the 100-meter race in the time of 12.2 seconds. During the years that have followed, Olympic sprint champions have come from Poland, Australia, and the Netherlands, as well as the United States. Surely the feats performed by Stanislawa Walasiewicz, of Poland (later Stella Walsh of the U.S.), and Francina Blankers-Koen, of the Netherlands, are among the great legends of women's track and field.

Stella Walsh, who was an Olympic Champion in 1932, competed for more than twenty-five years, ending her career with a good showing at the U.S. Olympic trials in 1956. Fannie Blankers-Koen, known affectionately as the "Flying Dutch Girl," had to modify her training schedule to give birth to the second of two children just prior to the 1948 Olympic Games. Though the world champion in the long jump and high jump, Mrs. Blankers-Koen entered different events at the

Olympics where she earned gold medals in the 100- and 200-meter races, the 80-meter hurdles, and in the 400-meter relay event.

The United States has had many outstanding sprinters over the years, and particularly during the past decade. Martha Hudson, Lucinda Williams, Barbara Jones, and Wilma Rudolph won the 400-meter relay in the 1960 Olympic Games. Miss Rudolph received two additional gold medals by winning the 100- and the 200-meter events. Edith McGuire and Wyomia Tyus were the class of the world in the Tokyo Olympics in 1964. Oregon schoolgirl Margaret Bailes and California co-ed Barbara Ferrell, along with Wyomia Tyus, have dominated the national and international sprint scene through the Olympic Games held at Mexico City.

Speed is an essential part of track and field. While it is possible to perform at top speed for only a few seconds, it is generally concluded that races up to 440 yards in length are primarily speed, or sprint, events. Indeed, the inclusion of the 440-yard race in this category constitutes one of the marked changes in women's track and field during the past several years.

Sprinting is primarily a strength event. This does not mean that sprinters are heavily muscled individuals; it only means that they are strong. Most ranking American sprinters during the past two or three decades have been slender, graceful girls. Certainly those who saw Wilma Rudolph at the peak of her career or Wyomia Tyus, Barbara Ferrell, and other outstanding sprinters in the 1968 Olympic Games recall the grace and beauty with which they ran. Their strength was so effectively utilized that every motion seemed effortless as they strode over the track.

SPRINT START

The basic problem of starting is to overcome the resting inertia of the body in the shortest possible time while placing the sprinter in the most effective position for the continued application of force. Since this is a technical problem, there have been numerous experimental efforts to determine the best starting form. These efforts have revealed certain fundamental principles about starting, though there still is considerable difference of opinion as to which sprint start is the best.

Some teachers are intent upon producing maximum speed out of the starting blocks; others sacrifice initial explosive speed for balance during the transitional strides between the starting blocks and the all-out sprinting effort. A third group seeks the best of each, namely, initial velocity and balanced sprinting form. To a large extent the end or goal that the teacher is seeking will determine the starting technique that she chooses. Differences in individuals also may affect her judgment.

The three most commonly used starting techniques are the bunch start, the medium start, and the elongated start. Each has its own merits and each has been used successfully by one or more top American sprinters. The bunch start usually is credited with putting the sprinter into a position which permits her to explode from the blocks. The elongated start permits the sprinter to step out of the rear block in a balanced running position. The medium start seems to combine the best elements of both the bunch and the elongated starts. Because of its adaptability, the medium start is discussed in detail following.

Placement of the Starting Blocks

Since it is no longer permissible to start from holes which are dug in the track, the sprinter should have starting blocks which are calibrated in inches and easy to adjust. These are set with the front block fixed at a point between sixteen and twenty inches behind the starting line. The exact distance is determined by the structure and preference of the runner. The rear block is next moved to the extreme back end of the sliding frame. To locate the rear block, the sprinter assumes a four-point starting position with her preferred foot in the front block (whichever foot feels most comfortable). She then places the knee of the opposite leg parallel to the toe of the front foot and slides the rear block up to meet the rear foot. The distance between her two feet when this procedure has been completed will be about fifteen inches. Beginners usually find that their initial exploration of the sprint start is uncomfortable. They should be encouraged to experiment for themselves, to make minor adjustments which fit their particular needs, and to practice until they can start with poise and security (fig. 4.1).

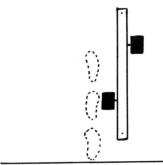

Figure 4.1. Placement of the starting blocks, showing the relative positions of the frame and the respective blocks in terms of foot lengths from the starting line.

Starting Procedures

1. *On Your Marks.* This is the command given by the starter prior to the race. Upon receiving the command, the runners move to their starting blocks. Most sprinters step in front of the starting line, stretch, and back into the blocks. The hands are placed on the track, at shoulder width, just behind the starting line. The preferred foot is placed against the front block, part of the weight is shifted to the hands, and the opposite foot and leg are extended rearward to release muscular tension. This foot is next placed against the rear block, and the weight is shifted to the supporting knee. The runner makes herself comfortable, permits her head to hang in a relaxed and natural position, and awaits the second command (fig. 4.2*a*).

2. *Get Set.* As this command is given, the sprinter takes a deep breath, rocks up and forward over straight arms, getting set for the starting signal. The weight is shifted to the hands as the shoulders move three to four inches ahead of the starting line. The driving muscles are placed on stretch, the front leg assuming an angle of about 80 degrees, the rear leg an angle of about 130 degrees. The hips are elevated slightly above the shoulders, the back is straight, and the head is held comfortably in line with the body. The eyes are focused ahead of the runner at a distance which permits her to hold her position without strain for a period of two full seconds (fig. 4.2*b*).

There are at least two modifications which girls may have to make in the set position. Both of these stem from their lack of strength. It may be necessary for girls to support their weight on the knuckles rather than on the fingers, and it may be necessary for them to minimize the forward lean. These adjustments will have an effect on initial speed out of the starting blocks, but when they are made, they will permit almost every girl to start from the four-point stance.

3. *Go.* Though there is some controversy over the focus of attention in the set position, the writers believe that the sprinter should concentrate on exploding out of the blocks. The gun merely triggers the action which is perceived in the mind. The action sequence (for the sprinter with the right foot back) is left arm, right arm, right foot, and left foot. The left arm, counteropposing the right-leg drive and step, is up and out in a forceful thrusting action. The right arm is up and back. The first stride is quick, though not choppy, as the foot contacts the track about twenty-four inches ahead of the starting line. The left leg continues to drive against the front block throughout this sequence of action (fig. 4.2*c*).

The sprinter must stay low during the acceleration period so that maximum force can be expended to drive the body forward. A good

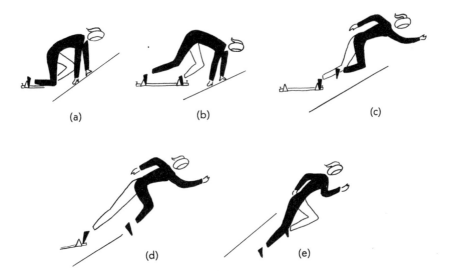

Figure 4.2. The sprint start. (a) "On your marks." Body weight is borne by the right knee and the arms. The head is relaxed with the eyes fixed on the track directly in front of the runner. (b) "Get set." The seat is elevated slightly higher than the shoulders, and the weight is shifted forward over the supporting arms. (c) "Go." Note the extreme lean as the sprinter drives forward, her focus of attention continues to be immediately ahead. (d) Vigorous arm action and an explosive pull and step by the rear leg enables the sprinter to move her center of gravity directly toward the finish line. (e) Strides are natural, with no attempt to shorten or extend their length.

starter will relax, use her arms vigorously, and keep her knees high (fig. 4.2*d*). Each stride will increase in length as the body gradually assumes a balanced running posture. Maximum acceleration is attained during the first fifteen or twenty yards. Beyond this point, the sprinter's attention is focused on a spot fifteen yards in front of her, and every effort is made to maintain forward progress with a minimum of tension (fig. 4.2*e*).

SPRINTING STRIDE

The sprinting stride is long and powerful. The weight is caught and transferred by the toes as extensor muscles of the feet, legs, and hips react explosively to expend their force almost directly through the body. Arm action continues to be vigorous and perfectly coordinated with the driving legs. The forward leg action is out, down, and back in a pawing motion. Each new base of support is established directly beneath the body to avoid a breaking action and subsequent loss of speed. It is essential that the sprinter continue to relax. Tension chokes off power and restricts the stride length (fig. 4.3*a-f*). Because beginners frequently tense up, teachers must find ways to help them run with little effort. Some teachers constantly remind their sprinters with signs and verbal commands—"relax, relax, relax." More than one sprinter has discovered that taking a breath twenty or thirty yards before the finish of the 100-yard dash helps her to relax.

FINISH

Races are frequently won and lost during the final two or three strides. For this reason a runner, and particularly a sprinter, should

Figure 4.3. Wyomia Tyus, Olympic sprint champion, leans forward into the finish yarn. (Photo courtesy of Don Wilkinson, Greeley, Colorado.)

run to a point beyond the finish line. This will prevent a last instant letdown and insure the maintenance of speed through the entire race. The actual finish of a sprint race may be negotiated in one of two acceptable ways. During the final driving surge for the tape, the runner may extend herself forward in an attempt to move her chest beyond those of her opponents or she may turn one shoulder toward the tape in a final burst of energy. Both of these techniques make it appear that one sprinter has crossed the finish line ahead of her more erect opponents and may well constitute a margin of victory. While leaning and turning are acceptable finishing techniques, a runner never dives for the tape. A dive may result in injury and certainly is slower than sprinting through the tape.

PRINCIPLES TO REMEMBER WHEN TEACHING GIRLS TO START AND TO SPRINT

Starting Principles

1. When starting mechanics have been explored and the beginner is learning to drive out of her starting blocks, she should concentrate on keeping her head down and her center of gravity close to the ground. The tendency to stumble during the first starting strides should not be compensated for by standing or driving the arms upward, but rather by an added effort to bring the legs through quickly so that a new base of support can be established.
2. Concentration in the set position should be on the motor response, not on the gun. Research has shown that listening for a sound does not produce a response equally as fast as concentration on the movement pattern itself.
3. Because girls tend to step out of the blocks and run through their arms (which hang down like an inverted wishbone), it is important that the driving, explosive nature of the start be emphasized and that girls be encouraged to use their arms vigorously.

Sprinting Principles

1. Running at all speeds involves a synchronous bilateral swinging of arms and legs. As leg speed is increased, arm speed must also increase to compensate for the added force of the heavier legs. All movement is forward or backward to minimize torquing or twisting during the run.

2. Sprinting action involves high knees, a slight forward lean, and a straight back. The head is held so that a line of force extends from the foot through the leg, the body, and the head at the instant of push-off. This principle holds true for starting as well as for running.

3. The sprinter should learn to run through the finish line. She must not let up until reaching a spot five yards beyond the finish line. The practice of finishing strong will eliminate many distressing losses at the tape.

4. The sprinter should avoid stopping suddenly. She should drive through the finish line, letting up gradually after the race has been completed. Such a procedure will help to prevent injury to the working muscles and will help the sprinter to stay loose through the entire race.

5. Every runner must relax. This fact is so important that considerable time and effort should be given to this phase of running. Some release from tension is a natural consequence of learning how to run. The ability to relax while applying peak effort, however, stems from the conscious attention of the runner. Drills requiring the sprinter to overtake and pass an opponent during the practice session often help a sprinter to concentrate on running faster with little added effort. Breathing during a race also may help the sprinter relax. In the 100-yard dash, a single breath should be taken at about the 75-yard mark. In distance as long as the 220, several breaths should be taken as a natural part of the race. (This point is made because some sprinters attempt to hold their breath during an entire 100-yard dash, only to find that they tense up near the finish line.)

STEPS IN TEACHING SPRINTING

After girls have experimented with the pattern course and have become aware that they control their running form, they should run with increased speed. They should be encouraged to stay relaxed, lift the knees a little higher, swing the arms a bit more vigorously, and expend their energy forcefully against the running surface. It is this greater force that moves the runner with increased speed, not a desperate, wild flailing of arms and legs.

Running a Line

The shuttle drill, with students sprinting back and forth across a football field along the yardage lines, teaches a girl to place one foot

Figure 4.4. Barbara Ferrell, Olympian, manifests the grace and symmetry of the powerful sprint stride. (Photo courtesy of Don Wilkinson.)

ahead of the other and apply her force in a straight line. In physical education classes, girls are asked to watch each other, to observe correct as well as incorrect form, and to make those comments which they feel to be valid. The teacher moves from line to line, observing each girl independently, encouraging and correcting as she goes.

Tandem Push

An effective technique for teaching girls to lean forward and to expend their force through their bodies is the tandem push. This drill involes working in pairs, one girl standing and facing the direction the pair will run. The other girl moves behind the first, grasps her by the waist with outstretched arms, inclines her body forward, and on a signal begins to run. The two accelerate slowly, the front girl mildly resisting the pusher. Each practices proper form, the front girl lifting her knees and swinging her arms, the pusher lifting her knees, leaning, and driving against the track.

The tandem drill can be used along the yardage lines of the football field, on the track, or in the gym. The length of the run should be about twenty or twenty-five yards. The teacher observes, encourages, and makes appropriate comments. During the drill, students learn how to expend energies effectively and in the process gain strength which is essential to running speed.

Sprint Start

Large groups of girls can learn to start from a long line, such as the sideline on the football field or the end line on the basketball court. Working in squads, several girls take their marks simultaneously. They have had the sprint start explained and demonstrated to them, and now they are ready to explore the start for themselves. The hands are placed behind the line, the knuckles giving support. The front foot is placed in a hypothetical starting block about sixteen inches behind the line; the opposite foot is placed so that the back knee is even with the toe of the front foot. The arms are straight, hands shoulder width apart; the weight is borne by the resting knee. The teacher, standing in front of the class, reviews these form fundamentals and checks along the line to make certain that each girl has assumed the proper starting position.

The second girl in each squad now steps forward and places one of her feet behind each foot of the girl who is at her mark. The command "on your marks" is given, and the starters rise to the set position with their weight thrust back against the feet of their squad mates. Once again the teacher reviews the key points: The hips are elevated slightly above the head, the head is held naturally without tension, the arms are straight, the front leg forms an angle of 80 degrees, the back leg forms an angle of 130 degrees, and the weight is shifted forward over the hands.

Each girl holds the set position for several seconds and then returns to her preliminary stance. The teacher calls each girl independently to the set position, comments on her form, and has her return a second time to the preliminary stance. When all of the girls in a group have had this individual attention, the entire group is given the commands "Get set" and "Go." They sprint fifteen or twenty yards, return to the rear of their squad line, and the process continues.

Start Resister

This drill places the sprinter in a position which demands a powerful expenditure of force against the starting blocks if movement is to occur. The starter thus learns to drive forward and upward, applying force through her center of gravity. She also becomes aware of the importance of arm action to the maintenance of balance and stability.

Figure 4.5. The start resister

Sprint Buildup

This is an excellent technique for teaching the sprinter to increase and decrease her speed with little or no obvious change in form or effort. The buildup may be run out of the starting blocks or from a standing start. The runner gradually increases her speed to a peak, then lets up in a long, smooth period of deceleration. When she has learned to change her speed effortlessly, she can experiment with several buildups in a series. These may be run on the track or on grass, though grass is preferable. When several buildups are run consecutively, the sprinter is performing what many coaches call the "in-and-out" drill. To the observer, she appears to be prancing over a series of hot spots in an exaggerated or animated manner. Perhaps this is exactly what she should be thinking—it's hot, get off . . . it's hot, get off—remembering all the time to lift her knees, to use her arms, to lean, and to relax.

Freewheeling Run

This drill is little more than a downhill sprint though it has proved to be an excellent practice condition for teaching beginners to "let go" and to speed up the actions of their arms and legs. To use the drill, a well-mowed, gentle slope must be located. The learner starts her run at the bottom of the slope, angling upward to minimize the climb. She is soon aware of the need to lean and to drive with her arms and legs. When she has proceeded up fifteen or twenty yards (and before she is too tired to profit from the run back down), she races back down the slope as if pulled by a cord around her middle. Her stride is longer than usual, and her legs are moving with greater speed. There is an exciting sense of ease associated with the freewheeling run, and girls who use this drill soon become convinced that they can move faster, and faster, and faster. If they persist at it, they will become stronger, their stride will become longer, and their speed will increase.

HINTS FOR THE 220-YARD SPRINT

The longest sprint event for girls and women is the 220-yard race. For the beginner, a sprint of this length is virtually impossible, and even the well-trained runner finds that she must utilize her energies carefully if she is going to have a strong finish.

There are two common approaches to the 220-yard dash—one involves the concept of maximum acceleration-minimum deceleration; the other involves an all-out effort during the entire race. While this latter approach is taken by most of the better male sprinters, it is not yet recommended for girls. A girl (especially the beginner) should attain her peak speed during the first fifty yards of the race, then with no obvious change of style, she should attempt to move mentally and physically into a relaxed, floating sprint while maintaining as much speed as possible. The length of the float will be determined by the strength and condition of the runner. Usually a final dash is begun thirty or forty yards before the finish line. If a girl is going to win this race or place among the winners, she must be up with her competition when the final sprint begins.

Since many 220-yard races are run in lanes around a curve, a runner often must sense where her opponents are and begin her final sprint with them. A sense of position seems to develop with experience. The beginner must recognize her limitations in speed, condition, and judgment and take her chances as they come. She must never, never look back, for to look back is to break stride, lose sprinting rhythm, and suffer defeat.

TRAINING SCHEDULE FOR THE BEGINNING SPRINTER

The following schedule would be appropriate for girls in physical education classes or for club performers who are just beginning. One should resist the urge to work too hard too soon. Enjoyment is important during this period when the performer is building the foundation for serious training later on.

M. Stride a distance of 180 yards several times, floating, sprinting, and floating during each run. This running should be done on the grass, with emphasis on proper body lean, high knees, and vigorous arm action. Stay relaxed.

T. Run several buildups from fifty to sixty yards in length, increasing running speed effortlessly with several strides at full speed followed by a gradual deceleration. Stride along a line several times, concentrating on foot placement, proper body alignment, high knee lift, and vigorous arm action. Set up the starting blocks and experiment with various starting positions. Drive out of the blocks a distance of fifteen to twenty yards.

W. If a gentle, grass-covered hill is available, practice on the free-wheeling drill. Jog obliquely up the hill, turn and stride down again. Repeat this drill several times. Stride through a 220. Rest and repeat. Take several starts with a gun, sprinting from 20 to 30 yards with a long, relaxed letup.

Th. Take several buildups on the grass, covering a distance of 100 yards with a relaxed increase in speed, a few full-speed strides, and a long, easy letup. Stride 75 yards at near-full effort. Join the long jumpers or hurdlers and give some attention to one of these events.

F. Warm up well, set the starting blocks and take several practice starts. Sprint 75 yards at top speed. Rest well. Sprint 180 yards at a speed which can be maintained with relaxed running form.

S. Thirty minutes of easy striding on the grass. Stretch well.

TYPICAL TRAINING SCHEDULES
FOR THE SKILLED SPRINTER

Early Season (February through March)

Assuming that the performer is working throughout the entire year, the so-called early-season program is aimed primarily at the development of running form, or rhythm, and stamina. Each day's activity will include a warm-up jog, conditioning exercises, and running.

M. Stride 330 yards at three-quarter speed (47 to 49 seconds) followed by two laps of easy shuffle for recovery.
Repeat 330 with recovery.
5 x 60-yard acceleration sprint with walk-back interval—running start.
Finish workout with ten minutes of easy shuffle on the grass.

T. Stride 220 yards at three-quarter speed (33 to 34 seconds), walk 110 yards, accelerate 50 yards, followed by one lap of walking for recovery.
Repeat five times.
Take ten starts out of blocks—20 to 30 yards.

W. 110 fast striding—220 shuffle.
220 fast striding—440 shuffle.
330 at three-quarter speed (47 to 49 seconds)—four laps of shuffle.
220 fast striding—440 shuffle.
110 fast striding—four laps of shuffle.
Finish by sprinting out of five turns.

Th. Stride 440 for form—shuffle two laps for recovery.
Take ten starts out of blocks—20 to 30 yards.
Work with long jumpers for fifteen minutes on pop-up jumping.
3 x 150 fast striding with walk-back recovery.
Finish with ten minutes of easy shuffle on grass.

F. 2 x 220 fast striding with walk-back recovery, followed by four laps of easy shuffle.

3 x 60-yard sprints with running start—one-lap shuffle recovery.

Ten minutes of form work over two hurdles.

2 x 180 acceleration sprints—one-lap shuffle recovery.

Finish by sprinting out of four turns.

S. One-half hour of easy striding, preferably in hilly, grassy area.

Competitive Season

M. Fast stride 330 (41 to 43 seconds)—five minutes of shuffle recovery.

4 x 150 acceleration sprints out of blocks with one-lap shuffle recovery.

One-half hour of work with sprint relay team (or comparable short, repetition acceleration activity).

T. 3 x 180 acceleration sprints from blocks at seven-eighth speed—two laps of shuffle recovery.

Fifteen minutes of work with either long jumpers or hurdlers.

Six gun starts, 40 yards—one-lap shuffle recovery.

Finish with ten minutes of easy shuffle on grass.

W. 2 x 220 fast striding with running start—two laps of shuffle recovery.

4 x 75 acceleration sprints from blocks with one-lap walk recovery.

Ten minutes of easy shuffle on grass.

One-half hour of work with sprint relay team, or

4 x 50 acceleration sprints from blocks with one-lap walk recovery.

Th. Stride 440 for form—shuffle two laps for recovery.

2 x 150 acceleration sprints from blocks—walk-back recovery—four laps shuffle recovery.

5 x 40-yard sprint starts with one-lap shuffle recovery.

F. Thirty minutes of easy striding and stretching.

S. Competition.

THE 440- OR 400-METER RUN

The 440 is a relatively new event for women, having been contested in the Olympic Games, for the first time, at Mexico City. Even so, the quarter-mile race already has evolved from the classification of a run to that of a sprint. Thus, coaches and athletes no longer approach the race as a middle-distance event in which there is a fast start, a long, relaxed float, and a final sprint to the tape. Rather, like the men, women are now following the principle of maximum acceleration-minimum deceleration as the best strategy for this distance.

The quarter miler is a sprinter who has developed the stamina necessary to maintain her speed throughout the length of this very demanding race. The trend, thus, is for girls with sprint potential, yet not quite being of championship caliber, to move up to this event. As late as 1964 there were few girls in the United States who had run 440 yards under sixty seconds. Then a sprinter named Janell Smith startled the track world with her time of 54.7 seconds, and the precedent was set for speed to dominate the event.

Though not victorious at Mexico City where Colette Besson, of France, and Great Britain's Lillian Board placed first and second in the 400-meter race, the United States trio of Kathy Hammond, Jarvis Scott, and Ester Stroy now rank among the top quarter milers in the world; and with the wealth of fine sprinters in this country, it is probable that we shall excel in this event as long as it is contested.

Strategy in the 440-Yard Race

It is to be remembered that this is a sprint, thus the performer utilizes all of the technical advantages that she can. She starts from blocks, following the principles which apply to the shorter 100- or 220-yard dash.

There are, however, two different approaches to the quarter-mile race. These might be modified according to the competition; still, sprinters moving up to the longer distance take one approach, whereas middle-distance runners moving down take another. In general, the sprinter does not start as fast as her more highly conditioned adversary but stays close to her throughout the first 350 to 400 yards, after which she seeks to win with a sprint to the finish. Following this strategy, the sprinter would likely run a race having a difference of two to three seconds between the first 220 and the last. (For example, if the elapsed time were 54 seconds, the split times probably would be 25.7 to 28.3 seconds.)

The middle-distance runner who moves down to the shorter event seeks to take advantage of her strength and stamina. Accordingly, she runs harder throughout the entire race. Her strategy is to take the "sting" or kick out of the sprinter and thus win with her fast opening pace. If a poorly conditioned sprinter can be pulled into this trap, she likely will be beaten. For the well-conditioned sprinter, however, this is an opportunity for a very fast race. (In this example, the split half times for a 54-second 440 would be approximately 25.3 to 28.7 seconds.)

TYPICAL TRAINING SCHEDULE
FOR THE BEGINNING QUARTER MILER

Since the quarter miler must possess a high degree of stamina, it is important that she participate in an extended period of preconditioning activity. This would include cross-country running, Fartlek, and general conditioning exercises. In pursuing the following training program, the performer should begin each day with a time of relaxed striding and stretching.

M. Overdistance work through a park, a golf course, on a beach, beside a lake—anywhere that will permit the beginner to forget herself and to run for fun. Time should be the major consideration, not distance. The beginner should try to run for ten minutes, then fifteen, then twenty, and so on, until she can run half an hour without stopping.

T. 5 x 220 in 36 to 37 seconds. Walk 440 yards between each.
Take several relaxed sprints out of the turn—50 to 60 yards—slow walk-back rest interval.

W. Drill on sprinting with emphasis on form, covering from 150 to 180 yards on the grass. Two to three minutes of easy shuffle rest between each.
Repeat six to eight times.
Finish with ten starts 20 to 30 yards.

Th. 3 x 330 easy striding (52 to 54 seconds). Ten minutes of easy shuffle rest between each.
Finish workout with five acceleration sprints 40 to 50 yards with walk-back rest interval.

F. 110 fast stride. 220 walk-rest interval.
220 in 32 to 34 seconds with 440 walk interval.
440 for form (no time), with five minutes of walking rest interval.

220 in 32 to 34 seconds with 440 walk interval.

Finish by fast striding 110 yards.

S. One-half hour of Fartlek running for stamina and fun.

TYPICAL TRAINING SCHEDULE
FOR THE HIGHLY SKILLED QUARTER MILER

Early Season (February through March)

 This schedule assumes that the performer has participated in pre-season conditioning of a general nature and now is ready to pursue the specific preparation essential for the 440-yard race. Note, too, that each day's activity is to be preceded by a jog of two to three laps, followed by ten minutes of stretching.

M. 4 x 440 in 70 to 72 seconds with two laps of easy shuffle between each.

5 x 150 acceleration runs with walk-back interval.

Finish workout with ten minutes of easy shuffling on the grass.

T. 2 x 5 x 220 in 35 to 36 seconds with walk-back interval between each 220.

Shuffle two laps for recovery between the two sets of five 220s.

10 x 70-yard acceleration runs with slow walk-back recovery—out of starting blocks.

Finish with ten minutes of easy shuffle on grass.

W. 3 x 330 fast striding (4 to 6 seconds less than best time) with one lap of walking between each.

Ten starts out of blocks, 25 to 35 yards—emphasis on form.

5 x 180 fast striding with slow walk-back interval.

Finish with ten minutes of easy shuffle on grass.

Th. Stride 600 yards for form—no time.

Shuffle two laps for recovery.

3 x 5 x 150 fast striding—with walk-back interval between each 150.

Shuffle two laps easily between each set of five. Finish with ten minutes of easy shuffling on the grass

F. 440 in and out.

110 fast stride—220 recovery shuffle.

220 fast stride—440 recovery shuffle.

330 at 5 to 6 seconds less than fastest time—two laps of recovery shuffle.

440 for form (no time) with five minutes of easy recovery shuffle.

330 at 5 to 6 seconds less than fastest time—two laps of recovery shuffle.

220 fast stride—440 recovery shuffle.

110 fast stride—finish with ten minutes of easy shuffling on grass.

S.   Two to three miles of Fartlek on the grass.

Competitive Season

Each day's activity is to be preceded by a jog of from 880 yards to a mile, followed by ten minutes of stretching. Note that the overload increases have occurred in different ways. Primarily this is to avoid too much repetition and boredom.

M.   4 x 440 in 63 to 65 seconds with five minutes of easy shuffle between each.

6 x 150 acceleration runs with walk-back interval—out of starting blocks.

Finish workout with ten minutes of easy shuffle on grass.

T.   660 in 1:48-1:50 followed by ten minutes of easy shuffle on grass.

5 x 220 in 28 to 30 seconds with one-lap walk between each.

Ten starts out of blocks—20 to 30 yards.

W.   440 in and out.

110 fast stride—220 recovery shuffle.

220 fast stride—440 recovery shuffle.

330 at 2 to 3 seconds less than fastest time—two laps of easy shuffle.

440 in 60 seconds—five minutes of recovery shuffle.

330 at 2 to 3 seconds less than fastest time—two laps of easy shuffle.

2 x 75 sprints with walk-back recovery.

Th.   2 x 5 x 180 fast striding with walk-back interval. Two laps of easy shuffle between each set of five.

Ten 60- to 70-yard sprints into the turn out of starting blocks.

Finish workout with ten minutes of easy shuffle.

F.   Fast stride 330 out of blocks—no time.

        Finish workout with twenty minutes of easy shuffle on the grass.

S.   Competition.

It is recommended by the writers that the serious athlete train on the day before competition except when entering the big meets of the year.

Chapter 5

Relay Races

Relay racing can be one of the most satisfying activities in the entire track and field program. The relay race involves speed, endurance, teamwork, and exciting competition. Indeed, the effortless coordination of the well-drilled relay team is a fitting tribute to the painstaking practice of its members.

This chapter includes a discussion of different types of relay events as well as an analysis of relay racing techniques and strategy.

TYPES OF RELAY RACES

Relay racing includes pursuit and shuttle events. At the secondary school level, girls run both shuttle and pursuit relays up to distances of 440 yards. In open competition the mile, 880, and sprint medley races are added for the more mature performers.

Pursuit Relay

Nearly every relay race involves teams with four members. In the pursuit race, girl number one starts and carries the baton to her second teammate. The second girl exchanges the baton with team member number three who passes it to the fourth and final runner. Each girl runs a specified distance, the same direction around the track, and exchanges the baton in a fixed zone twenty meters in length. The most common pursuit relays for women are the 440-yard sprint and the 880-yard medley. In the 440 relay each girl sprints 110 yards. In the 880-yard medley the first girl runs 220 yards, the number two and three girls run 110 yards each, and the anchor runner covers a distance of 440 yards.

Shuttle Relay

In the shuttle relay, the participants run alternately back and forth between two fixed points. Team members may exchange a baton; or the second, third, and fourth girls may start from the set position as their teammates cross a restraining line. Shuttle races usually include sprint relays of 220 or 330 yards in length or the longer 320-meter hurdle event.

Figure 5.1. The first girl in the relay race carries the baton in her left hand. In this instance she holds the baton with her thumb and forefinger, permitting her to use her three remaining fingers for support during the set position.

COMPONENTS OF RELAY RACING

Handling the Baton

Baton handling includes both general and specific characteristics. The general nature of the baton exchange is determined by the distance run, whereas the specific refinements of the exchange are largely a matter of coaching preference. In the shorter races, the exchange is nonvisual, with the incoming runner responsible for placing the baton in the hand of the outgoing runner. In races where fatigue is a factor (4 x 440 or 3 x 880), the exchange is visual, with both participating members sharing the burden of accuracy.

Figure 5.2. In the Dyson, or alternate-hand exchange, the lead-off runner carries the baton in her right hand, passing it to the left hand of her teammate running the second leg of the race.

Nonvisual Exchange

Successful coaches and teams have used a variety of exchange techniques to advantage. The two methods most commonly seen in recent years are the left-to-right-hand underhand exchange and the alternate overhand exchange (commonly called the Dyson exchange). Both of these methods have their strengths and weaknesses. These will be explored in the paragraphs which follow.

In the *left-to-right-hand exchange*, the lead-off runner starts with the baton in her left hand. She sprints along the inside of her lane until she approaches the passing zone; then she moves to the outside of her lane to exchange the baton. This precaution is taken to avoid running into the outgoing girl who, like the incoming girl, begins her leg of the relay by running on the inside of her lane. The actual exchange in this situation is made across the lane with a smooth, lifting motion by the left hand and arm.

Figure 5.3. In the nonvisual exchange, full responsibility for the handoff rests with the incoming runner.

In the nonvisual, or sprint, exchange, the two participating girls must operate with clocklike precision. The front girl stands at the end of the exchange zone, her right side turned toward her incoming teammate and her feet spread about shoulder width. As the incoming girl crosses a predetermined *go* mark, the standing girl turns and drives full speed ahead as if she were sprinting out of the set position. (For additional comments about determining the *go* mark, see section on Teaching Relay Racing Skills and Tactics.) When she has completed two or three full strides, she extends her right arm to the rear; the hand is spread, thumb toward the side and the palm facing the incoming runner. If the timing has been perfect, the two sprinters will make contact about five yards before they reach the end of the exchange zone. There will be no overlap between the two girls. The incoming runner merely swings the baton firmly up into the out-

Figure 5.4. The ready stance for the nonvisual exchange

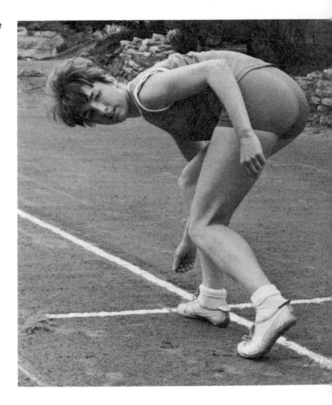

stretched hand to which her attention has been fixed. The outgoing runner grasps the baton securely, changes it to her opposite (left) hand, and sprints on to repeat the procedure.

After the exchange has been made, the incoming girl decelerates easily along the outside of her lane to avoid blocking the progress of other runners. The outgoing runner, on the other hand, stays close to the inside of her lane to avoid running extra distance around a turn. When using this style of exchange, the baton is received by the right hand, shifted across to the left hand during the first two or three strides, and passed off again to the right hand. The incoming runner always moves to the outside of the lane, and the outgoing runner always receives the baton and runs on the inside of the lane.

The advantage of this technique is its fixed pattern of exchange. Regardless of which relay leg a performer runs, she passes and receives the baton in a similar manner. Replacing a runner, or changing her order, thus results in a minimum of disturbance to the continuity of the team.

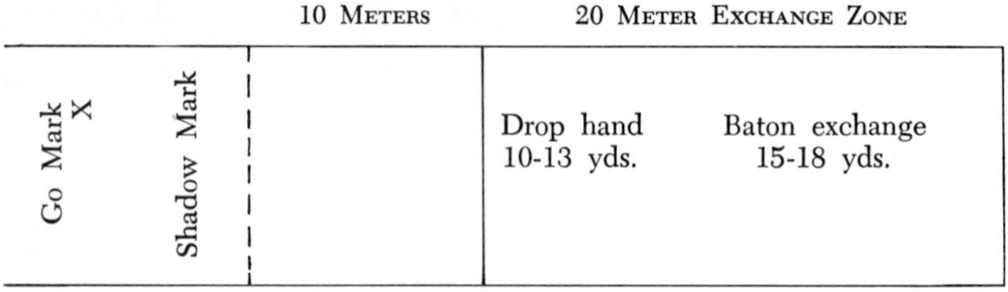

10 METERS		20 METER EXCHANGE ZONE	
Go Mark X Shadow Mark		Drop hand 10-13 yds.	Baton exchange 15-18 yds.

Figure 5.5. Approximate distances for initiating and executing the blind pass. The distance between "go" mark and the rear zone line where the receiver is waiting is determined by the speed of the two runners participating in the baton exchange. This mark is determined after extensive practice.

In the *alternate-hand technique*, the first and third exchanges are from right hand to left hand, with the second exchange being from left hand to right hand. Mechanics of the exchange involve a downward striking motion, with the baton being "slapped" into the upturned palm of the receiver's extended hand.

This technique has several advantages. One advantage concerns the second and fourth runners who receive the baton on the turn. With the right-to-left-hand exchange they are able to accelerate along the extreme outside border of their lane, then "cut" diagonally into the turn after receiving the baton. This latter maneuver provides space for three or four straight-line strides and offers an added margin for the attainment of speed.

A minimum of baton handling throughout the race is another advantage stemming from this technique. Each runner receives, carries, and exchanges the baton with either the right or the left hand. The chances of dropping the baton or forgetting to change the baton from the receiving to the passing hand are therefore minimized.

Perhaps the most important advantage of the alternate-hand technique is that it permits the acquisition of maximum free space between participating members of the relay team. This free space is the distance gained during each exchange and is the hallmark of the championship team. Indeed, the principle of relay racing does not necessarily concern itself with participant speed, but rather with baton speed. The secret is to get the baton moving as fast as possible as quickly as possible and to maintain or increase that speed throughout the race. Every yard of free space attained thus contributes significantly to the speed with which the baton is moved.

Precision in baton handling, which is an important key to success in relay racing, constitutes the main disadvantage to using the alternate-hand technique. This stems from the fact that replacement of team personnel is almost impossible without a prolonged period of drill on the specific factors involved. Thus when four reliable sprinters are available, the use of the alternate-hand technique is strongly recommended. However, when team personnel is uncertain, it is likely that the similarity of the left-to-right-hand pattern would constitute the safest approach to the relay event.

Visual Exchange

In the visual exchange, the burden of responsibility is on the outgoing runner, for the incoming runner frequently is tired and can neither catch the rapidly moving girl, who is fresh, or place the baton accurately in her hand. The outgoing runner, therefore, waits at the near end of the exchange zone and moves only when she is certain her teammate can reach her. The actual exchange is made at whatever speed the incoming runner is capable of producing. The outgoing runner merely turns toward her teammate and extends her right hand and arm as far rearward as possible while she is moving. In this instance, her palm is held upward, her fingers are relaxed, and her thumb is rotated toward the inside of the track. In reality the baton is just handed from one girl to another.

In longer races, a girl may carry the baton alternately in her right hand and then her left hand. This practice permits a girl to gain relief from the tension of gripping the baton, though it adds to the chances of the baton's being dropped.

Standing Exchange for the Shuttle Relay

The shuttle relay is run back and forth between two parallel lines. When batons are used, the receiver stands facing her incoming teammate with her right arm extended forward. The fingers are spread with the thumb toward the midline of the body, palm toward the runner. The exchange is made with a thrusting motion as the incoming runner pushes the vertically held baton into the right hand of the receiver. To facilitate the handoff and gain as much speed as possible, the receiver leans forward in a slightly bent-knee starting position. She grasps the free end of the baton and immediately sprints to the opposite exchange area, carrying it as she receives it. (Exchanges are made from right hand to right hand.)

Sprint Start for the Shuttle Relay

In the hurdle relay and some other shuttle events, all participants start from the regular sprinting position. The first runner starts with the firing of the gun, takes her hurdles in stride, and sprints the final several yards to the restraining line. The second and subsequent runners also assume a sprint starting position. Each girl comes to a set position when her teammate crosses a predetermined mark in front of the restraining line, and she holds this position until she receives a slap on the right shoulder as the signal to go. The timing in this maneuver would be similar to starting from the starting blocks.

STRATEGY IN THE RELAY RACE

It bears repeating that the key to success in relay racing is to move the baton with the utmost speed. To do this, a technique of baton exchange must be adopted which permits team members to accelerate quickly, to attain maximum free space at handoff, and to maintain peak velocity throughout the race. When these criteria have been met, four girls with an average time of 12.5 seconds for 110 yards (or 50 seconds flat for 440 yards) can move the baton over this distance in from forty-eight to forty-nine seconds. This is possible because of free space, that distance which can be gained between teammates when each is in full stride and reaching as far as possible toward the other during the handoff.

Other, more specific, comments about the strategy of relay racing are to be found below:

1. The placement of team personnel should follow a logical pattern.
   a. In sprint races held indoors it is wise to get the lead and force one's opponents to run wide around the turns. For this reason, the fastest starter should lead off with the hope that she can gain running room for her teammates who follow.
   b. The distance which the baton is carried by a runner also must be considered. In a typical 4 x 110 relay race, each runner starts from the ten-meter shadow line, accelerates to a point 15 yards

inside the exchange zone where she receives the baton and sprints to the next zone where the same circumstances eventuate. Diagraming such a race makes it obvious that the lead-off runner covers a distance of 115 to 118 yards with the baton. Runners two and three carry the baton approximately 110 yards, with runner number four carrying the baton from 102 to 105 yards. It is obvious that the lead-off runner must be a good starter who is strong enough to maintain her speed to the point of exchange.

c. The second and fourth runners must be able to accelerate out of the turn. (Some sprinters cannot do this because of the length of their strides.) The second runner also must be a good baton handler since she both receives and passes off during her leg of the race.

When using the alternate-hand exchange, the second and fourth runners assume a starting stance which permits them to look back along the left shoulder at their incoming teammate. Since this stance shifts the left foot rearward, it seems awkward to the girl who normally places her right foot in the rear starting block. Occasionally a runner cannot make this adaptation to her regular foot placement. The coach should be aware of this when selecting and placing team personnel.

d. The third runner also must be a good baton handler. Because this leg of the race begins on the straightaway, this is a good place for the long-striding performer who has trouble sprinting out of the turn.

e. The fourth girl is known as the anchor runner. Traditionally, it has been her responsibility to win the race for her teammates, the rationale being that the anchor runner is the fastest, thus she has the burden of catching or holding off her adversaries.

Though this rationale has some validity, it also is true that the anchor runner actually covers the least distance of the four members of the team. Because of this fact, it may be more important to find an anchor runner who can accelerate on the turn but yet cannot maintain her speed quite so long as a stronger teammate. The anchor runner also must be a "fighter," a girl who is courageous under pressure.

The placement of team members is not just a matter of whim, for a split second gained or lost during exchange may mean the difference between victory and defeat. The coach should consider all extenuating factors, and only after experimentation should she make her decision regarding the running order.

2. It is always wise to utilize the speed and strength of the fastest girls. This can be done by having them receive the baton at the near end of one exchange zone and carry it to the far end of another. Such a maneuver is especially effective in the medley relay where the first runner sprints 220 yards, the next two girls sprint 110 yards each, and the anchor runner must cover 440 yards. In this situation, the second runner would receive the baton just inside the exchange zone so as to capitalize on her greater speed in the shorter race. The second and third girls would exchange normally, though the third girl would sprint into the exchange zone when handing off to the anchor runner who, in this instance, would be covering the greatest distance at the slowest pace.

In every instance of relay racing, participants should take as much advantage of the passing zone as possible. They should exchange the baton early or late as the situation dictates. In sprint relays each performer should attain maximum possible speed at the hand-off. Both visual and verbal cues should be utilized to facilitate split-second timing. It is imperative that the coach recognize the importance of practice, for winning is frequently as much a matter of pride and precision as it is a matter of sprint ability.

TEACHING RELAY RACING SKILLS AND TACTICS

Teaching emphasis in the relay events is on handling the baton. Whether a large group or just two individuals are involved, the procedure is the same. The teacher explains the different types of baton exchanges, demonstrates them, and has the girls drill under her supervision.

Running in Place

One effective starting point is a drill in which two girls assume the relative positions of the incoming and outgoing runners so they may practice the exchange while running in place. This drill is used for both the visual and nonvisual pass, with the learners working together until they can accurately coordinate their movements.

Left-to-Right-Hand Exchange

When the stationary pass is perfected, the girls shift their attention to a half-speed exchange. One girl moves to the shadow mark and assumes a standing position with her feet spread shoulder width and turned slightly to the right. She looks back over her right shoulder, fixing her attention on the *go* mark which has been arbitrarily established fifteen feet away.

The other girl sprints toward the exchange zone; her passing the *go* mark constitutes a signal for the waiting girl to start. Each girl runs as fast as she can, continuing to run through the zone to determine how well their relative speeds match. If the incoming girl fails to catch the outgoing girl, or if she runs past her, they adjust their *go* mark accordingly. This skill is practiced until the two girls just come together but never really overlap.

The two girls now attempt to effect the exchange. They repeat their drill, and when the incoming runner is within "exchange distance," she calls "hand" to her teammate, who immediately extends the right arm and hand to the rear. The baton is lifted upward in a firm, positive movement and is placed into the grasp of the receiver. This first exchange is the most difficult exchange to make, but practice and attention to details will soon bring dividends in smoothly coordinated performance. (The same procedure would be followed when teaching the alternate-hand technique, except the mechanics would vary according to the placement of the runners. Note section on alternate-hand exchange.)

Modifications for the Physical Education Class

There are many drills for perfecting the baton exchange. These drills also can be used as a means of improving running form and endurance. Following are two drills that the writers have used successfully.

The Multipassing Drill. This drill is most effective when there are from twelve to sixteen girls participating. These girls are given numbers and are distributed equally among the four exchange zones. When an arbitrary *go* line has been established at each zone, the girl numbered one sprints toward girl number two and passes the baton to her. Girl number two receives the baton, runs to the next passing zone, and exchanges the baton with girl number three. The drill continues around and around the track, with a new girl receiving the baton at each station until all have completed a specific number of exchanges.

The teacher can station herself at any one exchange area and observe all of the girls during a period of several minutes. If there are several girls running, the teacher has ample time to make appropriate comments to each girl after she has exchanged the baton.

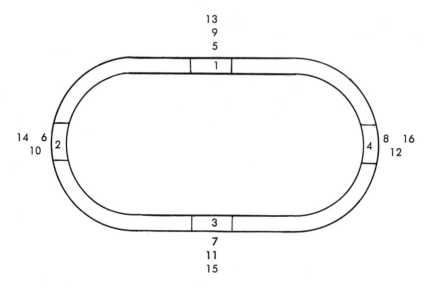

Figure 5.6. The multipassing drill

The multipassing drill also can be effectively adapted for team use. To do this, the teacher organizes two or more teams having five members, with the first and fifth girl on each team starting from the same exchange zone. The race is started, and the participants run and run and run, moving to a new zone each time they exchange the baton. When this drill is used, girls are challenged to run faster and to give close attention to the proper mechanics of relay racing.

One of the authors has used the foregoing team drill for many years and has found that it offers an extremely good incentive for pushing beyond the normal limits of fatigue. Girls love to run this way, and they tend to forget the hard work that they are imposing upon themselves.

THE SHUTTLE-PURSUIT DRILL. This drill incorporates the nonvisual exchange and the face-to-face exchange used in some shuttle relays and can be utilized out-of-doors or in the gymnasium (fig. 5.7). Here again five or more girls can participate, twelve being a very workable number.

The drill is initiated by the first runner at station A, who sprints to station B and exchanges the baton with a nonvisual pass. The second girl sprints to station C and exchanges the baton with the third girl, also using a nonvisual pass. The third girl sprints to station D

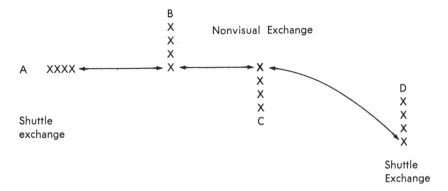

Figure 5.7. The shuttle-pursuit drill

and exchanges the baton with a face-to-face (visual shuttle exchange) pass with the fourth girl who sprints back to Station C to repeat the procedure.

The shuttle-pursuit drill is best adapted to a running distance of 100 feet or more. This drill gives a large number of girls baton-exchanging practice in a minimum amount of time.

Chapter 6

Hurdling

The hurdle event as known to modern man probably had its origin on the steeplechase fields of Great Britain. Form, determined by the formidable structure of the heavy barrier, involved a clearance technique little different from the vertical, or scissors, jump. By the early thirties, however, both the hurdle and the technique had been sufficiently modified so that Mildred Didrikson won this event in the good time of 11.7 seconds at the 1932 Olympic Games.

In a period of three decades following the 1932 Olympics, better hurdlers came from countries other than the United States. These included such outstanding performers as "the flying Dutch girl," Mrs. Blankers-Koen, Shirley Strickland, of Australia, Irma Press, of Russia, and Maureen Caird, the current Olympic Champion from Australia. During this period from 1932 to 1960, the Olympic record was lowered from 11.7 to 10.6 seconds, though not a single American girl was capable of running the eighty-meter race in less than 11.0 seconds.

The improvement in hurdle technique and performance records has been phenomenal during the past several years. Indeed, the improvement has been so great that the height of the hurdle has been modified to accommodate the skill of the contemporary performer. Among those whose skill has made these changes necessary are three outstanding American performers, Mrs. Cherri Sherrard, Miss Mamie Rallins, and Miss Pat Van Wolvelaere. Each of these performers has run the eighty-meter race in 10.7 seconds or better. Miss Van Wolve-

74

laere is the current world indoor record holder at sixty yards, whereas Miss Rallins holds the world indoor record for the fifty-meter, high hurdle race with a time of 7.0 seconds flat.

Someone has suggested that the hurdler must have the speed of the leopard, the spring of the deer, and the heart of the lion. Surely those who have observed the flawless form and the wreckless courage of the expert hurdler will agree. No other track and field event demands such a carefree approach to a purposefully imposed barrier. Perhaps no other event offers the same challenge or so great a personal reward as running at and over ten hurdles in the course of an all-out sprint race.

Hurdle races for girls are run at distances ranging from fifty yards to 100 meters. A hurdle race of 200 meters is run in open competition at the national and international levels. The height and the number of hurdles in a race are determined by the distance run. A schedule indicating the proper distances for hurdle placement is to be noted later in this chapter.

SOME BASIC CONSIDERATIONS

Many a casual observer has concluded that hurdling is so complicated that only the highly skilled athlete can participate in this event. While it is true that good hurdling form is developed through long hours of practice, it is equally true that the hurdler is a sprinter who has learned to accommodate her running form to the barriers which have been placed in her pathway. The object of the event is to win the race, and whatever the hurdler must do to accomplish this end in the fastest possible time should be the major objective of her training.

From this standpoint, hurdling form is largely an individual matter. Each participant, under the direction of her teacher, makes whatever modifications she must to sprint through the hurdle race. The most important of these modifications is an exaggerated lift of the forward leg to permit hurdle clearance, an aggressive drive into the hurdle, a sharp lean or bucking motion at the instant of takeoff, and trail-leg action which permits an explosive recovery. These and other techniques for hurdling are discussed in the pages that follow.

The Start

The start for the hurdle race is exactly the same as the sprint start, though it may be necessary for the hurdler to reverse her feet in the starting blocks to arrive at the hurdle with the preferred foot forward. Most hurdlers take eight strides to the first hurdle, in which case the back foot in the starting blocks is the lead foot in clearing the hurdle. When seven strides are taken, the forward foot in the starting blocks would be the lead foot over the hurdle.

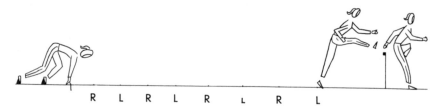

R   L   R   L   R   L   R   L

Figure 6.1. The start, stride pattern and clearance of the first hurdle. Karen Frisch, former world ranking hurdler showing medium start with excellent forward lean in the set position. Note the usual eight-stride approach to the first hurdle, with the rear leg in the blocks being the lead leg over the hurdle. The hurdle is cleared here with an exaggerated sprint stride which is made possible by the leg length of the performer and her perfectly timed forward lean, or bucking motion, into the barrier. Karen has come off the hurdle in good balance, her left knee well up and forward, permitting a normal following stride.

Some hurdlers elevate their hips slightly higher than the recommended height for the set position, and they use their arms more vigorously so that they can attain their maximum speed more quickly than a sprinter. A hurdler must arrive at the first hurdle balanced and ready for the lift forward and upward over the barrier; these modifications help in this respect.

The takeoff point for the hurdler (distance between the takeoff foot and the hurdle) should be about five or six feet from the barrier itself. Each girl should establish this point to fit her particular qualifications of speed and form. If a girl takes off too close to the hurdle, she tends to swing her foot and leg around and over the hurdle rather than lifting it sharply into the hurdle. If she is too far from the hurdle at the instant of takeoff, she tends to float over the barrier, losing precious time while in the air.

Lead-Leg Action

The first modification of sprinting form is the higher lift of the knee and thigh to permit hurdle clearance. This is accompanied by a bucking action of the trunk and a forceful drive against the track by the takeoff leg. All available forces are expended forward and slightly upward (not upward and forward). The lead leg is kept in perfect alignment, cutting sharply downward to the track immediately after the heel clears the top of the hurdle.

Figure 6.2. The hurdle clearance. (a) The runner approaches the hurdle with normal sprinting form. (b) A forward bucking motion permits an exaggerated leg lift. (c) The drive over the hurdle is initiated by a powerful extension of the takeoff foot and leg. (d) The hurdler stays as close to the top of the barrier as she can. Her only marked deviation from normal sprinting form is an exaggerated extension of the left arm. (e) Almost immediately after it passes over the hurdle, the lead foot is cut sharply to the track, and the knee of the trail leg is whipped forward and upward in preparation for the next sprinting stride. (f) The toes of the lead foot contact the track beneath the runner, her head comes up, and she focuses all of her attention on the next hurdle.

Trail-Leg Action

Action of the trail leg, described by the word *punch*, is a reflection of current thinking regarding this event. The action is unlike the "flattened split" required of the male high hurdler (or the short-legged female). Rather, the performer assumes a more upright position during hurdle clearance, with the thigh and knee extended slightly downward from the horizontal. Following a slight delay as the lead foot reaches for the track, the trailing knee punches upward, across the hurdle, toward the chest. The quick, high knee facilitates the sprint action so essential to this event. (Beginners have a tendency to rush the trail leg, bringing both legs over the hurdle almost simultaneously in a jumping-floating movement. This pattern seriously limits the length of the stride and forces the performer to lope between hurdles.)

Figure 6.3. Drill for teaching trail-leg action. The beginner jogs along beside several hurdlers, stepping just ahead of each with the lead foot, forcing herself to lift the knee of the trail leg sharply upward over the barrier.

Hurdle Clearance

Since the hurdler can only gain speed while in contact with the track, she should constantly strive to shorten the time it takes to clear the hurdle. One way to realize this objective is to avoid too much float during the period of clearance. Perhaps this can best be accomplished by working endlessly on the action sequence over the hurdle. Certainly a mastery of the clearance components is imperative to championship performance. (The expert requires from 0.1 to 0.2 of a second longer to clear the hurdle than to take a normal sprinting stride.)

Arm Action

Tall girls will find that with practice they can sprint over the hurdle with little modification in running form. Shorter girls have to lift their lead leg proportionally higher and buck sharply to clear the hurdle. Thus, while the tall, long-legged girl merely reaches toward the lead leg with the opposite arm to control her balance, the short girl finds it necessary to buck sharply and reach toward the lead leg with both arms. This double reach facilitates forward lean and lift of the lead leg. The arm on the same side as the lead leg should be carried as normally as possible, for the tendency to develop a side swing is common among beginners and heavy-legged hurdlers. An excessive side swing pulls the shoulders out of alignment and seriously affects the pattern of subsequent strides.

Figure 6.4. For the tall girl the stride over the hurdle is little more than an exaggerated sprint stride. (Action picture taken from 16 mm. movie film.)

The Stride Off the Hurdle

Getting over the first barrier is the most important problem facing the hurdler. If she arrives at her takeoff point in step and is able to come off the hurdle in a balanced, sprinting position, she very likely will run a smoothly coordinated race. If she has to stretch or is too close to the first hurdle, fails to buck, or swings her arms to the side, she likely will have trouble gaining either body control or momentum. For most girls the cut down should be about thirty inches in front of the hurdle with the lead leg landing beneath the center of gravity. The trailing knee, on the other hand, is lifted high and in toward the chest until the leg extends forward and downward in a long, powerful sprinting stride. This is a critical phase of the race since speed is dependent upon a normal sprinting stride off the hurdle.

If the girl is not leaning forward as she comes off the hurdle and her stride is not normal and powerful, she will lose her forward momentum, and the race becomes little more than a series of animated lopes.

The first barrier behind her, the girl now focuses her attention on the top of the hurdle just ahead. She continues to run her race as smoothly as possible, taking each hurdle as it comes, focusing her attention on the next barrier, and finally sprinting for the tape. Throughout the race she is relaxed and confident, expending all of her forces forward and maintaining her center of gravity at a constant height.

Figure 6.5. The stride off the hurdle. In this photo Virginia Husted demonstrates the balanced form of the skillful hurdler. Her head is erect, her weight is over her new base of support, and her left knee is high enough to permit a normal sprint stride toward the next hurdle. She has delayed bringing the trail leg forward until the lead leg has nearly made contact with the track.

TIPS FOR THE HURDLER TO REMEMBER

1. The hurdler must be loose. She should warm up well, running and stretching the muscles of her trunk, hips, and legs.
2. The hurdler does not run and jump the barriers which have been placed in her path but rather runs over them in a modified sprint. In reality she merely accentuates her normal sprinting rhythm every fourth beat.
3. Form is important and should receive endless drill, but the really good hurdler is the one who wins the race. Greatest emphasis, therefore, should be on speed and not merely form.
4. It must be remembered that hurdling involves the same bilateral movement as walking and running. The forward leg must be counter-opposed by the opposite arm. Then too, when one leg is extended, the other leg is recovering. Violation of this principle results in a series of awkward leaps with little or no coordination or speed.
5. Action is continuous throughout the race; there should be no letup, no floating over the hurdles.
6. The hurdler should take off far enough from the hurdle to permit a straight-ahead motion, the lead leg lifting directly into, passing directly over, and cutting directly down from the hurdle.
7. All extraneous movement should be eliminated by the hurdler. It is particularly important that her center of gravity be maintained at a constant height throughout the race. This can be accomplished by alternately bucking into the hurdles and rising to a full height while sprinting in between.
8. At the instant of takeoff, better hurdlers concentrate on lifting the thigh rather than the foot. The thigh lift results in a stepping action over the hurdle and the maintenance of sprint form throughout the race. An exaggerated foot lift, on the other hand, tends to produce a locked knee and a subsequent floating over the hurdle barrier.

TEACHING BEGINNERS TO HURDLE

Since the beginner must overcome a physical as well as a psychological barrier when learning to hurdle, it probably is best to follow the explanation and demonstration of the whole skill with specific practice on one of its parts. Most teachers begin with action of the trailing leg.

Before actual practice can begin, a girl must determine which leg is to be her takeoff leg and which is to be her trail leg. For nearly all girls, this is a simple matter of kicking an imaginary ball, the kicking leg being the lead leg and the supporting leg the trail leg. If a girl does not know which is her kicking foot, a slight push applied by the teacher would quickly reveal how she transfers her weight. The foot which is extended to catch the weight would likely be the lead leg over the hurdle. The supporting leg would be the trail leg.

Trail-Leg Action

With several hurdles properly spaced along the track, a number of girls can practice trail-leg action together. With their trail legs to the inside, they walk in single file past the hurdles. Forward progress is controlled as each girl attempts to adjust her strides so that the outside or lead foot falls several inches ahead of each hurdle. If a girl is sufficiently close to the hurdles, this action forces her to lift her trail leg up and over to avoid banging the side of the barrier. The movement skill which she is attempting to learn is a quick sequential act involving a step, a buck, and a pull. This drill can be speeded up the next time around so that the girls develop a sense of timing, first walking, then jogging, and finally running as they are able to. Because the quick whip action of the trail leg is so important, this drill should be a part of the daily schedule of all hurdlers, beginners and experts alike. They should work toward the development of quick trail-leg action, taking five short, light, prancing steps between the hurdles and an exaggerated drive step just ahead of the hurdles, followed by the explosive pull through of the trail leg.

Lead-Leg Action

Teaching lead-leg action poses a particular problem, for there really is no substitute for going over a hurdle. About the only thing that the teacher can do is to create a barrier which presents as little psychological disturbance as possible. This can be achieved by placing bamboo poles, lightweight tubes, or strings across the tops of two hurdles. The beginner thus hurdles a barrier which she can hit without injury to herself.

There is no substitute for practice, and no amount of discussion will reveal to the beginner what it really is like to stride over a thirty-three-inch barrier. Perhaps it is best at the outset to let girls "jump" the hurdle any way they want to; then when they have convinced themselves that it can be done, they will be ready to consider proper form.

It has been noted by the writers that most beginners crowd the hurdle in the fear that they cannot clear it with a normal sprinting stride. It thus becomes necessary to establish a takeoff mark which permits straight alignment of the lead leg. The teacher should stand beside the hurdle, observing each girl as she approaches, bucks, drives, lifts, and clears the barrier. The teacher's comments are brief and specific. They are aimed at helping individual girls adapt their sprinting form to the hurdle event.

Drill Over Two Hurdles

As soon as the beginner has developed some semblance of skill over a single hurdle, she should begin working over two hurdles. Though three strides are normally taken between each hurdle, the two-hurdle drill will involve five short, prancing steps. This short-step drill has several advantages: (1) It teaches a girl to lift her knees; (2) It enables her to adjust her stride so that she arrives at the hurdle at the correct takeoff point; and (3) It provides a practice situation in which she can exaggerate her forward drive into the hurdle. This latter point is extremely important, for the hurdler must have a feeling of building speed over every hurdle or she will tend to jump and float. (Some girls have found that by mentally thinking the words *quick, quick, quick, quick, quick, push, quick, quick, quick, quick, quick, push,* they can develop a rhythm which definitely contributes to a quicker hurdling response.)

Out of the Starting Blocks

The learner faces an entirely new situation when she attempts to take a hurdle out of the starting blocks. She is forced to adjust her stride plan so that she arrives at the takeoff point in a balanced, forward leaning position. It is difficult for her to keep her head down and to drive out of the starting blocks when she is uncertain where she is going.

The teacher must be patient at this point, helping the beginner to develop confidence in her ability to start properly and to arrive at the takeoff point in stride. Perhaps this can best be accomplished by drawing a line across the track where a hurdle normally would be.

With several practice starts the girl will see that she is ready and actually could stride over a real barrier.

Placement of the first hurdle for the learner should be determined by her particular stride pattern. There is no harm in moving the hurdle several inches up or back during the learning period. The main thing is to get the girl over the hurdle successfully so that she can be encouraged to start and sprint without any hesitation.

When a girl has learned to start and clear a single hurdle, she should begin working over two hurdles. The problem once again involves the development of confidence and poise on the part of the learner and patience on the part of the teacher. Hurdle placement should be modified again to meet the needs of each individual learner. The main objective is to get the girl out of the starting blocks and over the two hurdles. When this has been done, it is just a matter of time before she can run the full flight with relative ease.

Short-Step Drill

Girls who are learning how to hurdle frequently have difficulty in covering the distance between hurdles in three strides. Part of their difficulty is a reluctance to drive at the hurdles with an attitude of carefree confidence. The short-step drill has proved to be most effective in helping beginners to improve their skill, build their confidence, and forget their fears.

Actually this drill should be a part of every serious hurdler's training schedule. The drill usually is performed over a full flight of hurdles, the hurdler approaching the first barrier from a standing start. This and subsequent hurdles are taken with an explosive effort. Emphasis is on relaxing and driving, relaxing and driving, relaxing and driving. An equally effective training situation is the *hurdle shuttle drill*. This involves the placement of several hurdles (preferably five) side by side, though facing opposite directions. The hurdles are spaced according to the race for which the performer is training. From a standing start the hurdler short-steps the hurdles facing her, loops back, and short-steps the second flight. Repetition of this drill ten to fifteen times in an afternoon both sharpens technique and develops the endurance so essential to the hurdle event. (The hurdle shuttle drill also frees half the track for other training activities.)

The development of greater confidence and skill helps most girls to take the hurdles in three strides. Those who still have trouble stretching out should run many sprint races to build greater strength. They then can practice over hurdles which have been set closer than the normal distance. This kind of training schedule, with emphasis on form, speed, and strength, usually permits a beginner to push the hurdles farther and farther apart each week. She soon finds that she can forget her fears and sprint the entire hurdle race.

TABLE 6.1.   SPACING OF HURDLES

Length of Race	Number of Hurdles	Start to First Hurdle	Distance Between Hurdles	Distance from Last Hurdle to Finish
50 yards	4	39' 4½"	26' 3"	31' 10½"
70 yards	6	39' 4½"	26' 3"	45' 9"
80 meters	8	39' 4½"	26' 3"	39' 4½"
100 meters	10	42' 7½"	27' 10⅝"	34' 5¾"
200 meters	10	52' 5¾"	62' 3"	42' 7½"

TYPICAL TRAINING SCHEDULE
FOR THE BEGINNING HURDLER

Since speed and height are prerequisites to success in the hurdle event, tall (5' 7" or more), fast girls have a marked advantage over their shorter, less fast adversaries. Flexibility also is an important asset to the performer in this event, as is quickness. For this reason training schedules for beginners, as well as for experienced performers, give considerable emphasis to the development of sprint speed, supple hips, and explosive action.

The following schedule would be appropriate for girls in the physical education class. Each training session should be preceded by a jog of 440 yards, followed by ten minutes of stretching and strengthening exercises. (See chapter on conditioning—general exercises.)

M.   5 x 75 fast striding with walk-back recovery interval.
Work over four hurdles for form—short-step drill—ten repetitions.
Finish with two laps of walking and sprinting.

T.   3 x 110 fast striding with one lap of walking between each.
Five minutes of trail-leg drill, followed by ten starts over two hurdles.
Finish with four laps of walking and sprinting.

W.   5 x 75 sprints out of turn.
5—5 x 5 shuttle hurdle drills.

Finish with ten pop-up jumps at the long-jump pit (see long jumping).

Th. 2 x 150 fast striding with one-lap walk recovery.

Ten starts twenty yards without hurdles.

3 x 8 hurdles at top speed, followed by five minutes of recovery walking.

F. 2–4 x 75 fast striding—walk-back rest with a 440 recovery walk between sets of four.

Ten minutes of trail-leg drill.

Finish with fast stride of 220 yards.

S. For the serious performer, one-half hour of easy jogging on grass.

TYPICAL TRAINING SCHEDULE
FOR THE EXPERIENCED HURDLER

Early Season

Each training session would be preceded by four laps (1 mile) of easy jogging, followed by fifteen minutes of strengthening and stretching exercises. (See chapter on conditioning exercises—specific exercises for the hurdler.)

M. 5 x 220 in 32 to 34 seconds with slow walk-back recovery.

10–5 x 5 hurdle shuttle for form.

Twenty to thirty minutes of work with sprint relay team.

T. 5 x 75 sprints with slow walk-back recovery—out of starting blocks.

Ten starts over three hurdles.

Five minutes of trail-leg drill, followed by five minutes of lead-leg drill.

Finish with six laps of walking and sprinting.

W. 2–5 x 75 sprint buildups, with slow walk-back recovery. Easy shuffle of 440 between sets of five.

3 x 8 hurdles out of blocks, with two laps of walking between each race.

Finish with ten minutes of easy striding on the grass.

Th. 1 x 330 for strength.

Five starts without hurdles, followed by ten starts over three hurdles.

Twenty to thirty minutes of work with the sprint relay team.

F. 2 x 220 in 28 to 30 seconds with one-lap jog recovery.

Take ten pop-up jumps with long jumpers.

Finish workout with fifteen minutes of easy shuffling on the grass.

S. Thirty minutes of fast striding (150 to 200 yards) with slow walk-back recovery. Preferably on the grass away from the track.

Competitive Season

M. 2 x 220 in 26 to 28 seconds with walk-back recovery.

Ten minutes of trail- and lead-leg quickening drills.

Five starts over six hurdles spaced for 200-meter race.

Twenty minutes of work with the sprint relay team. Finish with 440 stride for form.

T. 3 x 150 fast striding with walk-back recovery.

3–5 x 5 shuttle hurdle (set for 100-meter distance) with two laps of shuffle between sets of five.

Ten starts over three hurdles (set for 100-meter distance)

W. 2 x 220 taking last five hurdles (out of starting blocks).

4 x 8 hurdles (set at 100-meter distance) with two laps of slow walking between each race.

Fifteen minutes of drill with high jumpers.

Finish with fast stride of 330 yards.

Th. 220 fast stride, followed by 440 shuffle.

Ten starts over four hurdles with emphasis on 100- or 200-meter race as desired.

Twenty minutes of work with sprint relay team.

F. Prolonged warm-up with emphasis on stretching.

Fifteen minutes of quickening drill over three hurdles.

Finish workout with ten minutes of easy shuffle on the grass.

S. Competition.

Perhaps it should be emphasized again that hurdlers are sprinters who merely have modified their sprint form to accommodate a series of purposefully imposed barriers. To be a really great hurdler, therefore, one must be a nearly great sprinter. The three top American hurdlers of the past decade, Mamie Rallins, Cherri Sherrard, and Pat Van Wolvelaere, are excellent sprinters. Each is capable of running 100 yards in less than 11.0 seconds. Moreover, each runs the anchor leg on the sprint relay team for her respective club.

On the other hand, girls with only fair speed, and yet who have great flexibility and determination, can perform very successfully in the hurdle event. They may even win most of their races, beating better sprinters, if they are willing to give careful attention and hours of practice to the little details of style.

Chapter 7

Middle-Distance Runs

Long considered a distance event for women, the 880-yard run has now become a middle-distance race in theory and in practice. First contested internationally during the 1928 Olympic Games held at Amsterdam, the 880 was not run again in Olympic competition until the 1960 games at Rome. Since that time, however, this event has become extremely popular and often is considered the premier event of the women's track and field meet.

During the past decade, several outstanding middle-distance runners have been developed in the United States. In the early 1960s both Sandra Knott, of Ohio, and Leah Bennett, who competed for the University of Hawaii, pushed the American record near the 2.10 mark. In 1965, Marie Mulder, a schoolgirl from Sacramento, manifested the growing interest of American girls and women in the 880 event by placing second to Tamara Schelkanova in the dual meet between the United States and Russia. Miss Mulder's time of 2:07.3 was a new American record.

Presently there are several fine middle-distance runners in the United States. Most notable of these are Mrs. Doris Brown, an Olympic performer with a best time of 2:02.9, and Madeline Manning, who won the Olympic gold medal with her record time of 2:00.7. Perhaps more than any other runners in the United States, these ladies represent the difference between the distance-runners' approach and the sprinters' approach to the middle-distance event—Mrs. Brown, the international cross-country champion, moving down to the shorter, faster race, and Miss Manning, a former quarter miler, moving up to the longer, slower race. The approach which each of these athletes has taken to prepare herself for the middle-distance event is pertinent to all who aspire to participate in the 880-yard or 800-meter run.

SOME GENERAL COMMENTS
ABOUT THE MIDDLE-DISTANCE RUN

Currently the 880 is one of the most popular events on the women's track and field schedule. Girls are becoming aware that they can retain their feminine characteristics and still train as hard as they

Figure 7.1. The standing start used by middle-distance runners.

must to compete in this demanding event. Moreover, girls are recognizing that there is a certain satisfaction in disciplining their lives toward a worthy goal. Certainly the first responsibility of the teacher and the coach is to inspire the interested girl to think in terms of some future goal and to work with great anticipation toward its attainment.

Once a girl has become convinced that she wants to train for the middle-distance event, she should receive careful guidance. She should be told frankly that she must work hard to develop both speed and endurance. There is only one way that this can be done and that is to *run* and *run* and *run*. She should then be protected against herself and permitted to increase her activity only as she is able to absorb greater amounts of work. The route to success in middle-distance running is long and arduous. Constant training, attention to details of form, work on speed, the development of pace, and an understanding of racing strategy—all are essential to the half miler. With these things in mind the authors have written this chapter, seeking to provide for the reader a detailed analysis of middle-distance running form and pertinent information about training girls for the middle-distance event.

Middle-Distance Running Form

As indicated earlier, middle-distance runners tend to approach their event either as sprinters or as performers with a great deal of endurance. In general, the sprinter is content to be a follower during most of the race, running off the shoulder of her slower adversary until she chooses to apply a final burst of speed with which she hopes to win. Endurance runners, on the other hand, tend to be leaders, setting a pace which is too fast for their opponents, thereby winning by virtue of superior strength. While these differences do exist, performers in this event tend to manifest certain similar patterns of form.

Nearly all girls in this event are relaxed runners. They move economically with little displacement of their centers of gravity in either the vertical or the lateral plane. These girls run with relatively long strides, though they do not drive so vigorously as the sprinters. During most of the race, the middle-distance runner tends to assume a nearly vertical posture, carrying her arms at something less than ninety degrees. Most middle-distance runners have a slightly flexed supporting leg. The foot contacts the running surface directly beneath the body, the weight is caught on the toes, shifted for an instant to the heel, and it is moved forward again as the foot is extended. (Though there is no discernible delay or rocking motion as the weight is shifted from toe to heel to toe, this action permits an instant of relaxation and delays the onset of muscular fatigue.)

If a single sentence were to be used to describe the middle-distance runner, this sentence would have to include the word *flowing*, for girls who excel in this event possess a rare ability to run in a flowing and graceful manner.

Development of Pace

The ability to run on pace is important to successful performance in the middle-distance race. This statement has many implications,

TABLE 7.1. TYPICAL EVEN-PACE SCHEDULE FOR THE 440- AND 880-YARD RUNS
(Minutes and Seconds)

110	220	330	440	660	880
20 s	40 s	60 s	1.20	2:00	2.40
19.75	39.5	59.25	1.19	1:58.5	2.38
19.5	39	58.5	1.18	1:57	2.36
19.25	38.5	57.75	1.17	1:55.5	2.34
19	38	57	1.16	1:54	2.32
18.75	37.5	56.25	1.15	1:52.5	2.30
18.5	37	55.5	1.14	1:51	2.28
18.25	36.5	54.75	1.13	1:49.5	2.26
18	36	54.	1.12	1:48	2.24
17.75	35.5	53.25	1.11	1:46.5	2.22
17.5	35.	52.5	1.10	1:45	2.20
17.25	34.5	51.75	1.09	1:43.5	2.18
17	34	51	1.08	1:42	2.16
16.75	33.5	50.25	1.07	1:40.5	2.14
16.5	33	49.5	1.06	1:39	2.12
16.25	32.5	48.75	1.05	1:37.5	2.10
16	32	48	1.04	1.36	2.08
15.75	31.5	47.25	1.03	1:34.5	2.06
15.5	31	46.5	1.02	1:33	2.04
15.25	30.5	45.75	1.01	1:31.5	2.02
15	30	45	60	1:30	2.00

This table should be read as follows: A performer attempting to run 880 yards in 2 minutes 40 seconds, with an even distribution of effort throughout the race, would cover 110 yards in 20 seconds, 220 yards in 40 seconds, 330 yards in 60 seconds, 440 yards in 1 minute 20 seconds, and 660 yards in 2 minutes even. A race run in this manner would be referred to as an even-pace race. By repeated practice runs over fixed segments of a given race, a performer develops a sense of pace and is better able to utilize his energies efficiently during competition.

though perhaps none is more meaningful than the fact that a change of pace or speed is in effect a change in the nature of a given skill. Running at one rate of speed is different than running at a faster or slower pace, both with respect to learning and in all-out performance.

Pace judgment stems from practice at a specific tempo over distances of varying lengths. A girl learns to judge her pace by repeated running against a watch. When she has attained a sufficiently high level of strength and endurance to work without undue stress to her mind and body, she should give careful attention to the development of her pace.

The first step in pace training is the establishment of a theoretically best, though realistic, time for the distance which a girl expects to run. She can get some idea of this goal by keeping an accurate record of several practice runs during early season. If, for instance, she averaged 2 minutes 40 seconds for the 880, it might be logical that she could run this distance in 2.30 with continued practice. An even-pace schedule for this theoretical time thus would be 75 seconds for the 440, 37.5 seconds for the 220, and 18.75 seconds for the 110. (See Table 7.1, p. 92.)

A training schedule for the middle-distance runner should always include some pace judgment work. The distances run may vary to avoid boredom, but pace should receive constant attention during the entire running season.

The Development of Endurance

According to Doherty, endurance is a word; it is not an entity or a thing.[1] It is, together with speed, strength, skill, and the like, a modifiable condition, the effects of which are noted in the muscles, the heart, the lungs, the nerves, the mind, and all else that is part of man, giving rise to improved human performance. The consequences of improved endurance are both general and specific. Since man is totally integrated, every activity has some effect on his total being. In like manner, that which affects all of him tends to affect most that part of him which works hardest to overcome an imposed resistance. What this means to the middle-distance runner, or to any track and field participant for that matter, is that all kinds of activity have an effect on the body, and some kinds of activity have a more profound effect on some parts of the body than on others. This is to say that

---

1. Kenneth J. Doherty, "The Nature of Endurance Running," *Journal of Health, Physical Education and Recreation* 35, no. 4 (April, 1964), p. 29.

training must include activities which are both general and specific if an individual is to adapt most effectively to the increased demands of intense competition.

Endurance training is a long-term process. The performance records of highly successful middle-distance runners indicate that they trained for several years before reaching their maturity as athletes. Indeed, the average age of the successful middle-distance runner is considerably higher than that of successful sprinters and jumpers.

Espenschade has stated that it takes a minimum of two years of practice to develop acceptable endurance levels for intense track participation.[2] Other track and field authorities would concur, adding that even two years is not long enough unless an individual is willing to discipline her life rather severely. Even these statements are inadequate and misleading, for they deal only with time, disregarding the more important content of the training program.

Modern concepts of endurance training look to the future. A training program is designed to produce high levels of endurance by carefully guided, progressive overloading over long periods of time. Such a program seeks small but continuous adaptations to ever-increasing overload demands. The Swedish system of Fartlek, or speed play, is an excellent example of such a program as it attempts to develop endurance through weeks and months of increasingly larger bouts of running activity. The Fartlek system puts the runner in the woods or on the seashore where she becomes interested in the objects of nature and pushes on oblivious of fatigue. She thus runs and runs and runs, ever-adapting and running farther and farther and farther. Running alone is not enough, however, for a runner adjusts to certain conditions of speed and duration. To be most effective she must, on occasion, practice her skill at as near performance level as possible. She thus combines speed play with periods of interval training, a program which includes carefully determined bouts of running, jogging, and resting in a given unit of time.

The interval system assumes that overload can be attained by controlling the factors of speed, distance, and time. For example, a girl training for the 880 may run that distance three times during an afternoon at less than pace. She may run the 660 three times during an afternoon faster than her pace for an 880, or she may run many shorter races at her 880 pace. Each session is different, though the purpose

2. Anna S. Espenschade, "Women and Competitive Sport," *Proceeding of National Institute on Girls' Sports*, University of Oklahoma, Norman, Oklahoma (November 4-9, 1963), pp. 19-22.

is the same: to push the barriers of mind and body farther and farther toward human limitation.

Example of Interval Training for 880-Yard Run with a Best Time of Two Minutes, Thirty Seconds

1. Run three 880s at two minutes forty seconds with ten minutes' rest between each race.
2. Run three 660s at one minute fifty-six seconds with ten minutes' rest between each race.
3. Run three 440s at one minute twenty seconds with five minutes' rest between each race.
4. Run eight 220s at forty seconds with three minutes' rest between each race.

Note that the first two examples involve overloading by running over pace, whereas the third and fourth examples involve overloading at pace. The factors of distance and time produce the overload effect. The continued use of overload involves an increase in the number of races run, a shortening of the rest period, an increase in distance run, greater speed per unit of activity, or a combination of these. The objective, of course, is to impose greater demands upon the body during any given unit of time.

Since the discussion has thus far been oriented toward the development of a specific kind of endurance, namely, the ability to persist at running, it might be well to mention other types of developmental activities. These would be used for general conditioning and probably would be included as part of the off-season training schedule for the middle-distance runner. Note that each of the activities mentioned involves large muscle groups, and participation in them produces a rather rapid rise in the cardiorespiratory rate.

1. Continuous bouncing on a trampoline.
2. Rapid running in place.
3. Calisthenic exercises involving rapid movement of the arms and legs, especially the jumping jack and inverted bicycling.
4. Badminton, doubles play in volleyball, field hockey, speed ball, and other running-striking games.
5. Rope-skipping.
6. Swimming, water polo, and other vigorous water sports.
7. Walking. A serious track and field athlete will forget that she has access to an automobile. She will walk whenever and wherever she

can, moving briskly on the flat, pushing up hills, and welcoming stairs.

PERFORMANCE TIPS
FOR THE MIDDLE-DISTANCE RUNNER

1. Speed, endurance, and pace judgment are the essential elements of middle-distance running. The wise teacher will stress each of these components in the training of her girls.
2. Middle-distance running form is generally more vertical and less vigorous than the form used by the sprinter. The girl in these events runs with a long, relaxed stride, using a toe, foot, toe action to catch, balance, and transfer her weight from stride to stride.
3. The girl who plans to win should work for good position from the start, set her pace so as to distribute her energies evenly throughout the race, and keep within striking distance of her best competition. Moreover, she must be alert at all times, recognizing that she can make only one serious bid for victory and that this should be made when it can be carried through to the finish line.
4. The sprinter type can lay back and beat her opponent in a final dash for the tape, whereas the girl without a kick must be far enough ahead to outlast her opponents in the final bid for victory. On the other hand, the 440 and 880 should be considered even-pace races with the participants running as fast as they can all the way. The 440 definitely should involve maximum acceleration-minimum deceleration with the runner slowing down very gradually throughout her race. In the longer 880 the same principle applies, though most races reveal a time differential of two to four seconds between the two halves of the race, the second half generally being the slower of the two.
5. Training for the middle distances is hard, and frequently lonesome, work. A teacher, therefore, should develop a varied and exciting schedule, matching her girls in competition so they have a chance to win. Excitement and winning usually are satisfactory balm for fatigue.
6. The third quarter of a middle-distance race usually is the hardest part of a race. A wise runner will buffer her psychological letdown by pushing hard during this phase of the race.
7. The middle-distance runner should recognize that the energy cost for increasing her pace is far greater than that which is essential for maintaining her pace. She should keep up with her best competition and plan to make one strong move for victory. This move

should preferably be made when she comes off the final curve into the straightaway (she never passes on a curve if she can possibly avoid doing so).

8. Since the purpose of running is winning, a girl should be mentally and physically prepared to forget her pace, her plans, and her form if she must come on to win in the stretch. The best adage when behind at the end of a race is "any port in a storm"—do what you must to win.

TEACHING BEGINNERS TO RUN THE MIDDLE-DISTANCE RACES

Perhaps the most important responsibilities the teacher has to the girl who chooses to enter middle-distance competition are these: to keep her encouraged, to bring her along slowly, and to help her to learn pace judgment. It has been the writers' experience that girls respond to the challenge of running distances if they can run in pairs or even groups of like-minded individuals. Perhaps a park or a golf course is the best place to get them started. They are given some hints about running form and then left alone to run on the grass in their regular tennis shoes. Distance or time is no concern at the outset, though the teacher encourages the beginner to push a bit farther each day. Excessive soreness should be avoided at all cost.

When a girl begins to loosen up and develop a rhythm of her own, she is ready for some simple speed work. This should be added to the schedule at the discretion of the runner. The idea is to jog along, singing, laughing, having fun, and then suddenly to dash forward as if chasing a sunbeam. The whole atmosphere of the training session is carefree and joyous, with sporadic bouts of sprinting, bounding, walking, chasing, and fleeing. As the girl improves her form and condition, these sprinting bouts can become more frequent and longer, though there seldom need be any great sense of urgency about the workout.

The development of pace judgment should be the next objective. This must be done on the track and should follow several weeks of pre-track conditioning on the grass. The first pace race may well be over a distance of 220 yards. The teacher has each girl run the distance at about three-quarter speed and estimate her time after she finishes the race. She repeats this process until she can predict her time within an error margin of plus or minus two seconds. She then extends her pace-runs to 330 yards, repeats the process, and finally moves up to the 440-yard run.

Figure 7.2. There is little body lean in the middle-distance running style. The head is erect, eyes at shoulder level. The lead leg reaches comfortably forward, downward, and rearward. The foot of the recovery leg is elevated above the horizontal to shorten the extremity. This action makes possible a fast recovery of the swinging leg with a minimum of energy expenditure.

Racing strategy can be developed only through competition. Girls who want to run the middle distances should be permitted to do so when they have conditioned themselves properly and when they are participating against girls of comparable ability. Times are relative; a closely contested half mile at three minutes is as exciting to many people as a race which is run in near record time. The conditions of the race, the problems of strategy, the excitement, and the element of suspense are about the same, and a girl can learn what she needs to know about running under these conditions nearly as quickly as she can in a national-caliber meet. The main thing is to run, to run often, and to run with the intent to learn.

RACING TACTICS FOR MIDDLE-DISTANCE RACES

It is a well-accepted principle among track authorities that a middle-distance race should be run as near to even pace as possible. The runner therefore attempts to set her pace early in the race and ignores her competition. If she is good enough, has planned well, and can distribute her energies as she chooses, she should run to a victory. If these ideal conditions do not exist, as is frequently the situation, a girl may be forced to change her tactics and run just to beat her competition.

Since some races are started in lanes and others from scratch, it is difficult to cover all of the tactical situations which may arise in an 880-yard run. A middle-distance runner should remember, however, that if she is going to win, or place among the winners, she must keep up with her best competition. She should start briskly and work for good position early in the race, settling down to a pace that keeps her in contention at all times. To compensate for the psychologically difficult third quarter of her race, a girl should pick up her pace as she passes the midpoint. Failure to push through this hard place may result in the loss of a yard or two which cannot be regained against an equally talented opponent.

When it is possible, a middle-distance runner should know her opposition. She should be aware of their strengths and weaknesses, having a fairly good idea of how each might best be beaten. The girl who has a strong kick may well win by keeping up throughout the race and then making a quick bid for victory as she moves off the turn and into the final straightaway. The runner who does not have a strong kick must rely on her superior pace and her ability to move far enough ahead to hold her competition off in the dash for the finish. In either situation, the wise runner follows her own stride pattern rather than falling into the pattern of her opponent.

While it is impossible to determine what percentage of the middle-distance runners' success can be attributed to the power of positive thinking, experience seems to show that most real victories are won in the mind before they are won by the body. Thus what a runner thinks about her ability and the ability of her opponents is extremely important. To have beaten an opponent in a previous race is usually a psychological advantage for the winner. The wise teacher is conscious of this fact and does not mismatch her girls. When they have a chance to make a favorable showing, she lets them run, but when they are likely to suffer little but discouragement and self-defeat, she keeps them out of the race. A good time or a smashing victory is a great incentive to the middle-distance runner. When she is badly beaten or performs poorly, the practice miles are longer and the discomfort more intense.

TYPICAL TRAINING SCHEDULE
FOR THE BEGINNING MIDDLE-DISTANCE RUNNER

All runners would precede their formal training session with a period of relaxed jogging. This is a time for becoming mentally ready for the work to follow as well as a time for loosening stiff and tired muscles. Middle-distance runners should perform stretching and strengthening exercises along with their teammates. This is particularly important for those girls whose arms and shoulders become tired and tight near the end of their race.

The following schedule would be appropriate for the beginning club runner as well as for the serious performer in a physical education class.

M. Overdistance work through a park, a golf course, on a beach, beside a lake—anywhere that will permit the beginner to forget herself and to run for fun. Time should be the major consideration at the outset, not distance. The beginner should try to run for three minutes, then four, then five, and so on, until she can run ten or fifteen minutes without stopping.

T. Run several buildups.
Run five 220s in 35 seconds each with five minutes of rest in between.
Train down with several relaxed sprints.

W. 110 fast stride with 220 walk recovery.
220—35 seconds with 440 walk recovery.
330—55-60 seconds with 660 walk recovery.
440—80 seconds with two laps of walking for recovery.
220—35 seconds with 440 walk recovery. Finish with fast stride 110 yards.

Th. 3 x 440—75 to 80 seconds with ten minutes of walking between each.
Finish with several sprint pickups—50 to 60 yards.

F. Stride 1,320 yards for form (no time to be kept).
Finish with ten minutes of easy shuffling on grass.

S. Thirty minutes of fun running away from the track.

TYPICAL TRAINING SCHEDULE
FOR THE EXPERIENCED MIDDLE-DISTANCE RUNNER

Begin each session by jogging one to two miles, to be followed by ten to fifteen minutes of stretching and strengthening exercises.

Early Season

It is strongly urged that all persons preparing for the middle-distance event train twice daily. The following schedule is predicated on the assumption that the performer is running from two to four miles each morning.

M. 3 x 440 at pace with two laps of recovery jogging between each. Easy stride 660 yards, followed by ten minutes of shuffling. Finish with ten 75-yard sprint pickups.

T. 2 x 1,320 for form (no time to be kept) with ten minutes of shuffling between each.

W. 2 x 660 at race pace with one mile of easy jogging between each. Ten minutes of easy shuffling.
    5 x 220 fast striding with one lap of recovery jogging between each.

Th. 5 x 330 at 1 to 2 seconds faster than race pace with two laps of walking between each.
    Finish with ten minutes of jogging on the grass.

F. 110 fast stride with 220 shuffle.
    220 fast stride with 440 shuffle.
    440 at pace with 880 shuffle.
    440 at pace with 880 shuffle.
    220 fast stride with 440 shuffle.
    110 fast stride followed by ten minutes of shuffle on grass.

S. Fartlek—30 minutes.

Sun. Early morning run as usual with complete rest in the afternoon.

Competitive Season

The writers are strong believers that track and field athletes should train daily, including the day preceding competition. Therefore, during the spring season the Friday schedule will be somewhat lighter if there is a meet on Saturday, but there will not be a complete day of rest prior to competition until the important national and international meets held during the summer.

33482

M.   5 x 440 at pace with three laps of shuffle between each. Finish by sprinting out of ten turns.

T.   3 x 660 at pace with ten minutes of shuffling between each. Finish by shuffling ten minutes.

W.   110 fast stride with 220 shuffle recovery.

220 fast stride with 440 shuffle recovery.

330 at 1 to 2 seconds faster than pace with two laps of shuffle recovery.

440 at pace with four laps of shuffle recovery.

440 at pace with four laps of shuffle recovery.

330 at 1 to 2 seconds faster than pace with two laps of shuffle recovery.

110 fast stride—shuffle 220—110 fast stride to finish.

Th.   220 at pace—110 shuffle—110 fast stride—440 shuffle.

Repeat four to six times, as able, to contain the overload demand.

Finish with ten minutes of shuffle on the grass.

F.   660 at pace with two laps of shuffle recovery.

220 at 35 with 220 shuffle recovery.

220 at 33 with 220 shuffle recovery.

220 at 30 with ten minutes of shuffle recovery.

S.   Competition.

The reader is reminded that there is nothing necessarily sacred about work. At the present time, too many coaches like to boast about the quantity of work that they have imposed on their runners. This business of coaching is precise. One only asks what one knows the performer can produce—with some pain, yet with a sense of containment. For this reason, careful records must be obtained and scrutinized in order to impose overload demands which are realistic and yet intense enough to keep the athlete constantly working at, or near to, the edge of her capacity.

Chapter 8

Distance Running

In recent years distance running has become extremely popular with girls and women. This new interest stems in part from the fact that runners are finding that they can withstand vigorous training without damaging their bodies or losing their feminine charm. Such a change in attitude should lead to significant improvement in the existing records for the 1,500-meter and mile runs.

Russia seems to have been the first country to emphasize distance running for women, with Valentina Postnikova setting a world record of 5:56.8 for 1,500 meters in 1922. By 1936, women in several countries were running long distances. Diane Lather, of England, was first to run the mile under five minutes. Her best time of 4:45.0 stood as a world record for many years.

In 1962, Marie Stephen, of New Zealand, lowered the 1,500-meter record to 4:19.0. Ann Smith, an English girl, broke this record with the excellent time of 4:17.3 during the summer of 1967. Several weeks later, running virtually alone on a cold October day in Sittard, Holland, Maria Gommers set the current record of 4:15.6.

The first 1,500-meter race contested at a national meet in the United States was won by Sacramento schoolgirl Marie Mulder in the good time of 4:36.5. This record stood for one year, with Doris Brown setting the current U.S. mark of 4:20.2 at Frederick, Maryland, in 1966. The following spring, competing in the Canadian National Indoor meet at Vancouver, British Columbia, Mrs. Brown set a world record for the mile run in the time of 4:40.4.

Since the enthusiasm among girls and women for distance running is such a marked change from the mood which prevailed in the United States prior to the 1960s, very little has been said or written about the subject. This chapter is therefore an attempt to present information which is pertinent to a clearer understanding of the conditions that motivate the female to run, as well as information concerning the factors which should contribute to her success in the distance events. In preparing this chapter, the writers have drawn heavily upon ideas expressed by selected authorities on distance running for men as well as upon more than two decades of personal experience working with outstanding female performers.

WHY DO WOMEN RUN LONG DISTANCES?

Perhaps more than any other group of athletes, distance runners are unique. There is a kinship among them unknown to those who have never committed themselves to an intense, almost intolerable, burden of work. One was particularly conscious of this kinship during the banquet following the international cross-country race at Barry, Wales. For the first time in its long history, the international body had invited women's teams to compete, and on this occasion an American girl had won. When she received her award from the Mayor of Barry, runners from around the world, male and female alike, gave her a moving ovation. This was not an ordinary thing but the recognition of a champion by fellow runners who personally shared the pain which she had tolerated to become the greatest of them all.

This experience tended to crystallize the idea that there is a certain "mystique" about distance running. This is an activity for which words become extremely inadequate. It involves the total experience of commanding one's body, of sensing a oneness with the beauty and form of nature, of being a part of the eternal rhythm of the universe. Perhaps more than anything, the distance runner desires to be free, running across an open field, through a scented wood, or beside the crashing sea. For some deeply satisfying reason, these are persons who thoroughly enjoy just running.

When writing about his first sub-four-minute mile, Bannister commented frequently about running and nature. As a college athlete he found it necessary on occasion to leave the track, to run for the sheer joy of running alone, without purpose or plan, across hill and dune "into the sun." "There are many reasons for running," he said, "but no explanation is satisfying that does not take account of feelings; of beauty and power."[1]

Most women who run long distances seem to do so with deep feeling. They are sensitive to beauty, to the colorful leaves of fall, the crunch of fresh fallen snow in winter months, and the buds and blossoms of spring. It is this joy, this sensitivity to wind songs through the trees, the beauty of brooks and flowers, the flowing pattern of moving feet, which quickens their desire to run on and on and on.

PHYSICAL CHARACTERISTICS OF THE SUCCESSFUL DISTANCE RUNNER

While success in the distance events probably stems less from physical than from psychological factors, there is evidence that body form has some relationship to performance. Writing in the *United States Track Coaches Quarterly Review*, December 1966, Carter and Sucec reported that long-distance runners tend to manifest a rather specific muscle-fat relationship, that is, the major difference between college and Olympic distance runners is that the Olympic performers are less endomorphic.

One facet of the preparation and training of the United States women's team for the 1968 Olympic Games was an appraisal of each performer's radioactivity as measured in the medical laboratory at Los Alamos, New Mexico. Though essentially concerned with other factors, the "Human Body Counter" provided data about each performer's muscle-fat relationship. These data tend to support the findings reported by Carter and Sucec by revealing that the top American female distance runners manifest a high degree of ectomorphy. By subjective appraisal, they were all feminine in appearance, though definitive measures showed that their ratio of muscle per kilogram of body weight was higher than most men of their size.

There seems to be little doubt that girls and women of different sizes can excel in distance running. To be highly successful, however, the performer must train in such a manner that her muscle mass predominates over the subcutaneous body fat. This does not mean that a woman must change her essentially female body form. It merely means that the serious performer has run enough to burn off all unnecessary fat.

1. Roger Bannister, *The Four Minute Mile* (New York: Dodd-Mead & Co., 1957), p. 57.

PSYCHOEMOTIONAL CHARACTERISTICS
OF THE SUCCESSFUL DISTANCE RUNNER

Dedication

Almost anyone who so desires can succeed at distance running. While sprinters definitely are granted some special gift by nature, as perhaps are jumpers and throwers as well, distance runners can attribute their success to dedication and hard work. Because words convey different meanings to different people, the following incident is related for the purpose of defining dedication as an essential characteristic of distance running success.

From the bustle of life to a place called Merthyr Mahr on the rugged coast of Wales come men and women to prepare themselves mentally, physically, or spiritually for some great task which they have to perform. The site is an old farm with its fields close to the sea, cut across by a cold river which tumbles down from the fog-shrouded hills nearby. The central building is a barn that has been improved to house those who come to this place to rest, to train, to think.

Some years ago at Merthyr Mahr, a lone man was seen running along the seashore, through the fields, across the river. On and on he went, pushing himself until the pain was obvious, and it seemed as if he could scarcely take another step. This was a fascinating manifestation of commitment, continuing for more than an hour. When the young man had finished running and was recovering from his ordeal, he was asked why he punished himself as he did.

"For ten years," he answered, "I have been training this way. It is my way of life to arise at 6:00 A.M. each morning and run through the streets of my town; to change, eat, work, and repeat this routine again in the afternoon. Then on weekends I come here where I can dedicate myself fully to my training."

"Ten years!" was the reply. "How do you justify this use of time, this very narrow and austere life?"

"That is easy," he answered, "for during each of those ten years I have improved, and so long as I improve I shall continue to use my time this way."

This is dedication, extreme perhaps, and yet this is what it takes to be truly great in the distance running events—a kind of dedication that is able to look ahead, to bridge the gap between the present and the future, between desire and fulfillment.

The wise coach recognizes that few persons possess the kind of dedication necessary for great success. She also knows that though speed potential may be limited, one's capacity for commitment likely is not. Thus she nurtures each spark of dedication, building on the initial spark until she has helped to strengthen the will of her runners as well as their muscles. She does this in many ways, one of which is setting and resetting meaningful goals while patiently working toward their realization.

Tolerance for Pain

Long-distance running is both pleasurable and painful. Perhaps the acquisition of anything worth having carries with it a burden of pain. It is this burden which quickly erodes the initial commitment of many a wishful seeker. The great distance runner, on the other hand, welcomes pain, knowing that this is an essential adjunct to success.

Women have a remarkable capacity to bear pain. This is particularly true when they have come to know the significance of the pain which they are asked to bear. The wise coach thus teaches the runners that the barriers of mind and body are a great distance apart and that aching lungs, leaden feet, and fatigue-taxed brain are really the rewards of a special kind of human endeavor.

While it is a mistake to seek pain just for the sake of pain itself, and some coaches are making that mistake these days, every runner of any consequence has known pain. Indeed though it is probable that all of the performers in a well-run long-distance race have known some pain, the pain which the winner experienced was greater than that experienced by others in the race.

Need to Succeed

Almost every person who attains a significant achievement seems to be motivated in part by a need to succeed. In athletics this often is called the "burn," or the "inner urge," which drives individuals toward personal fulfillment. The discerning coach looks for this characteristic in her candidates for the distance races, recognizing that herein lies a potent source for the "steam which drives the human machine."

Sensitivity to the Beauty and Freedom of Nature

Most persons who run long distances experience great satisfaction in striding freely over hill and dale. How often one can see the female performer run joyfully off to some obscure place to see the autumn leaves or discover the first wild flower of spring. The miles slip unnoticed beneath her feet. She returns tired, perspiration soaking her sweat suit, and yet delighted with what she has done, what she has seen.

One lady runner, known to the writers, lives in the woods where her husband has painstakingly built for her a sawdust track on which to train. She knows every foot of her track, the form and shape of every tree and vine. The moods of the seasons are hers to enjoy. It is her sensitivity to beauty, her awareness to buds and blossoms, the wind songs in the trees which give her daily strength to run.

Acceptance of Solitude

Early one morning following an international track and field meet some years ago, a lone figure was observed running along an empty city street. A closer look revealed that this was no ordinary runner, but rather it was Jim Ryun, world record holder in the mile, who less than twelve hours earlier had run the fastest 1,500-meter race of all time. Ryun, like the marathon runners who were seen jogging along a narrow mountain trail above Mexico City after the 1968 Olympic Games, had learned to accept solitude. Every serious distance runner is willing to run the long, lonely, extra mile. Few runners have become champions without doing so; all learn early that this is a price which they must pay.

Doris Brown is a housewife, a teacher, and a runner. To fulfill all of her obligations, she arises daily at 5:00 A.M., prepares breakfast for her husband, and then runs several miles through a park near her home. Most days from October to May are wet, and it is still dark when she runs; the solitude is very great.

Many promising runners never realize their potential because they are unable to accept solitude. They enjoy the races, the fun of being on a team, but they cannot bear to be alone.

COMPETITIVE CHARACTERISTICS
OF THE SUCCESSFUL DISTANCE RUNNER

Perhaps it is presumptuous to establish any kind of hierarchy with respect to the importance of those characteristics which seem to identify the highly competitive distance runner. On the other hand, experience leads one to believe that when all such characteristics are considered, the one which is most important is "desire"—or the will to win.

The Will to Win

Every true victory is first an act of the will, and then an act of the body. In every race of consequence there comes that instant when the pain of flesh is greater than one believes it possible to bear. This is the time of ultimate decision when leaden legs and aching lungs and fatigue-dulled brain cry out for relief. This is the time when the lesser fail; when the champion fights against the agonizing hurt. This is the time when a great runner moves by the instinctive drive to survive—by the impelling power of the human will.

Persons who would run long distances competitively must face this time of truth. To avoid it in practice, or during the race, is to ask too little of oneself. To accept it without struggle is to condition oneself for defeat. To face it is to agonize—again and again and again. Very probably every runner in a difficult race struggles with her will, yet the winner struggles most, pays the greatest price of pain for her victory.

Though individuals differ markedly in their capacity to act on the strength of their will, experience seems to indicate that "will power," like muscle power, can be improved. In some subtle way the will to win is intimately related to one's purpose for running. Though this is a very personal thing—this purpose for running—it is aptly described by Nietzsche's thought that "he who has a why can bear almost any how." In like manner, girls who run for reasons which are deeply important to them are willing to hurt, to thrust back the barrier of pain, to succeed by the sheer force of their will.

Ability to Relax

Almost without exception, distance runners are characterized by their ability to relax. Their gait is pleasing and graceful as they seem to just flow around the track. For the most part, relaxation is a gift of nature; yet like other dimensions of human performance, this factor too can be improved.

Experience seems to show that confidence and relaxation are closely related. Thus a performer running at a pace which she can "handle" or against opponents with whom she feels she can adequately compete tends to be relaxed. A quickened pace, however, or the imminent fear of defeat may well cause the performer to become mentally and physically tight. Once this has happened, it weighs on the person's mind, and the vicious process of thinking-becoming causes it to happen again and again and again.

Wise coaches nurture their runners like a tender plant. They apply gentle pressure. Seldom, if ever, do they yell. They enter young runners only in those races where they have some reasonable chance of success. Nervous runners are reassured by the confident smile of the coach. No athlete is permitted to dwell on failure; rather, all are encouraged to think positively about their training, their ability, and the strategy of each race.

Other ways of helping a runner relax during competition include training at different speeds and actually "rehearsing" segments of a given race. An example of the latter would be to practice passing and being passed, preferably off the final turn where tension from this tactic most frequently occurs. Lowering and shaking the arms during the course of a race also tends to keep the performer loose.

Wise Use of Racing Tactics

To some the distance race may appear to be the monotonous circling of a quarter-mile track. To the perceptive person, however, distance running is sheer drama, the supreme tactical struggle between individuals of iron will and superbly conditioned bodies. Indeed, the winner of any race beyond 220 yards often is the person utilizing the soundest tactical procedures.

In general, there are two different approaches to the distance race. These are often identified by the terms *front running* and *kicking*.

Front running is a procedure utilized by the performer who likes to lead or who has great endurance though only nominal speed. This runner seeks to set a fast pace early in the race, take the kick out of her adversaries, and win by her superior strength. While this strategy works if the opposition are forced to run faster than they should, it more often ends in defeat. Front running, therefore, is a tactic to be used with caution—perhaps when one is attempting to set a record or when convinced that this is a gamble which must be taken to win.

Most distance runners prefer to be followers. Psychologically, it is less difficult to follow than to carry the burden of the pace. It also is an advantage to know what one's opponents are doing. The wise performer thus maintains contact with the leader, kicking for the finish at the instant of her own choosing. The very act of passing is often sufficiently traumatic to insure victory.

Serious runners also should have some general plan for each new race. Such a plan takes into consideration the strengths and weak-

Figure 8.1. Doris Brown setting the pace during the 1969 meeting between the United States, Russia, and the British Commonwealth. Note the relaxed running style of these world-class performers. (Photo courtesy of Jeff Johnson. Reprinted by permission of **Women's Track and Field World**.)

nesses of each opponent, the tactics which they normally employ, the purpose for running this particular race, and so on. One value of such a plan is that it gives the runner confidence in her preparation; another is that it occupies her mind when fatigue might well take command. Like a well-trained soldier going into battle, the successful distance runner leaves little or nothing to the whim of chance.

Following is an extended discussion of a race plan which contributed to the "making" of a world champion and the setting of a world record for the indoor mile.

On Saturday night, February 19, 1966, Roberta Pico, of Canada, was the odds-on favorite to win the Achilles International indoor mile run at the Agradom stadium in Vancouver, British Columbia. Miss Pico had had an excellent season, and following a tremendous three-quarter-mile time trial the previous week, her coach openly predicted that she should set a new world record in the Achilles meet.

TABLE 8.1.   RACE PLAN FOR ACHILLES INDOOR MILE
February 19, 1966

Race Plan (Elapsed Time)	Actual Elapsed Time	Actual Lap Time	Leading Runner
27	24	24	Pico
54	49	25	Pico
1:21	1:15	26	Pico
1:48	1:45	30	Pico
2:15	2:13	28	Pico
2:42	2:43	30	Pico
3:09	3:10	27	Pico
3:36	3:35	25	Pico
4:03	4:00	25	Pico
4:30	4:25	25	Brown
4:55	4:52	27	Brown

Doris Brown, of Seattle, also had had a fine season, though due to the limited publicity afforded to women by the local press, her efforts had gone virtually unnoticed. The situation was therefore perfect for an upset—a prerace favorite convinced that she would be running without serious competition; a challenger with great, though unknown, ability and a burning desire to win.

Since Pico was after a record, it was anticipated that she would choose to lead. The strategy was to follow, with Doris pushing, but not passing, while setting the pace from behind. It was assumed that Pico would be pleased to have someone with her, though too proud to let her pass, and this assumption proved to be correct.

At the gun, Pico sprinted into the lead with Brown running easily off her right shoulder. One lap, two, then three, and as predicted, it had become a "one-woman race." "Oh, the little lady with glasses [as commentator Ron Delaney put it] is running very courageously, but it is just a matter of time until she too will be badly outclassed!"

The race plan called for an even pace, faster than world record time, with Pico carrying the total burden of the lead. If it worked, Brown was to move quickly to the front at the end of lap ten, surprising Pico and forcing her to finish by running outside around the final two turns.

Table 8.1 (above) shows that this strategy worked even better than anticipated. By lap nine Pico had so "extended" herself that she began to falter, and Brown sprinted into the lead. She won the race by more than fifty yards and set a new world indoor mile record of four minutes and fifty-two seconds.

Judgment of Pace

Current physiological evidence indicates that the most efficient means of expending energy under anaerobic conditions is at a steady, or even, pace. Thus during a race of 880 yards or longer, the performer attempts to cover each segment of the race in a nearly similar time. Pace segments in the quarter mile (440 yards) are usually selected for this appraisal.

Careful study of the time sequence posted by runners in dozens of races at 880 yards or longer revealed to the writers that the first half of these races usually was run faster than the second half. In the 880 or 800 meters run in world-class time (2:06 or better), the differential between the first half and the second half usually was from one to three seconds. Three noteworthy races of the 1968 track season which substantiate this point of view are noted below:

National A.A.U. Outdoor Championship meet, 1st—Brown   62.5-62.5 (2.05:0)
United States Olympic Trials,   1st—Manning 60.0-63.0 (2.03:0)
Olympic 800-meter final,   1st—Manning 59.6-61.3 (2.00:9)

It is interesting that Nikolic's world record performance of July, 1968, also was run at a remarkably even pace, 60.5-60.0 (2.00:5), though in that instance the second half of the race was faster than the first.

Most authorities agree that even-pace running becomes increasingly more important with the length of a race. Thus to be successful in the mile or 1,500 meters, an individual must develop a very keen judgment of pace. While most women have not had sufficient experience at these distances to have developed a sense of pace comparable to topflight men, it is significant that Brown achieved near-even pace in both her world record outdoor 1,500-meter race of July, 1966, and her world record indoor mile of February, 1967. Split times for these races were as follows:

1,500 Meters 68.5-71.0-70.0 (4.20:2)
Mile   67-70-74-69.4 (4.40:4)

More recently (July, 1969), competing in a three-way meet between the United States, Russia, and the British Commonwealth, Doris Brown ran 1,500 meters in 4:16.8. Split times for this race were 67-71.3-71.5 and a final 320 yards at approximately 68-second quarter-mile pace

(1,500 meters are 120 yards short of a mile). This was obviously a remarkably even-paced race. Based on the evidence now available, it appears that women should attempt to run the first half of the mile race some two to five seconds faster than the second half.

Pace judgment can be developed in several ways. Coaches should understand and utilize those ways which are applicable to their system of training, making certain that each of their runners accrues a keen sense of pace. (See section on Training Methods.) The wise coach also teaches her runners that there are times when it is necessary to change one's pace, for while pace judgment is important, *maintaining contact with one's strongest opponents is indispensable*—frequently the difference between winning and just running a well-paced race.

MECHANICS OF THE SUCCESSFUL DISTANCE RUNNER

For years the writers have contended that running is a lost art— lost both in the sense that so many persons run poorly and a great many others do not run at all. Actually, this need not be, for running is largely natural. Each individual who chooses to run should seek to apply certain basic principles, though these should not be rigidly applied to anyone.

Surely one could not have watched the Olympic Games without seeing that both the male and female distance runners varied markedly in their individual style; and yet the discerning viewer noted certain common characteristics as well. Successful distance runners tend to run in a nearly perpendicular position. They carry their hands above the waist and swing them easily from the side to the midline of the body. The stride of the successful runner is moderate; the heels are carried slightly above the knee rearward; the thigh is somewhat less than parallel to the ground forward. The full foot strikes the track with each step, driving the performer forward in a relaxed and rhythmic manner. The head is carried above the thorax, with the eyes gazing forward along the track.

Certainly coaches must be concerned with running mechanics and should attempt to correct such serious faults as overstriding, running on the toes, swinging the arms excessively, and the like. Yet in my mind primary coaching emphasis should be on the development of a style which is effective for a specific individual. This is time-consuming, but it is also rewarding in terms of ultimate success, whereas attempting to force all runners into some preconceived pattern can be intensely frustrating and frequently leads only to failure.

CHARACTERISTICS OF THE
SUCCESSFUL TRAINING PROGRAM

While it is probable that all coaches who work seriously at the development of distance runners utilize methods or techniques which are uniquely their own, the basic elements of the programs advocated by these coaches are essentially the same. These are elements from the systems of training known as Fartlek, interval running, and long-distance, or marathon, running.

Fartlek is a program developed by Gosta Holmer, formerly the chief Olympic coach of Sweden. This program grew out of the need to train runners in a geographic area where the summers were short and the winters long and severe. The word *Fartlek* thus describes a kind of "speed play" in which individuals run through the woods, along a sandy beach, or in the open fields, moving with a zest which reflects the freedom of the spirit and the beauty of nature. Running of this kind is not without direction, however, as individuals are urged to change their pace—sprinting, striding, walking—working-recovering, working-recovering, ever striving toward greater speed and endurance.

Interval running is a system of training developed by Dr. Woldemar Gerschler and his colleague, the eminent cardiologist Dr. Herbert Reindel. Perhaps the most popular of all systems, interval training involves repeated runs of fixed distance with the aim to raise the heart rate to 170 to 180 beats per minute. Actually, interval running utilizes five different variables to obtain the objectives being sought. These variables are as follows:

Distance of each effort (100 yards to a mile)
Number of repetitions of each effort (5 x 220, 10 x 110, etc.)
The pace, or time, in which each effort is completed
Length of the rest interval (walking, jogging, or resting)
The ease with which the total program is completed.

Interval running is without question the most precise of all training systems currently in vogue. By utilizing this method it is possible to keep accurate records and thus determine the progress of each athlete. On the other hand, interval training tends to produce boredom, making it necessary to vary the schedule so that each day's work is fresh and challenging.

Long-distance or marathon running is a program popularized by Arthur Lydiard. Here again the germ idea was related to a special kind of topography, as men were encouraged to run great distances beside the sea or over the rolling hills of New Zealand. Where Fartlek would change the pace, marathon running would continue at a fixed pace, covering from ten to twenty miles each day seven days of the week.

According to Mr. Lydiard, marathon running is the backbone of all training programs and constitutes the foundation upon which other systems can build for success.

Because these brief comments are overly simplified, the serious coach will want to study each program in depth, extracting those things which are pertinent to her particular situation. Be assured that this is the way all coaches learn—by reading, discussing, experimenting, adapting, and the like.

Because no two situations are exactly alike, each coach will have to make adaptations of her own. The important thing is to catch the whole picture—seeing each runner as an individual, knowing why each individual wants to run, setting goals for individuals which are realistic, understanding as much as possible about training techniques, and acting on this knowledge to develop a program which encompasses both the present and the future.

The general developmental program for distance runners competing for the Falcon Track Club is outlined below. Definitive information concerning each segment of the cyclic program follows:

September 1-December 1	Cross-Country Running
December 1-January 1	Active Rest
January 1-February 15	Circuit Training—modified
February 16-March 30	Fartlek and Repetition Running
April 1-May 31	Interval Training—endurance
June 1-August 31	Interval Training—speed

Cross-Country Training includes three basic elements—long-distance running, speed work, and hill work. All runners should be encouraged to train twice daily, with the first workout to be an overdistance run for fun. Usually this involves running for time rather than distance with from forty-five minutes to an hour as the goal.

The afternoon training session is more formal with specific areas or times or distances prescribed for each athlete. Once or twice a week the runners work on hills, alternately leading and catching up under "competitive" conditions. Since many cross-country races are won and lost on hills, a great deal of attention should be given to this phase of the race. Performers should be instructed to lean forward, shorten their stride, and "drive vigorously" up all hills.

During the cross-country season, Doris Brown frequently runs from 100 to 150 miles a week. Judy Oliver, age eighteen and youngest of our better distance runners, presently runs from forty to sixty miles each week without residual fatigue. Vicki Foltz, on the other hand, does more repeat work on her own one-quarter-mile track through the woods. While just doggedly running mile after mile is not the whole answer to success in distance running, this kind of dedicated activity certainly contributes to success.

Active Rest. During this portion of the season, distance runners should be encouraged to take a complete change of pace. While some choose to run "on their own," others play team games, swim, or participate in activities such as badminton. This phase of the program is aimed at providing psychic as well as physical rest from the daily demands of structured activity.

Modified Circuit Training. Assuming that strength is an essential adjunct to running, we have developed an indoor training circuit which includes gymnastic activities, extensive stretching, stair running, and the lifting of weights. This program is based on the writings of Morgan and Adamson who first explored circuit training at the University of Leeds in England. Following a pretest, an appropriate "overload" is established for each athlete, who then trains on her own. Subsequent testing is done each second week with modifications in the circuit occurring at that time. A final test is given to determine gains and provide an incentive for maximum effort during the training period.

Because biophysical changes are transient, runners should exercise the arm and shoulder girdle muscles throughout the entire year. Examples of the kinds of activities appropriate for this purpose are rope climbing, parallel bar dips, prone press with fixed weights, chinning the bar, and throwing the medicine ball.

Fartlek and Repetition Running. Because women have so little opportunity to run indoors, one ought assume that those meets which are available to them are primarily "practice" sessions. Thus formal training for the outdoor season actually begins during the middle of February. The first six-week period is committed to "speed play" and repetition running. Each runner is given a specific work load, though records are not obtained. This is a transitional period when the athlete is preparing herself for the precise work necessary to develop pace endurance, pace judgment, and speed.

During this period, the runner works at Fartlek on the flat, grassy areas, accelerating over distances from 50 to 150 yards and recovering at a jog; or she does repetition striding on the track, covering distances between 100 and 300 yards with walk-back periods of rest. In addition to the relaxed repetition training, each girl completes twice weekly an extended run of three to six miles.

Interval Running (endurance). Interval running aimed at the development of endurance usually involves the repetition of distances representing one-fourth to two-thirds of the length of the race for which the person is training. At the outset, the time for each effort approximates the expected pace at a later date (*i.e.*, the first "big race" of the season, the best anticipated time for the season, etc.). The work volume for each training session usually represents approximately two to three times the length of the race for which the performer is preparing herself. The exact components of interval work are very precise, however, and must be carefully determined for each runner. The following schedule prepared for Doris Brown is provided here to help clarify the rationale described above:

EARLY SEASON (APRIL-MAY)   PREPARATION FOR MILE RUN

DATE	WARM-UP	STRIDING	PACE	REPS	RECOVERY
M.	Long-grass run with periods of fast striding (minimum of six miles)				
T.	1-mile jog	220	34	4	Jog back
		Stride 880 easily			
		(Repeat four sets of four 220s with 880 between each set)			
		Shuffle ten minutes			
		Finish workout with ten 150s at three-quarter speed			
W.	1-mile jog	1320 run-through			
		110	sprint		220 shuffle
		220	34		440 shuffle
		440	68-70		880 shuffle
		880	2:20-24		880 shuffle
		1320	3:34-38		1-mile shuffle
		Repeat 220-110			
		Finish workout with ten minutes of shuffling			
Th.	1-mile jog	440	68-70	3	Walk 440
		Stride 880 easily			
		(Repeat two sets of three 440s)			
		Shuffle ten minutes			
		220	32	1	Shuffle back
		220	30	1	Shuffle back
		220	28	1	Shuffle back

F.   Thirty minutes of easy striding and stretching

S.   Competition

Sun.   Active rest. Swimming, hiking, etc.

    Interval Running (speed). When speed is emphasized, practice intervals are from one-eighth to one-half the length of the race for which the person is training. The time for each effort is faster than race pace. The total volume varies with the speed and the number of repetitions run. In the examples which follow, it should be noted that training efforts other than just repetition work are provided for the purpose of developing speed-endurance.

COMPETITIVE SEASON
(JUNE-AUGUST)   PREPARATION FOR MILE RUN

Date	Warm-Up	Striding	Pace	Reps	Recovery
M.	Jog through Rogers Park	220	30-31	4	Shuffle back
		Shuffle one lap			
		(Repeat five sets of four 220s with shuffle between each set)			
		Ten minutes of shuffle			
		330	48	1	440 shuffle
		330	46	1	440 shuffle
		330	44	1	
T.	1-mile jog	440	65-66	8	Walk 440 between each
		Speed drill for finish of race. Stride first 220 in 34.			
		Maintain pace through turn and then simulate sprint to the finish line.			
		Finish workout with ten minutes of shuffle on grass			
W.	1-mile jog	880	2:15	2	Five minutes of shuffle
		Ten minutes of shuffle			
		Finish workout with 10 by 75-yard sprints			
Th.	Five sand banks	440 run-through			
		110	Sprint	1	220 shuffle
		220	Fast stride	1	440 shuffle
		330	47-48	1	880 shuffle
		440	66-68	1	4-laps shuffle
		Repeat 330-220-110			
		Ten minutes of shuffle			
		Repeat 440 run-through			

F.   Fifteen minutes of easy striding and stretching

S.   Competition

Sun. Complete rest

The reader is reminded that the foregoing schedules were prepared for a highly skilled, well-conditioned athlete. Schedules are therefore relative to particular persons and imposed at particular times during the season. This is an important factor, since all training schedules, to be meaningful, must be prepared for individuals.

When working with any person who aspires to be a distance runner, it is essential that rather definitive information be accrued about the strength, speed, and endurance of that individual. This can be done following a preliminary period of "general conditioning." The runner is timed over distances of 100, 220, 440, or even 660 yards. By comparing these times with those obtained from other runners, or by knowledge gained through experience, the coach can then prepare a tentative training schedule for the person in question.

Following are times for 220 yards whereby one could make a preliminary judgment of an individual's race potential. A time of twenty-four to twenty-five seconds would indicate definite sprint potential; twenty-five to twenty-six seconds would indicate marginal sprint potential, or sufficient speed to succeed at the quarter mile; twenty-six to twenty-eight seconds would seem to indicate that the performer's "best race" would be the 880-yard run, whereas twenty-nine to thirty-two seconds, or slower, would indicate natural speed best adapted to the mile run.

When preparing the tentative training schedule, it is essential that the coach take into account the fact that the development of cardio-respiratory endurance is a long-term process. *The training schedule therefore should impose gradually increased overload demands.* By keeping careful records of each day's activity and by conducting an occasional time trial, progress can be measured and the training regime modified as deemed necessary.

Regardless of the ability level at which a coach is working, it is profoundly important that she remember at all times that her runners are human beings. Doherty reminds us of this fact again and again in his book *Modern Training for Running*. He advocates the "holistic" approach, taking into consideration the attitudes, hopes, feelings, and aspirations of runners, as well as their physical ability. When guided by this point of view, we approach our calling in as orderly and scientific a manner as possible, recognizing that there are times when we act on intuition as well. Like the pilots of the northern bush, there are days when we need to "fly by the seat of our pants"—days when we consider people more sacred than programs and modify our schedules accordingly.

While there is much more that could, and perhaps should, be said about distance running, the writers choose to close with this final thought to ponder. This thought has grown out of the deeply moving experience mentioned earlier concerning the lonely runner at Merthyr Mahr in Wales.

What is the ultimate value of running—of the tedious days, the tortuous hours of training? Winning? No, not winning, for all who run cannot win. Perhaps then it is some more important thing—some intrinsic thing, some uniquely personal, yet wholly ennobling, thing. Perhaps it is the *striving toward some worthy goal, the struggle to be better, the stretching forth of flesh and spirit and will* which is of greatest value.

Brian Mitchell, in his essay on character and running, expresses this idea rather clearly. He wrote:

If the athlete who is habitually last, intends to be first, that is all that matters. Some men will never be first actually and visibly; a one legged high-jumper will not get over seven feet. But that is to measure as the world does. If a man intends to be first, and knows absolutely the meaning of that word intends and does not just "say" that he is going to be first, or "wish" that he could be, then he will be like Ernest Hemingway's old man and the sea. That really is the psychology of the athlete. The rest is special detail and particular knowledge.[1]

TRAINING SCHEDULES FOR THE BEGINNING DISTANCE RUNNER

Early Season

This schedule assumes that several weeks of preliminary jogging have preceded any formal training on the track. One way to build a sound foundation is to have the beginner walk and jog through her own neighborhood until she can jog a distance of fifteen blocks. Another is to walk and jog for time until the performer can jog continuously for a period of ten minutes.

1. Brian Mitchell, "Character and Running," in Fred Wilt, *Run, Run, Run* (Los Altos, Calif.: Track and Field News, Inc., 1964), p. 253.

Day	Warm-Up	Distance	Pace	Reps	Rest Interval
M.	Jog four laps easily	440	80	4	Slow walk back

Jog easily for five minutes

Finish with several short sprints—with walk-back rest

(Each week add an additional 440 until a second set of four are being run following the five minutes of jogging recovery.)

T.	Jog four laps easily	220	37-38	4	Walk back

Jog easily for five minutes

		220	37-38	4	Walk back

Jog easily for five minutes

(Each week add an additional 220 until a third set of four are being run following the second five minutes of jogging recovery.)

W.	Jog four laps easily	880	2:40	2	Four laps of walking

Jog easily for five minutes

Finish by sprinting out of several turns

(Each week add one or two sprints. The fifth week of training add a third 880 after the second five-minute jog interval.)

Th.	Jog four laps easily	110	Sprint	1	Walk back to start of 220
		220	Fast stride	1	Walk 440
		330	60	1	Walk two laps
		440	80	1	Walk four laps
		330	60	1	Walk two laps
		220	Fast stride	1	Walk 440
		110	Sprint	1	Five-minute jog

(Each week repeat a longer segment, i.e., 110-220-330, etc., until running two 440s with four laps of walking between each.)

Finish by striding three-quarter mile on estimated race pace, without keeping time

F.	Jog four laps easily	110	Fast stride	10	Walk-back recovery

Jog easily for five minutes

		330	65	1	Walk two laps
		330	60	1	Five-minute jog

S.		Jog two to three miles			
Sun.		Fifteen minutes of Fartlek—or take a hike thirty minutes or more			

Competitive Season

Day	Warm-Up	Distance	Pace	Reps	Rest Interval
M.	Easy stride one mile	440	80	4	Jog back
		Jog easily for ten minutes			
		440	80	4	Jog back
		Jog easily for ten minutes			
		440	80	4	Jog back
		Finish workout with several short sprints			
T.	Easy stride one mile	220	35-36	4	Jog back
		Jog easily for five minutes			
		220	35-36	4	Jog back
		Jog easily for five minutes			
		220	35-36	4	Jog back
		Jog easily for five minutes			
W.	Easy stride one mile	880	2:40	3	Four laps of walking
		Jog easily for ten minutes			
		Finish workout with several short sprints			
Th.	Easy stride one mile	110	Sprint	1	Double-distance jog
		220	Fast stride	1	Double-distance jog
		330	56-58	1	Jog two laps
		440	80	1	Jog four laps
		440	80	1	Jog four laps
		330	56-58	1	Jog two laps
		220	Fast stride	1	Double-distance jog
		110	Sprint	1	
		Jog easily for five minutes to finish workout			
F.		Ten to fifteen minutes of easy striding and stretching in anticipation of competition on Saturday.			
S.		Competition			
Sun.		Thirty minutes of easy striding and stretching			

The writers advocate no rest the day prior to early season competition; one day of rest during mid-season competition; and when competing in a major meet, two days of rest is advocated. In the event that the runner trains twice daily (and every serious distance runner should), the morning turnout should involve overdistance work with a greater emphasis on speed-interval work in the afternoon.

Chapter 9

Cross-Country Running

Not to be confused with cross-country training (a type of over-distance work pursued by every serious distance runner), cross-country for girls and women is one of the most rapidly growing competitive activities in America. The first national championship in cross-country was held at Seattle, Washington, in 1965. Winner of this event was youthful Marie Mulder, competing for perennially strong Will's Spikettes of Sacramento, California. The 1966 national champion was Olympian Sandra Knott who had moved up to this longer race from her favorite event, the 880-yard run.

In 1967 Doris Brown of the Falcon Track Club won her first national cross-country championship. Following her U.S. victory, Doris won the international cross-country championship for women, beating

Figure 9.1. The beauty and freedom of cross-country running

the outstanding Lincoln twins of England over a rugged 2.5-mile course at Barry, Wales. The 1968 U.S. cross-country champion was Vicki Foltz, a teammate of Mrs. Brown. Running in Blackburn, England, the U.S. team of Brown, Foltz, Linda Mayfield, Lori Schutt, Cheryl Bridges, and Natalie Rocha won the international title, with Doris Brown winning the individual championship a second time.

Doris Brown again won the U.S. cross-country championship in 1969, with Falcon Track Club teammates Vicki Foltz and Judy Oliver placing second and sixth respectively. The U.S. team of Brown, Foltz, Oliver, Maria Stearns, Maureen Dickson, and Cheryl Bridges won the international championship at Clydebank, Scotland. Doris Brown established herself as the world's leading long-distance runner by winning the international championship a third straight year.

The cross-country season in the United States lasts from October to December. Races are contested at distances from three-quarters to two miles over terrain varying from concrete streets to narrow, wooded trails. The most appropriate course for girls and women, however, is the well-mowed surface of a rolling park or golf course.

In Europe the cross-country season extends through March. On the continent, cross-country courses are usually flat, with long, open stretches of grass. In Great Britain, the cross-country course is typically rough, with steep hills and obstacles not unlike those found on an equestrian field.

PHYSICAL CHARACTERISTICS
OF THE CROSS-COUNTRY RUNNER

Since distance runners usually double as cross-country performers, the physical characteristics manifested by these athletes have been discussed in the chapter on distance running. One additional characteristic, however, should be considered. That is the characteristic of physical

toughness. Because of the variation in terrain, the rough running surface, and the steepness of the hills, cross-country performers must be strong. Much of the time and energy utilized in their training should be aimed at the development of general toughness and physical strength.

PSYCHOLOGICAL CHARACTERISTICS
OF THE CROSS-COUNTRY RUNNER

Again it is safe to say that those characteristics which tend to describe the distance runner also tend to describe the cross-country performer. It is true, however, that not all successful distance performers enjoy cross-country running, nor do all successful cross-country runners like to compete on the oval track.

In a very real sense, the cross-country runner is a unique individual. She thoroughly enjoys just running and likely would do this even if it were not possible for her to compete. Particularly, she likes to run in open places, with the challenge of an occasional hill, or even a fence or stream to jump. These are the athletes who become bored by the monotony of interval training and who often ask if they can get away from the track to run alone through the woods or beside the crashing sea.

MECHANICS OF CROSS-COUNTRY RUNNING

The mechanics of cross-country running vary with the terrain. On flat, open areas the performer utilizes a relaxed, economical style. The body is essentially erect, with the eyes focused from fifteen to twenty yards ahead. The arms are carried loosely, with the elbows fixed at near ninety degrees. The partially flexed hands swing from the side rearward to the mid-chest forward. The running stride is relatively short. There is little knee lift. Foot action involves a ball-heel-ball sequence.

When running up hills, there is a marked modification of style. The performer assumes a decided forward lean in order to utilize the powerful gluteal muscles in hip extension. Arm action is vigorous to accommodate the driving legs. Eye focus is approximately five yards in front of the runner. The energy expenditure in running up hills demands weeks of specific preparation for effective execution.

Downhill running also requires special modification. Indeed, running downhill can be the most fatiguing and mechanically ineffective segment of a race if the performer has not learned the proper technique for this activity. Since balance often is a key factor in downhill running, the novice tends to markedly shorten her stride to control

Figure 9.2. Brown leading Lincoln, of England, and Mullen, of Ireland, during international cross-country race at Barry, Wales. Note the great interest of the European in cross-country running.

forward progress. This tendency, of course, is inappropriate. The stride actually should be lengthened when running downhill, with the arms carried away from the body for purposes of balance. Successful performers learn to "roll" their hips when running downhill, thus lengthening their strides in a somewhat freewheeling action. To perfect the mechanics of downhill running, as well as those essential to running uphill, the cross-country performer must practice many hours on hilly terrain.

TRAINING TECHNIQUES
FOR CROSS-COUNTRY RUNNERS

Marathon training is the foundation for success in all long-distance running. The cross-country runner should participate in this type of training at least two, perhaps three, times each week. It is not too much to expect that girls and women can run from five to ten miles during a workout of this type. For most effective results a fixed course should be followed. Times should be recorded to provide an incentive for working up to capacity. Recorded times are indicative of improvement, though for psychological reasons time should not become the preoccupation of the performer.

Fartlek, or fun running, also should be a part of the weekly schedule. The wise coach looks for different and exciting places for her runners to train. Sometimes this demands bussing the team to an entirely new area, yet the rewards of such activity far outweigh any inconvenience incurred. Boredom is a constant threat to the all-important mental attitude of the runner and must be avoided at all costs.

Hill work has already been emphasized. It is important, however, to recognize that hill work involves more than just running up and down an inclined plane. Hills are the places where cross-country races are won. Hills must therefore become a special kind of challenge to the serious performer. She should believe that she can catch and pass any adversary on a hill. A good drill for developing mental toughness on hills is to start one runner fifteen to twenty yards behind the pack and have her sprint to catch up before reaching the top. This drill might well be used at least one afternoon each week.

Hill work also should involve some type of strengthening activity, such as running stairs or upward through loose sand. This is painful and the uncommitted hate it, but the serious performer looks forward to a weekly challenge of this kind.

Speed work should be performed at regular intervals. The rationale here is that cross-country is partially a foundation for track, thus sprinting is a wise expenditure of time. Moreover, short-interval speed work is different than running endless miles and often is the change of pace which sharpens one's desire to return to marathon running another day.

Novelty Reemphasized

Surely one of the keys to the successful preparation of cross-country runners is the integration of novelty into the training program. While each kind of training activity already described is essential, novelty must be a primary concern of the serious coach. Several examples of the types of variation which might be utilized follow. The reader is encouraged to explore these and to develop novel ideas of her own.

Since cross-country is a team event, runners are encouraged to train as often as possible in a group. Two training sessions each day are advocated, with the morning session mostly fun. Follow-the-leader is an example of fun running, with individuals leading the group in their particular "thing." Running in Indian file with the last man taking the lead at some designated signal is an effective way to initiate this activity.

Cross-country golf, or segment running, is a good means of attaining motivation through variation. When this scheme is used, a long course (perhaps even an actual golf course) is divided into several segments of varying length. Through experimentation, times are affixed to each segment which, if equaled in practice, constitute par for that leg of the run. Differentials of five-second increments also are established so that each runner can score herself on par, one stroke, two strokes, three strokes over par, or under par, as the situation might be. By keeping score each time the cross-country golf course is run, improvement is readily noted.

Obstacle courses have a special appeal to most cross-country runners. These might involve different running surfaces such as sand, short grass, dirt roads, or leafy trails. Fences, walls, a stream to jump, or sharp turns also are effective. Some coaches even prepare a different obstacle course for each training session. Small cards with directions are affixed to trees or posts. The performers run a given segment, read the new directions, and run on to the next station. This is similar to an activity done by foresters who are learning to use the map and compass. It is particularly effective because it keeps runners alert, giving them little time to worry about fatigue.

Team relays constitute another excellent means of motivating individuals to work to their capacity. These can be conducted in various ways, though one which some coaches have found to be particularly appealing is the *zenderlaf*, or continuous run for time. The course for such a training session is established by placing flags at varying intervals throughout a park. The number of flags is determined by the number of runners. At the outset, one runner from each team is stationed at each flag. At an appropriate signal, the lead-off performers run to the next flag, passing a baton to their respective teammates. The pace for each runner is determined largely by the distance between flags and the overall time for the continuous run. The winning team covers the greatest distance in a predetermined period of time. For best results the course should be open so that team positions are never in doubt.

STRATEGY IN CROSS-COUNTRY RUNNING

Because of the nature of this activity, strategy is in some ways less specific than when running a fixed distance on the track. On the other hand, strategy is an integral part of every race and often is the difference between victory and defeat.

Perhaps the most obvious strategy in cross-country is the need for keeping the team together as a group. This means that each runner must maintain contact with her closest teammate. When this contact is broken, she does not panic but works on the opponent who separated the group, with every intention of moving up one position at a time. This approach of setting immediate, realizable goals is particularly important for the young runner. It keeps her alert and builds the team spirit so essential to success.

Figure 9.3. Team-grouping, essential to success in cross-country

Because there is a high degree of specificity in every activity, it is always wise to explore the cross-country course before an important competitive event. Such an exploration should provide information concerning potential bottlenecks where precious time might be lost if caught there with the "pack." Hazardous turns or obstacles should be noted, with time expended in determining how to best negotiate these during the competitive race. Hills should also be carefully explored for the purpose of fixing an appropriate racing pace.

The importance of pace was discussed in the chapter on distance running. It is mentioned here to give emphasis to the fact that the even distribution of energy becomes increasingly essential with the length of the race. The wise runner starts fast to get out of the pack, then settles into her rhythm at a tolerable pace. She does not necessarily want to be the "rabbit," or leader, but assumes this role if she must. There is no need to panic so long as she uses her strength wisely, either leading or maintaining contact in her mind.

Because distance running is largely an act of the will, attitudes are particularly important in this event. Successful runners, therefore, seldom give the impression of being fatigued. By acting fresh they weaken the confidence of their less-experienced adversaries. When discussing her first international cross-country victory at Barry, Wales, Doris Brown stated, "I heard her [Rita Lincoln] breathing heavily and felt that this was the psychological time to pass." And pass she did, and as so often is the result of passing in this kind of race, the runner who is passed tends to become discouraged while the passing runner gains immeasurable psychic strength.

TRAINING SCHEDULES FOR THE CROSS-COUNTRY RUNNER

Early Season

Separate schedules are not provided for the beginner. It is assumed that all candidates for the cross-country team have participated in some kind of preseason conditioning program. Too, the difference between the training schedules for the beginners and experienced performers is more a matter of quality than of the kind of activity which they would pursue.

M. Overdistance running. Five to six miles over flat, grassy terrain. Conclude workout with ten minutes of exercise in the weight room or gymnastic area, with emphasis on arm and shoulder strength.

T. Thirty to forty minutes of work on hills, preferably repeated runs of 75 to 100 yards, both up and down an incline of ten to fifteen degrees.

W.   Fartlek. Forty-five minutes of speed play over essentially flat terrain. This is a good time to run Indian file with different leaders doing their "thing."

Th.   Same as Monday.

F.   Speed work. Preferably on the grass. A football field is excellent for this activity, with the athletes sprinting the lines across the field.

S.   A good day for novelty. Drive the team several miles out of town and let them run back. Go to a lake shore, the ocean, a wooded area—anything to change the pace.

Sun.   Active rest. Take a hike, swim, or play some game which involves general bodily activity.

Competitive Season

M.   Recovery run of six to eight miles, followed by extensive stretching.

T.   Thirty minutes of vigorous training on a steep incline, preferably a sand bank. Rest periods should allow some ninety-five percent recovery—or a heart rate decrease to 140 beats per minute.

Complete the turnout with fifteen minutes of relaxed jogging.

W.   Fartlek. One hour of speed play over varying terrain, including long inclines. short, steep hills, flat stretches, and so forth.

Th.   Novelty day. See section on novelty activities earlier in this chapter.

F.   Fifteen to twenty minutes of easy striding and stretching. This may be a good day to explore the course over which Saturday's race will be run.

S.   Competition.

Sun.   Complete rest.

Perhaps it should be emphasized again that cross-country is a team sport. For this reason most training sessions should be team-oriented. Care should be taken to avoid the establishment of a "pecking order" while developing the all-important team pride.

Part III

Jumping Events

Courtesy Mr. Don Chadez and *Women's Track and World*

Chapter 10

High Jumping

Records show that girls and women have been competing in the running high jump since as early as 1910. The first recorded national record was set at a height of 4 feet 9 inches. A Canadian athlete named Ethel Catherwood established the first Olympic record with a jump of 5 feet 3 inches set at Amsterdam in 1928. Subsequent Olympic champions have come from Hungary, South Africa, Romania, Czechoslovakia, and the United States. The current world record holder is tall Iolanda Balas, of Romania, who has a best jump of 6 feet 3¼ inches.

While the United States has had three Olympic champions in the high jump, this event has been rather sorely neglected by the vast majority of American girls. Only recently have there been more than a dozen jumpers in this country who cleared 5 feet 5 inches or better in a given season. Russia, on the other hand, has for several years produced twenty or more athletes each season with best jumps over 5 feet 8 inches.

Most notable of the current American high jumpers are Estelle Baskerville and Eleanor Montgomery, both of Tennessee A. and I. University. Beginning as age-group performers in the Cleveland recreation program, these two young ladies represented the United States both at Tokyo and Mexico City. Miss Montgomery is the current American record holder with a jump of 5 feet 11 inches.

High jumping is a ballistic event. The jumper approaches the crossbar with catlike caution; her strides are calculated and deliberate. Then as if all fear had been abandoned, she springs up, turns in mid-flight, and rolls over the bar. To the sensitive observer, this is an act of grace and beauty. The drama of the high jump is a reminder of man's age-old quest for momentary freedom from the restrictions of earth.

For girls who have never jumped, either upward or forward, there are other factors to be considered. How fast do they run, which foot do they kick up, where do they take off? Some girls wonder if they really want to jump, for jumping seems so difficult and the landings so hard. This chapter has been written for girls who want to jump as well as for girls who are not so sure. Included in this chapter are a brief discussion of four styles of high jumping, a detailed analysis of the straddle jump and the Fosbury Flop, and hints for teaching the beginner.

STYLES OF HIGH JUMPING

High-jumping styles have changed rather markedly during the past several decades. The scissoring, bloomer-clad girl has been replaced by the trim, graceful athlete who crosses the bar in layout position. Emphasis on lifting the center of gravity to its highest point still remains, but the techniques for controlling the center of gravity at that height have changed. Some jumpers still scissor, and for most beginners this is a good route to learning, but the serious performer turns onto her side, back, or stomach when over the crossbar to take advantage of the height that she is able to attain.

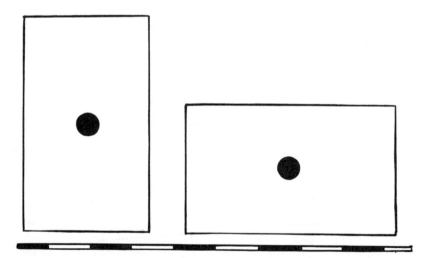

Figure 10.1. Relative heights of the center of gravity in the vertical or horizontal position.

A block of wood may well explain the reasoning behind the transition in jumping styles. If the block in figure 10.1 represents a jumper, it is obvious that considerably more lift is required to move the vertical block over the bar than to move the block which is lying in a horizontal position. A girl who scissors therefore expends greater force at a given height than a girl who is able to assume a horizontal position. Moreover, the vertical scissors jump imposes a lower ceiling upon ultimate performance than a jump in which the layout position is assumed.

Scissors Jump

There are two major differences between the scissors style of jumping and the western or straddle roll, namely, the relationship of the kick-up leg to the bar and the position of the body at the time of bar clearance. In the scissors, the inside leg is kicked up and the body passes over the bar in a near-vertical position. In the western or straddle roll, the leg away from the bar is the kick-up leg and the body passes over the bar in a layout position.

A right-footed jumper using the scissors style approaches from the right side of the jumping area at an angle of approximately thirty-five degrees. She takes several relaxed strides, plants her outside foot a distance of one arm's length from the crossbar, and kicks up forcefully with the inside leg. All of the body parts move along the line of approach, with no stepping or leaning toward the bar. At the lower heights the bar is cleared in a vertical position, and the jumper lands

Figure 10.2. The scissors jumping form. In the scissor jump the performer stamps with the outside foot, kicks up with the inside foot, and clears the bar in a vertical or semivertical position.

on the kick-up foot. As she goes higher, however, the scissors jumper tends to lay back to facilitate bar clearance, causing her to land forcefully on the seat.

By starting the beginner with the scissors style, it is possible to allay her fear of jumping while teaching her the important fundamentals of stamping, kicking, and springing upward. (All descriptions given hereafter will assume the jumper to be right-footed, *i.e.*, she kicks up with her right foot.)

Western Roll

When a right-footed girl uses the western roll, she approaches the bar from the left side at an angle of approximately forty-five degrees. Her approach is relaxed, with her last two strides slightly longer and faster than the others. As the left, or inside, foot strikes the takeoff point (a spot approximately one arm's distance out from the bar), the right leg is kicked forcefully upward. The arms are thrust upward and then extended across the bar.

When height has been attained, the jumper, using the western roll, turns onto her side. The inside, or lifting, leg is drawn quickly upward, the hip and leg are flexed, and the knee is tucked into the chest. At the instant of bar clearance (which is part of a continuous sequence of movement), the bent knee is snapped forward, then downward, to join the lower arm in turning the jumper into the pit. The kick-up leg follows through and remains extended as the jumper lands on the outstretched hands and the takeoff foot.

The whole action is little more than a glorified hop. It does, however, teach a girl to stamp, to kick, to lay out, and to roll over the bar. Many teachers believe that the western roll is the most effective transition to the more complicated straddle style of jumping. They also believe that this "glorified hop" teaches the beginner to drive upward better than any other jumping style.

Straddle Roll

There are many variations to the straddle form of high jumping. These include the dive straddle, the straight-leg kick-up, and the bent-leg kick-up, with modifications. All straddle jumpers take off from the inside foot, with the free leg being used somewhat as a pendulum to impart lifting force to the body mass. The most common characteristic of the straddle form is the layout over the crossbar. In this instance, the performer faces the bar during clearance, as opposed to the side opposition of the western roll or the back layout utilized by the "flopper."

"Fosbury Flop"

One of the words which best describes life is *change*. Certainly one of the more fascinating dimensions of the life and history of track and field is the change which has occurred in performance technique during the past half century. The most recent of these changes in technique is the evolution of the "Fosbury Flop."

Careful analysis of this new style of jumping reveals a remarkably economical performance skill. Perhaps more so than any other style, this back-clearance technique permits the performer to expend a greater percentage of her force in a purely vertical direction. This is possible since little eccentric thrust is needed to produce an adequate turning effect. Moreover, action of arms and legs seems to insure a maximum utilization of all lifting forces because the performer is able to "hang" large portions of her body below the crossbar during the time of clearance.

COMPONENTS OF THE STRADDLE ROLL

Approach

Good jumpers have approached the bar from all angles, though the recommended angle for the straddle jump is thirty to forty degrees. The length of the approach is forty or fifty feet, with the jumper taking five or six full strides. Her approach is relaxed; the final two strides are longer and faster than those that precede. Most jumpers use a single check mark to fix the starting point. The strides beyond this mark are taken with a detached confidence as the jumper mobilizes all of her energies for the plant and explosive spring.

Takeoff

Ideally the last stride is longer than the others, with the foot planted along the line of approach. (Few girls are able to attain this ideal, however, as they anticipate the jump, turn their foot slightly inward, and lean toward the bar.) The longer last stride tends to lower the center of gravity and permits the girl to gather for the spring. The takeoff foot is planted with a stamping motion, the heel striking the ground ahead of the toes so that the body rocks up and over the driving leg. It is imperative that the jumper's center of gravity be over her leg at the instant the lifting force is applied. The final application of force is off the jumper's toes.

Better jumpers take off from a point approximately twenty-four inches from the crossbar (measured at a right angle to the crossbar). This takeoff point is usually opposite the near jumping standard so that the flight of the performer carries her over the center of the crossbar. The landing point for better jumpers is approximately thirty-six inches beyond the crossbar and from two to three feet from the far jumping standard. The linear distance covered from point of takeoff to point of landing is from eight to ten feet.

Leg Swing

Ideally the kick-up leg should be straight, but since few girls have been able to master this technique, they should strive for a kick which

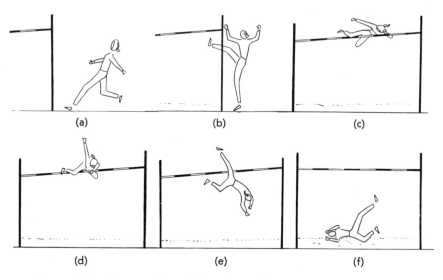

(a)   (b)   (c)

(d)   (e)   (f)

Figure 10.3. The straddle roll. (a) The stride before the jump is faster and longer than the preceding strides. The heel of the takeoff foot is driven into the ground to permit a transfer of forward momentum upward into the jump. (b) A powerful kick-up is coupled with a forceful extension of the takeoff leg to propel the body upward. (c) The layout over the crossbar is the most economical style of clearance. (d) The right leg is dropping toward the landing area, though the right arm is carried above the shoulder to counterbalance the trail leg. (e) The jumper has turned her head inward and is reaching toward the landing area to facilitate the roll around the bar. (f) Trail-leg clearance is attained by rotating the thigh away from the crossbar and rolling onto the back. (This view is from the approach side.)

carries the leg's center of gravity to the highest possible point in the shortest possible time. In other words, the kick-up is a ballistic act which helps to lift the jumper from the ground.

Good jumpers kick up along the bar rather than into the bar and are able to attain a maximum leg lift. Their explosive power and flexibility permit them to completely extend the kicking leg before they leave the jumping surface.

Arm Action

The arms have an important function in the high-jump event. During the approach they are used in the normal running action. As the final stride before takeoff is negotiated, both arms tend to fall behind the body in a semiflexed manner. This action helps to counterbalance the exaggerated extension of the forward leg and places the arms in a position from which they can be driven explosively upward at takeoff. Initially both arms follow the line of flight of the body mass. As maximum height is attained, the inside arm is placed against the abdomen, while the outside arm reaches over the bar, then downward to assist in the roll.

Once the turning pattern has been established, the outside arm is driven ballistically upward again. This action, or force, produces a counteraction, or force, which facilitates trail-leg lift (see action-reaction, chapter 1).

Bar Clearance

High jumping is a skill having two distinct parts, the lift and the crossbar clearance. The good jumper leaves the ground before she begins to turn into the bar. She recognizes that lift is the most important aspect of jumping, and she attempts to drive her chest and shoulders as high as she possibly can. Once she has left the ground, however, there is nothing that she can do to attain any greater height. Her full attention is now turned to clearing the bar in the most economical way possible.

The turn and layout come after height has been attained. With the chest, shoulders, and arms above the bar, the jumper drops her right side toward the pit, extending her body in the face-down position. The bar is cleared in a perfect layout. the left arm pressed to the chest and the right arm carried at the side. The jumper rotates around the crossbar by turning her kicking foot sharply inward and by looking back under the bar to the takeoff pad.

Figure 10.4. In the dive straddle the upper body precedes the lead leg over the bar. The right arm, having contributed to the turn, will now be driven upward to provide an interacting force essential to trail-leg lift. The left arm is held against the abdomen to avoid contacting the crossbar.

Figure 10.5. One of the most common problems in the high jump is failure to retain the straddle position and subsequent contact with the crossbar by the trail leg. The performer shown here has learned to retain her straddle by consciously rotating the trail leg up and away from the crossbar.

Landing

It is imperative that all straddle jumpers rotate far enough to land on their kick-up foot and the outstretched hands. Girls who knock the bar off with the second leg find it to their advantage to rotate even farther, landing on the right shoulder or even the back. It goes without saying that the pit should be well filled with loose shavings for this event.

COMPONENTS OF THE "FOSBURY FLOP"

Approach

The approach angle with the back-clearance style is approximately forty-five degrees. The speed of approach tends to be faster than that used by most straddle jumpers, contributing significantly to the potential success of each jump. Unlike the straddle jumper, the "flopper" takes off from the outside, rather than the inside, foot. As in all styles of jumping for height, eccentric thrust at takeoff produces the rotary motion which causes the performer to turn around the crossbar.

Takeoff

An instant before takeoff the body has settled slightly over the bent (outside) jumping leg. To initiate takeoff the inside leg is driven upward toward the opposite shoulder. This forceful action contributes both to the lift and to the turn which places the back toward the crossbar (this description assumes a left-side approach with the left leg inside and the right leg outside at the time of takeoff). The flexed right arm swings vigorously upward and to the right, adding its lifting, turning force to that of the left leg. The left arm seems to just hang loosely alongside the body. The actual takeoff is effected by a powerful extension of the right foot, knee, and hip.

Crossbar Clearance

There is nothing that can be done after the performer leaves the ground to alter her line of flight or add to her ultimate height. Actions which occur in the air, therefore, merely complement forces which have been initiated at takeoff. The rotation started on the ground carries the performer back-first over the crossbar. Were nothing done to control this motion, the jumper would continue to turn to a landing on her head. To prevent this from happening, the performer, during the layout, forcefully lifts her knees (action), resulting in subsequent flexion of the neck and shoulders (reaction) and a negating of the tendency to turn. This lifting of the legs also insures their clearance over the crossbar.

Landing

The landing constitutes the danger of this style and must be given careful consideration. As indicated above, the "flop" style jumper is, in effect, negotiating a back sommersault over the crossbar. While the parabola or path through which she turns is fixed, the speed with which she turns is not. Turning speed is controlled by shortening or lengthening her body lever or by producing a new force which is in opposition to the rate and direction of the turn. In the "flop," both of these controlling factors are used.

Near the peak of the jump, when the body is just beginning to lay back over the bar, the head is lifted and the knees are bent with the feet pulled up beneath the buttock. This shortening of the radius speeds the turn. Then when the trunk has passed over the crossbar, the knees are sharply lifted, imposing a second force which decreases the rate of turning. Moreover, during descent the legs are completely extended, lengthening the lever again and further decreasing the rate of the turn.

When coupled together in proper sequence, these actions control the speed of turning and provide for a safe landing on the upper back and shoulders. Needless to say, the landing area for such a jumping style must be soft and sufficiently large to protect against any chance of injury.

THINGS TO REMEMBER
WHEN TEACHING THE HIGH JUMP

1. The jumper should approach the bar in a relaxed and confident manner, not rushing but using as much speed as she can effectively transfer into lift. (Remember the law of inertia.)
2. The high jump has two distinct parts. These are the lift and cross-bar clearance. The jumper should give primary attention to getting lift; then she should shift her attention to the turn. This is a wise principle to follow with individual jumps as well as with the ex-

penditure of time in learning how to jump. (Even though the jump is a two-part movement from a mechanical standpoint, it must be performed as a coordinated whole.)

3. The last stride before jumping should be longer and quicker than all other strides. The longer stride lowers the center of gravity, shifting it behind the takeoff leg, and permits the jumper to gather for the spring. Force is applied when the center of gravity has moved forward over the driving leg. The actual jump is as near vertical as possible.

4. The body tends to follow the head. The rolling motion stems from an inward rotation of the head and shoulders, coupled with a downward thrusting action of the appropriate arms and legs (in the western roll the left arm and left leg; in the straddle roll the right arm and right leg).

5. Girls have a particularly difficult time retaining their straddle or legs-apart position while jumping. The straddle therefore should be emphasized during every practice session so that the trail leg is carried away from the bar during the landing.

6. The lifting force for high jumpers is determined by the factors of strength, distance, and time. The best jumpers will likely be those girls who can most effectively control these factors. They will be strong and will apply their force through a long power stroke as explosively as possible.

7. The jumper should kick vigorously to a point above the bar. A vigorous kick-up or leg swing will in effect lighten the body mass, and if coordinated with the drive of the takeoff leg, will produce the greatest possible body lift.

8. Teach fundamentals first. If some girls seem to perform well using variations, analyze these girls individually. If they are successful in spite of their style, encourage them to use proper form. If the variations which they are using are sound for them, then help them to perfect that style which suits them best. Remember that the physical education teacher works with individuals.

9. Research studies have tended to show that maximum potential lifting strength is available when the leg is flexed at an angle of ninety degrees. There is, however, great variation in potential strength and actual strength in human beings. Most female performers do not have sufficient leg strength to even approximate this optimum takeoff position. For this reason serious attention should be given to leg-strenthening exercises and to determination of the best takeoff position for each individual jumper.

TEACHING BEGINNERS TO HIGH JUMP

From an understanding of the learning process it is known that a beginner should learn one skill at a time. Since both the scissors and the western style have something to offer the beginner, it is the belief of the authors that these styles of jumping should be explored before the straddle roll is presented.

Determining Takeoff Foot and Kicking Leg

Two techniques are commonly used to distinguish the stamping leg from the kicking leg. One is to have the girls take several hops to a line and then hop over the line to a landing on the opposite foot. The other is to ask the girls to kick a ball. The hopping foot usually is the takeoff foot and the kicking leg is the kick-up leg when jumping for height. Several practice jumps will soon convince a girl whether or not she is stamping and kicking with the proper feet.

Teaching the Scissors

Scissoring is a natural movement pattern. After the lines of approach have been established and a general takeoff point identified, most girls can copy a scissors demonstration. They should begin jumping over a crossbar which has been set about twenty-four inches above the ground. If the bar is set much higher, some will shy away and will not get over it.

The teacher stations herself at the side of the jumping pit so that she can observe each girl independently. She makes certain that all jumpers are stamping with the outside foot and kicking up with the inside foot. As the girls begin to get a feel for jumping, they are encouraged to stamp harder and to kick higher, getting as much clearance over the bar as possible. Most girls can learn to scissor in one or two sessions. They are then ready to move to the opposite side of the approach area and explore the western roll.

Teaching the Western Roll

The takeoff foot and kick-up legs are the same for the western and straddle rolls as they are for the scissors. They are used differently, however. The jumper using the western roll springs off the inside foot (foot nearest the bar), passes over the bar, and lands again on the same foot. As was previously stated, this is a modified hop.

To teach this movement, have the beginner approach the bar from a distance of about fifteen feet. (If there are several girls, they can proceed in a single file.) She takes her initial jumps without a crossbar or any special concern about her run up. All the beginner thinks about is springing up from her inside foot and landing safely in the shaving pile. This is repeated several times.

The next drill is practiced away from the jumping pit on any flat surface. The beginner is instructed to spring from her takeoff foot, kick into the air with the opposite foot, make a half turn, and land again on the takeoff foot, facing the opposite direction. (This is exactly what the jumper does when she uses the western roll; she springs, kicks, turns, lands in a manner similar to a ballet dancer.) When the kick and turn have been mastered, the beginner returns to the jumping pit where she attempts to hop over a bar eighteen to twenty-four inches above the ground.

Practice on the layout follows. A handkerchief is placed in the jumping pit to the left side of the jumper and almost directly beneath the bar. She is instructed to ignore the handkerchief until she has attained her height and then to look down and reach for it in a sudden thrusting movement. This action will lower the shoulders, placing the body parallel to the crossbar and permitting the jumper to take full advantage of all her height.

When these skills have been mastered, the jumper should raise the bar to about four feet so that she can determine the takeoff point realistically. For most jumpers this point would lie between three and four feet in front of the crossbar. When this point has been established, it will remain the same for jumps at every height.

The final aim of the jumper is a smoothly coordinated action sequence which insures the attainment of maximum height, economical crossbar clearance, and a safe landing. Such a movement sequence is made possible only by extensive practice and a careful adherence to details. Girls who work at it will develop coordination and timing.

Teaching the Straddle Roll

Techniques for teaching the straddle roll are similar to those for teaching the western roll. The angle of approach and the takeoff foot are the same in these two jumping styles. They do vary, however, in leg swing (kick-up), style of clearance, and landing form.

Since it is assumed that the straddle roll would be taught to only those girls who have explored the scissors and western styles of jumping, the first new skill to be introduced would be the layout and turn over the bar. This might best be accomplished by having the girls experiment with a dance step, the *tour jeté*, away from the jumping area. In both the *tour jeté* and the straddle roll, the performer leaps off one foot, turns in the air, and lands on the other foot facing the opposite direction. Practice without a bar teaches the leap and turn, but only practice over a bar teaches a girl to lift her trailing leg.

Following several attempts at the *tour jeté*, the jumpers return to the pit and attempt to kick and turn over a bar which is about twenty-four inches above the ground. When most of the girls have cleared this height, the bar is gradually elevated. The teacher should watch the girls carefully to determine the point at which the height produces so great a barrier that each loses her jumping form.

Individual practice assignments are then given to each girl at a point just below her critical height. This will force each girl to work near her capacity, requiring her to kick and to spring vigorously. Any-

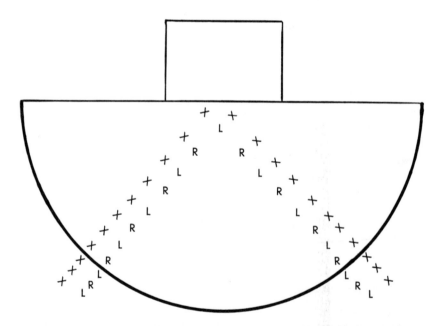

Figure 10.6. High-jumping pit and approach area. Shown is the 10′ x 16′ landing pit, the approach apron, the angle of approach, and the stride pattern for the right-footed jumper. The approach from the right side is for a scissors jump. The western and straddle forms are from the left side. Note that the stride is lengthened as the jumper nears her takeoff.

thing less will permit a girl to be lazy, and she will not learn the proper mechanics for straddle jumping.

The beginner must next learn to lay out and roll around the crossbar. One way to teach this is to place a white mark on the approach apron near the point at which she takes off. She is instructed to jump, and upon attaining her height above the bar, to turn her head sharply inward so that she is looking back at the white mark. This action, coupled with an inward rotation of the kicking foot, helps to lower the shoulders and turn the body around the bar.

The arms, which have been extended during the kick-up, also assist with the turn and layout. The left arm is pressed to the chest at the peak of the jump, though the right arm is extended across the bar and then thrust downward along with the left arm and right leg into the pit.

The final actions of the straddle jumper are the extension and quick pull-away of the trailing leg. These are facilitated by having the girl lie in the pit on her back and extend the straight left leg toward the sky. She next attempts to effect this movement as she is rolling over and away from the bar. The practice thus involves the flat foot stamp, the leg swing, lift, turn, layout, and roll-away to a landing on the right shoulder or back, with the trailing leg extended upward.

It is again true that no amount of work on the elements of jumping will produce a smoothly coordinated straddle roll. The serious jumper will begin with the whole skill, drill on each of the parts as necessary, and then give careful attention to blending all of these parts or elements into the movement pattern as a whole. If she is persistent, she will be rewarded for her efforts and enjoy that momentary thrill of being freed from the restrictions of the earth.

Teaching the "Fosbury Flop"

Mechanically the "Fosbury Flop" is closely related to the scissors technique. Indeed, it now seems strange that in the evolution of jumping, the back-clearance style did not become fully developed before the advent of the eastern, western, or the straddle rolls. The "flop," in essence, is a scissors jump with a quarter-turn outward, coupled with other modifications which control the body in flight. (Undoubtedly, the landing area has had much to do with the development of jumping techniques. The evolution here has been from sand to wood shavings to foam rubber to large, air-filled bags.)

Figure 10.7. Cathy Hamblin, teen-age member of the 1968 U.S. Olympic team, turns into the bar during a trial jump at Mexico City. Cathy was one of the first female performers to utilize the Fosbury Flop. (Photo courtesy of Don Wilkinson.)

Initially, the learner must determine her jumping and her kicking legs. In all probability, these will be the same as those used in the scissors jump. The next step is to master the quarter-turn which places the back toward the crossbar. This should be learned at a suitably soft landing area without obstructions of any kind. Using a short approach, the performer initiates a nearly vertical jump, driving the inside leg and the outside arm outward (toward the right, or opposite, shoulder). The landing which follows is on the seat, with the body held in a pike position.

As skill and confidence are developed, the learner should explore the effects of shortening and lengthening her body levers as well as the consequences of interacting forces on the speed with which the

Figure 10.8. Debbie Brill, of British Columbia, clearing the bar at 5′ 6″. Note the body parts draped beneath the bar with this back-clearance style. (Photo courtesy of **Women's Track and Field World.**

body turns in space. She should try jumping higher and higher, learning to control her turn so that the landing is always on the upper back and shoulders. When this has been accomplished, the crossbar is placed at a comfortable height, and the performer continues to practice her newly learned skills.

TRAINING SCHEDULE FOR THE
BEGINNING HIGH JUMPER

Begin the workout session with a jog of 440 yards, followed by fifteen minutes of conditioning exercises.

M. Place crossbar twelve inches below best effort and take several short-approach jumps (three or four strides) with an emphasis on explosive lift.

Raise crossbar six inches and take four full-approach jumps for height.

Work on in-and-out running for twenty minutes.

Weight training.

T. Stride 180 yards, rest, and take several sprints from 50 to 60 yards. Set up one or two hurdles and work on hurdle form for fifteen minutes.

Pass the baton with sprinters for ten minutes. Train down with relaxed striding on the grass.

W. Warm up well, emphasizing hip flexibility and leg swing.

Set the bar twelve inches below best effort; after clearing this height twice, raise it one inch. Repeat until the bar is three inches below best effort. If the jumper is having a good day, let her continue upward until she has missed three times. If she seems to be off form, leave the bar at the lower height and have her take several jumps, concentrating on a smoothly coordinated lift, layout, and turn.

Weight training.

Th. Stride 220 yards, rest ten minutes and repeat.

Take several starts with the sprinters.

Join the long jumpers and work on pop-up jumps for height and form.

Train down with ten minutes of relaxed striding on the grass.

F. Set the crossbar twelve inches below best effort and practice for fifteen minutes with two-step approach. Rest.

Raise the bar to a height three inches below best effort and take six jumps for form.

Pass the baton for ten minutes, ending the training session with relaxed striding on the grass.

Weight training.

S. Fartlek running on grass, followed by extensive stretching.

TYPICAL TRAINING SCHEDULE FOR THE EXPERIENCED HIGH JUMPER

Early Season

M. Jog two laps, followed by fifteen minutes of stretching.

5 x 50-yard sprint buildups.

Five minutes of recovery shuffle.

Fifteen minutes of kicking drill. (The performer takes a normal approach, stamps and kicks a ball or similar object suspended twelve to eighteen inches above highest competitive jump.)

2 x 220 fast stride with walk-back recovery.

Weight training with emphasis on ballistic, leg-extensor exercises.

T. Warm up as indicated.

Work for fifteen minutes over four hurdles set at regular distance.

Five minutes of recovery shuffle.

Set bar nine inches below best competitive jump and take several short-approach jumps with emphasis on lift.

Move bar up three inches and continue jumping with concentration on form (20 to 25 jumps total).

Finish workout with 5 x 50 sprints—walk-back recovery.

W. Warm up as indicated.

5 x 50 sprints with walk-back recovery.

Five minutes of recovery shuffle.

5 x 75 sprints with walk-back recovery.

Five minutes of recovery shuffle.

3 x 220 fast stride with walk-back recovery.

Weight training.

Th. Warm up as indicated.

Set bar six inches below best competitive effort and take several jumps for form.

Raise bar two inches and jump six to eight times.

Raise bar two inches, jumping until this height is cleared three times. (If form has "decayed," lower bar two inches and clear three times.)

Set bar two inches above best competitive effort and make three attempts at this height.

Finish workout with ten minutes of easy shuffle.

F. Warm up as indicated.

Work over four hurdles for ten minutes, followed by 3 x 70-yard hurdles at seven-eighths speed.

Five minutes of recovery shuffle between each hurdle race.

Weight training.

S. Thirty minutes of Fartlek running and stretching.

Competitive Season

M. Twenty minutes of easy striding and stretching for warmup.
220 fast stride—walk 220.
150 sprint—walk 220
75 sprint—walk 440.
75 sprint—five minutes of easy recovery shuffle.
Ten short-approach jumps at a height cleared with comfort—concentrate on rhythm and lift.
Finish with ten minutes of easy shuffle.

T. Warm up as indicated.
5 x 75 sprints with walk-back recovery.
Fifteen minutes of high-kicking drill from regular approach.
5 x 75 sprints with walk-back recovery.
Finish with ten minutes of easy shuffle.

W. Warm up as indicated, stretching as on day of competition.
Jump for height, starting nine inches below best competitive effort.
Clear three times, raise the bar two inches and again clear three times. Continue until one height has been missed three times, then lower the bar two inches and take several additional jumps.
Shuffle two recovery laps—stretch again and take three jumps at bar set two inches above best competitive height.

Th. Warm up as indicated.
5 x 75 fast stride.
Five minutes of recovery shuffle.
Work over five hurdles set at regular distance for ten minutes.
Five minutes of recovery shuffle, followed by movie analysis (if movies of previous meets are available).

F. Competition.

S. Active rest with twenty to thirty minutes of easy striding and stretching.

PERFORMANCE TIPS FOR COMPETITOR AND COACH

1. Early-season preparation in the high jump should be aimed at the development of skill and toughness of muscle. During the competitive season, emphasis should be given to lift and toughness of mind.

Great effort in any area is first an act of the will and then an act of the body.

2. The argument over a straight versus a bent lead leg becomes largely academic so long as the performer kicks up with maximum force at the instant of takeoff. (The long lever possesses maximum mass, the short lever maximum velocity, each tending to compensate for the other.)

3. The rhythm in the high-jump approach should at first be relatively slow, concluding with three or four relatively (accelerated) fast strides. The legs tend to run out from under the arms, the trunk, and the head. The lay-back and subsequent compression of the "leg springs" are essential to vertical lift.

4. The essence of high jumping is the attainment of maximum height; form is of no consequence except that it contributes to this end.

5. When coaching watch the high jumper from all angles.

   a. From the right side one should observe a full foot plant, heel striking the takeoff surface ahead of the toes. One should note a lay-back, perhaps as much as thirty degrees off the perpendicular, with twenty- to thirty-degree flexion in the jumping leg.

   b. From the rear, one should look for any tendency to turn the jumping foot inward from the line of approach—for any marked tendency to lean into the bar with subsequent loss of vertical lift.

   c. From the left side one should look for the high point of the jump—any tendency to strike the crossbar while either ascending or descending. In the straddle roll one should look for the upward thrust of the right arm during layout (action) with subsequent lift of the trailing leg (reaction).

   d. From the front the height of the kick-up leg should be observed. The focus of the eyes should be noted at some point above the crossbar.

6. The high jump should be approached as a total, sequential event. In the straddle roll every effort should be made to eliminate arching the back during bar clearance. This is a common error, usually occurring when the performer is attempting heights near or above her psychological barrier.

Chapter 11

Long Jump

Performance in the long jump has improved markedly since F. Crenshaw established the first recorded American record of 15 feet 3 inches in the year 1912. By 1929 the twenty-foot barrier was exceeded with the talented Kinue Hitomi, of Japan, jumping 20 feet 2 1/2 inches at Seoul, Korea. The first American to jump more than twenty feet was Margaret Matthews who set a national record with her leap of 20 feet 1 inch in 1958.

The long jump was introduced into the Olympic schedule during the 1948 games held at London, England. When world record holder Francina Blankers-Koen was unable to participate because of the recent birth of a child, this event was won by Olga Gyarmati, of Hungary, at the modest distance of 18 feet 8¼ inches. No Olympic champion has since jumped less than twenty feet.

During the past several years, international competition in the long jump has been dominated by Tatyana Shchelkanova, of the U.S.S.R., and Mary Rand, of England. Miss Rand established an Olympic record of 22 feet 2¼ inches at Tokyo in 1964. The world record of 22 feet 10 inches was set by Miss Shchelkanova in 1966.

Manifesting great durability in an event often considered too strenuous for women, Willie White has won the U.S. long-jump championship several times since her first victory in 1959. Miss White was a member of the U.S. Olympic teams of 1960, 1964, and 1968. Her best jump of 21 feet 6 inches is the current American record. The only other American to consistently jump more than twenty feet is Martha Watson, of Tennessee A and I University

The long jump is an event in which the performer attempts to combine maximum speed with maximum height to attain the greatest possible horizontal distance. It is in a sense a jump for height at the end of a sprint. The performer in this event thus is competing not only with her opponents but with the forces of inertia and gravity as well.

Most good long jumpers are girls who possess both speed and spring. They usually are well coordinated, having the ability to change their direction quickly and expend their forces explosively. Though not all girls can achieve championship performance, most girls can, within the wide latitude of their ability, develop a satisfactory degree of jumping skill. This chapter includes a detailed discussion of long-jumping technique and gives the teacher some ideas for introducing this event to beginners.

SOME COMMENTS OF A GENERAL NATURE

Though there is much common agreement about proper long-jumping technique, there also are points upon which there is considerable disagreement. These points are related to the problem of effectively coping with inertia and gravity. In general they involve three major questions: (1) How much speed should the long jumper attempt to utilize? (2) Should she concentrate on height or distance at the takeoff? (3) Should she "hang" or run in the air during her flight?

Some coaches advocate great speed and a run off the board with distance as their major emphasis. Others advocate controlled speed, with a float just prior to the takeoff so that the jumper can obtain maximum lift. The jumper who sprints over the takeoff board strikes the board with a slightly flexed leg. When lift is her primary concern, a girl will flex her leg noticeably before the takeoff.

Differences in carry stem primarily from differences of opinion regarding the best procedure for controlling the body in flight and adjusting for the landing. Some teachers conclude that the hang or vertical sit permits the jumper to keep her feet up longer and carry a greater distance. Other teachers feel that running in the air gives the jumper a better sense of timing and permits her to recover more economically.

It is readily acknowledged that there are good arguments for both points of view and that excellent jumpers have capitalized on the best of each style. In spite of this fact, the authors believe that primary emphasis should be given to approach speed, with height and stride in flight of secondary importance. Indeed, perhaps the major change in long-jump technique during recent years is the lengthening of the approach for the purpose of attaining greater speed. Most successful jumpers now think in terms of sprinting off the takeoff board, rather than springing upward and outward as was the case some years ago.

ANALYSIS OF LONG-JUMPING FORM

Approach

It is possible to attain maximum running speed in thirty or forty yards. While the long jumper does not want an approach which she cannot control, she should run sufficiently far to develop good, relaxed speed. It is important for her to mentally achieve a sense of floating so that she can gather for the jump.

A good jumper will approach the takeoff board from a distance of approximately 120 to 130 feet. She will use two check marks, one at the start of her run and a second mark about 50 feet from the takeoff board. She begins her approach with a short step, striking check mark number one with the takeoff foot. She increases stride length and speed to the second mark which she also strikes with the preferred foot. From the second check mark to the takeoff, the jumper mentally lets up and begins to gather for the stamp and spring. There is no loss of speed, but rather a sense of shifting from a drive to a float, in preparation for the explosive effort off the board.

The last two strides of the approach are usually slightly shorter than the preceding strides. During these strides, the jumper holds her head up and her shoulders back. Her eyes are focused on a spot well above the horizon. She strikes the takeoff board with a flat foot, and her center of gravity is directly above the slightly flexed takeoff leg.

Takeoff

The takeoff is the most critical phase of the long jump, for once the body has left the ground there is nothing that the jumper can do to change the flight characteristics of her center of gravity. She must therefore be in perfect balance, and she must apply her force through the body in a forward and upward trajectory.

Though the highly skilled jumper seems to sprint off the board and into flight, analysis of movies reveals that she changes her course

Figure 11.1. The long jump. (a) The foot plant with knee flexion and the center of gravity over the base of support. (b) The jumper strides off the board, expending her force upward through the chest. (c) The head remains erect as the jumper strides gracefully in the air. (d) The legs are lifted into the tuck position and the arms swing forward in preparation for the landing. (e) The jumper contacts the landing area with her heels first. The knees are relaxed. (f) She swings her arms up and over, helping her to fall forward into the jumping pit.

of action by dipping and lifting in an explosive effort. The head, shoulders, and chest are driven upward, and the free leg follows through in an exaggerated running motion. There is a complete extension of the takeoff leg as the arms swing in their normal bilateral pattern.

The jumper who applies her force too soon (before the center of gravity has moved over the takeoff leg) will tend to stop her forward momentum and impose a backward rotation to the body. This results

Figure 11.2. The stride off the board is aimed at attaining both forward speed and maximum possible height. Note that the left arm and right knee are driven forcefully upward to supplement the explosive extension of the takeoff leg.

in a jump which is fairly high but causes the girl to land on her seat. If, on the other hand, the center of gravity has moved ahead of the lifting leg, a forward rotary effect is imposed on the body, and the jumper will tend to fly low and land on her hands and knees. It is absolutely essential, therefore, that the timing of the jump be perfect and the force be expended forward and upward to as near a twenty- to thirty-degree angle as possible. (In actual practice jumpers seldom achieve an angle greater than twenty degrees.)

Perhaps the major distinction between the beginner and the skillful athlete is the difference in the lift which each obtains off the board. The beginner tends to lunge forward in a desperate search for distance, whereas the expert gets up and rides her greater height to victory.

Flight in Air

Though it is difficult for some jumpers to maintain their run in the air, this style of carry is generally concluded to be superior to the hang.

Figure 11.3. Willye White, American record holder, four-time Olympian, preparing to pike for her landing. (Photo courtesy of Don Wilkinson.)

A description of the run in the air must begin at the takeoff. If the left foot is the takeoff foot, the right leg naturally follows through with a high knee lift which is very similar to the stride over the hurdle. The leg is then thrust out and back, the foot is carried up behind and forward again, just as if the girl were running on the ground. The opposite, or lifting, leg follows through in the normal bilateral manner.

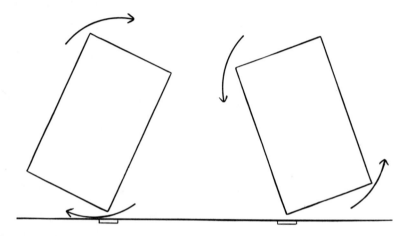

Figure 11.4. Rotary effect when the center of gravity is ahead of, or behind, the lifting force.

After the jumper has attained her height, she prepares to land by modifying her arm action rather markedly. The arms which have been used normally during the takeoff now swing down, back, up, and over to pull the head and shoulders forward. This is an abnormal movement and is difficult to learn. If the jumper is going to pike for a landing, however, she must use her arms in this manner.

Landing

The proper landing requires considerable abdominal strength, excellent body control, and courage. If these elements are possessed by the jumper, she terminates her run in the air with a smoothly coordinated lift of the legs and a forward bend of the trunk. This motion does not alter the flight of the jumper, but it does permit her to take full advantage of her optimum line of descent.

The expert jumper contacts the landing area with her heels, tucks chest to knees, and falls forward onto her hands. She has used her speed and spring to the maximum degree, achieving excellent lift off the board, a balanced stride in the air, and a landing which absorbs the last of her force without loss of distance or harm to the body.

THINGS TO REMEMBER
WHEN TEACHING THE LONG JUMP

1. The approach must be long enough to permit the jumper to achieve the maximum speed she can control. Moreover, the approach must be relaxed, making it possible for the jumper to apply her force at the proper instant.
2. The takeoff is essentially a stride forward and upward off the take-off board. The lifting force should be applied as the center of gravity passes over the takeoff leg.
3. The takeoff foot should be flat and the takeoff leg slightly flexed an instant before the body is propelled upward and forward.
4. The long jumper should concentrate all her efforts on combining optimum height with optimum speed.
5. The training schedule for the jumper should include activities aimed at the development of strength (particularly in the abdominal area), explosive power (especially in the takeoff leg), and sprinting speed.
6. The long jumper must recognize that the approach, takeoff, flight, and landing are parts of a complex skill. Part practice should therefore seek the development of habits which will stand up under the stress of speed and competition.

TEACHING THE LONG JUMP

The beginner must first identify her takeoff foot. If she is right-handed, she very likely will stamp or take off from the left foot. The indecisive girl should kick an imaginary ball, assuming that the supporting foot is the takeoff foot for the long jump.

With the takeoff foot in mind, the beginner is encouraged to explore the long jump for herself. Her only instructions are to approach the landing area with a short run up, stamp on the preferred foot, and try to jump forward and upward. She must, of course, be close, enough to the jumping pit to land in the sand. When a sufficiently soft landing area is available, it may be well for the beginner to land on her seat during these exploratory jumps. This drill teaches the idea of lifting the legs and extending them forward preparatory to landing.

Soon after starting the modified approach practice, a beginner should attempt the run in the air. Since this is not an easy coordination, she will need a great deal of patient encouragement; but if she is persistent, she can learn to "bicycle" off the board and into the carry. To facilitate the learning of this difficult skill the learner might assume a cross-support position on the even parallel bars, bicycling her legs as would be the situation were she midway between the takeoff and landing. Another effective device is to take off from a springboard, attaining sufficient height to permit a hitch kick before landing. When the beginner is able to maintain her balance and negotiate the hitch kick from the short, pop-up jump, she is ready to work from a longer and faster approach.

Determining the Jumper's Check Marks

Perhaps the best place to determine what a girl's check marks should be is the track itself. The teacher places a line across the track and moves to a point about ninety feet from this line. The learner is instructed to begin her approach by stepping forward onto the line with her takeoff foot, to build her speed gradually, and to sprint past this point without any letup. The teacher marks the exact spot at which the girl's takeoff foot strikes the ground and has her repeat this procedure several times. The teacher then measures the distance from the line to the midpoint of the cluster of stride marks which she has identified. Distance is transferred to the long-jump runway, and the girl is ready to recheck her marks.

The recheck is accomplished by starting the run at the far end of the runway, striking the first check mark with the preferred foot and sprinting along the runway, over the takeoff board, and into the jumping pit. If the jumper is ahead of the takeoff board, she moves her first check mark back; if she is behind the takeoff board, she moves her mark forward. She should be aware that these marks are only tentative and that her stride pattern will vary from day to day and from surface to surface. Added training and greater strength also will have an effect on the jumper's approach, though this basic distance will provide a ready point of reference for future practice sessions.

Learning to Lift

Some beginners have found that jumping over a height barrier helps them to obtain the desired lift at takeoff. One drill for teaching beginners to jump upward involves the placement of a bar or pole across the jumping pit. This bar should be several feet from the takeoff board and from two to three feet high. When placed too close, such an obstacle forces the performer to jump up rather than out, thereby minimizing, rather than maximizing, horizontal carry.

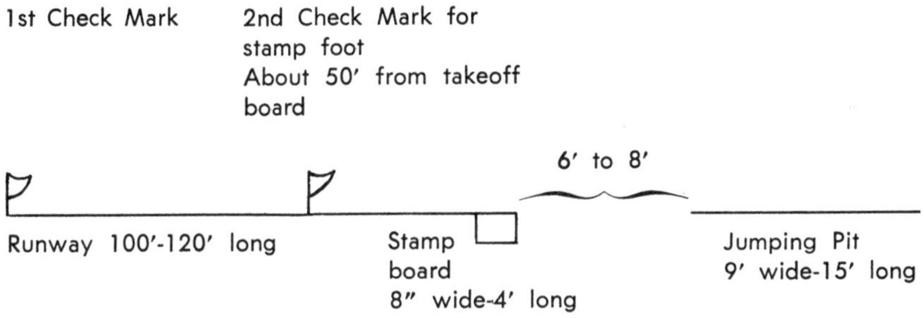

1st Check Mark

2nd Check Mark for stamp foot
About 50' from takeoff board

6' to 8'

Runway 100'-120' long

Stamp board
8" wide-4' long

Jumping Pit
9' wide-15' long

Figure 11.5. Relative position of check marks, the length of the approach, and dimensions of the takeoff board and landing area.

The true flight of the long jumper is a parabola similar to the flight of a projectile. If she is forced to attain her height too soon, this pattern is destroyed and she falls sharply back to the landing area. If, on the other hand, she leaves the takeoff board at the proper angle, she will reach her high point out away from the takeoff board and descend in a long, gentle curve.

Long jumping is a movement pattern that requires a great deal of skill. The girl who aspires to be a long jumper must be willing to work hard at other events. She likely would find it to her advantage to train with the high jumpers and the hurdlers where the drive up and the push-off force her to use her takeoff leg in an action similar to that required in the jump for distance.

STANDING LONG JUMP

According to the rules of this event, the participant jumps from an inclined board onto mats or other safe material. She is permitted to curl her toes over the end of the takeoff board, though they may not touch the floor beyond. Since this is a power event and all of the driving force is produced by muscular action, a girl must take advantage of the mechanical principles which apply. The girl having strong legs may bend her knees about ninety degrees to attain maximum force. If her legs are weak, she will bend or flex them only about twenty degrees, for though a deeper bend is potentially more powerful, only the stronger performer can utilize this superior mechanical form.

The jumper attempts to stay relaxed by rocking slowly backward and forward. When she is ready to jump, she flexes her knees, drops her arms, and in a smoothly coordinated effort thrusts her arms upward in perfect timing with the explosive extension of her legs. This action drives the body upward and forward at an angle of about thirty degrees. The chest and shoulders are extended and the legs are carried in a flexed position during the flight. The landing is effected by piking forward and spreading the feet to gain distance. The shock of falling is dissipated into the joints of the ankles, knees, and hips. (This latter point is most essential because the girl who remains rigid may injure herself or lose her balance and fall backward onto her hands or seat.)

SOME COMMON ERRORS IN THE RUNNING LONG JUMP

1. Rushing at the takeoff board with such speed and tension that there is no time for mentally gathering and lifting.
2. Taking a last stride which is too long or too short, in which event the long stride breaks forward momentum tending to rotate the jumper backward. The short stride, on the other hand, causes the jumper to dive off the board to a landing on hands and knees.
3. Failure to keep the feet and legs up during the final part of the flight is a common cause of losing distance.
4. Some long jumpers do not give adequate attention to the adjustment of their check marks. They develop a habit of changing their stride pattern or looking down at the takeoff board during the last twenty to thirty feet of their approach and are unable to mobilize their entire effort for an explosive lift-off.

TYPICAL TRAINING SCHEDULE
FOR THE BEGINNING LONG JUMPER

It is well to keep in mind that the beginner must increase her strength and speed as well as learn a complicated motor skill. For this reason, specific time should be allocated to each of these factors. Where time is limited, speed and skill should receive maximum attention, with strengthening activities introduced into the schedule whenever possible.

M. Jog two laps, followed by fifteen minutes of stretching and calisthenic activity.

5 x 75 sprint buildups with slow walk-back recovery. (Avoid all-out sprinting until later in the season.)

Five minutes of easy shuffle on grass.

Fifteen minutes of pop-up drill off springboard with emphasis on a single hitch kick.

Finish with several short sprints up an inclined area.

T. Warm up as indicated.

3 x 150 fast stride with 220 walk-back recovery.

Five minutes of recovery shuffle.

Join the sprinters and take ten starts from blocks (25 to 35 yards).

Five minutes of recovery shuffle.

Work on strengthening activities with special emphasis on abdominal muscles.

W. Warm up as indicated.

Place check marks on the track and run through several times at regular approach speed, adjusting as necessary.

Five minutes of recovery shuffle.

Take ten pop-up jumps for form. Concentrate on sprinting off the board, driving the chest outward and upward.

Jump three to five times for distance from full approach.

Finish workout with five minutes of recovery shuffle.

Th. Warm up as indicated.

Fast stride 220—shuffle 220.

Sprint 150—shuffle 440.

Sprint 110—shuffle 440.

Sprint 50—followed by five minutes of recovery shuffle.

Work over four hurdles for ten minutes, concentrating on powerful lift-off action.

Work on strengthening activities with special emphasis on abdominal muscles.

F. Warm up as indicated.

Take ten starts with sprinters (20 to 30 yards).

Ten minutes of recovery shuffle.

Take ten pop-up jumps for form. Concentrate on landing coordination, keeping the legs up, extending the heels, piking sharply forward to attain maximum distance.

Take several full-approach jumps for distance.

Finish workout with five minutes of recovery shuffle.

S. Twenty minutes of striding and stretching.

Strengthening activities, followed by additional easy striding on grass.

TYPICAL TRAINING SCHEDULE
FOR THE SKILLED LONG JUMPER

Early Season (February through March)

Every turnout is to be preceded by fifteen to twenty minutes of striding and stretching activity. See both general and specific conditioning exercises (chapter 16). Concentrate on abdominal strength.

M. 5 x 75-yard sprint buildups with walk-back recovery.

Five minutes of easy shuffle recovery.

Ten pop-up jumps, emphasizing one hitch kick with landing in stride position. (This teaches the performer to drive the chest upward off the board and to negotiate one full stride in the air.)

Take five full-approach jumps for distance. Finish workout with ten 50-yard sprint pickups.

T. 220 fast stride with walk-back recovery.

Repeat 220 fast stride.

Five minutes of shuffle recovery.

10 x 5 low hurdles set at regular distance for stride consistency work.

Five minutes of shuffle recovery.

Finish with 5 x 75 sprint pickups.

W. Run through long-jump approach on the track ten times.

Five minutes of shuffle recovery.

Take several pop-up jumps with concentration on sprinting off the board.

Take three full-approach jumps for distance.

Complete workout by striding through 330.

Th. Three by 150 fast stride with walk-back recovery.

Five minutes of shuffle recovery.

Take ten starts 30 to 40 yards with sprinters.

Five minutes of shuffle recovery.

Finish workout by taking several high jumps at a height six inches below maximum height.

F.   Thirty minutes of acceleration work on grass. (Fifty- to sixty-yard sprint pickups with slow walk-back recovery—stretch and repeat.)

S.   Twenty to thirty minutes of easy striding and stretching.

Competitive Season

Each training session is to be preceded by fifteen minutes of striding and stretching. Give continued emphasis to strengthening the abdominal muscles.

M.   150 stride-through—walk back.

150 run-through—walk back.

150 sprint-through—five minutes of shuffle recovery.

Take ten pop-up jumps for form. (Concentrate on landing with legs held high in pike position.) Take three jumps for distance.

Five minutes of recovery shuffle.

Work for fifteen minutes with sprint relay team, or finish workout with 5 x 75-yard sprints.

T.   Stride through 330 for strength-form.

Five minutes of recovery shuffle.

Take ten starts with sprinters—30 to 40 yards.

Five minutes of recovery shuffle.

220 stride-through—walk 440.

220 run-through—walk 440.

220 sprint to finish workout.

W.   Set check marks at long-jump approach and run through several times.

Take several pop-up jumps for form.

Stretch well for recovery, to be followed by eight to ten long jumps for distance.

Finish with ten minutes of easy shuffle on grass.

Th.   2 x 110 sprint buildups with walk-back recovery.

Place check marks on track and run through at regular approach speed several times.

Work for fifteen minutes with sprint relay team, or finish turnout with five by 50-yard sprints.

F.   Fifteen to twenty minutes of easy striding and stretching.

S.   Competition.

PERFORMANCE TIPS FOR COMPETITOR AND COACH

1. Confidence on the takeoff board is essential to the wreckless abandon which is necessary for a maximum expenditure of energy in the long jump. Coach and athlete should always approach this phase of the training program with a positive attitude—working, working, working until a sense-feel is developed, assuring the performer of success. Repeated running through one's check marks and other "stride consistency" work are effective at this point.

2. While approach speed is emphasized by most contemporary long jumpers and the phrase "sprinting off the board" is used to depict the action of takeoff, it must be remembered that lift, which is essential to maximum distance, is attained by an extension of a partially bent takeoff leg. This lifting action is explosive, demanding great strength and perfect timing. Specialized exercises and hundreds of jumps are required to produce the results desired.

3. Watch the takeoff foot on the board. For lift to occur there must be a heel-ball-toe action sequence.

4. To avoid boredom and unnecessary fatigue, the serious performer will vary her training program. The high jump and hurdle events are particularly valuable in this respect since they give emphasis to vertical lift and to consistency of stride pattern, both of which are essential to long-jump success.

5. On the day of competition give careful attention to the conditions of weather, running surface, and the like. Take several full-speed approaches before actually jumping so that all necessary adjustments can be made and the event can be entered with complete confidence.

6. It is important during the latter portion of the approach that the long jumper look up, think up, and then drive forward and upward off the board.

Part IV

Throwing Events

Chapter 12

Throwing Events

The successful teacher is aware that the human body is best adapted to those activities involving speed and range of motion and least well adapted to those demanding great power. Moreover, she is conscious that skillful performance is often dependent upon specific postural adjustments by the performer. In "throwing," for instance, the weight of the implement and the length of the approach determine the nature of the "throwing" technique. Each of the throwing events therefore has a different motor pattern. These patterns have been modified from time to time, but their general form is consistent owing to years of study and experimentation and the relatively fixed structure of the human body.

In reality, the softball throw is the only "typical throwing event" in track and field. The javelin, because of its length, becomes more of a pull; the discus becomes a whip; and the shot, which is the heaviest of all implements thrown by women, becomes a thrust. In this and the next three chapters, the throwing events are discussed in detail.

SOFTBALL THROW

The competitive softball throw is an excellent event for girls and a natural lead-up to throwing the javelin. Since the softball is comparatively light, very young girls can participate in this event and in so doing improve their strength and coordination. Then too, early exposure to throwing may lead to personal satisfaction, causing girls as they mature to want to explore other throwing events.

Analysis of the Softball Throw

The throw is made from a running approach, with the performer utilizing a transitional step to attain maximum force from body momentum and muscular strength. A good throw is a ballistic act. The performer approaches the scratch line with as much speed as can be transferred into the throw; she hops or glides into the throwing position, breaks her progress with the outstretched foot, and literally explodes. The distance which the ball will travel is fixed at the instant of release and is a result of both velocity and trajectory.

The velocity which is imparted to the ball is determined by the "captured speed" of the approach, the distance through which the force is applied, and the speed with which the arm is moved. The trajectory is determined by the angle at which the ball is released. To utilize these factors effectively, the girl must develop a high degree of flexibility and coordination and timing.

Throwing seems an unnatural movement pattern for most girls because they are required or permitted to throw so little. At present there does not appear to be any simple means of instructing them to throw properly, though perhaps a knowledge of the mechanical principles involved will provide some clues to more effective performance.

It has been stated on several occasions that any force which is exerted to propel either the body or some implement held by the body must be initiated from the base of support. As a first principle of throwing, a base must be established which gives the performer adequate support and balance. For a standing throw, the base should be slightly wider than the shoulders. When throwing from a run, the base must be extended to provide for a transfer of momentum from the run to the object to be thrown. The beginning performer frequently establishes a base which is too short, thus restricting her range of motion, upsetting her timing, and forcing her to throw with the arm alone. A throw which is made predominantly with the arm may result in injury to the elbow or shoulder.

A second principle essential to effective throwing is a backward body lean and rearward extension of the throwing arm to obtain full range of motion. The ball should travel in a wide arc from a point well back and down near the hips to the point of release well above the right shoulder. As the thrower approaches the final scratch line, she takes a glide hop which permits her to lay back over the rear foot. She is at this instant in a position which places her left side toward the direction of the throw. The trunk is bent rearward so that the body tends to form a bow. Anatomically this is the most powerful throwing position for light objects. The sudden forward rotation of the hip, rearward thrust of the free arm, and powerful forward flexion of the trunk—all impart great momentum to the arm. Without these adjustments the throw would be a flat snap delivery, imparting little velocity to the ball.

A third principle necessary to effective throwing is the attainment of a relaxed elevation of the elbow. Since most girls tend to rotate their throwing arm through a short, flat arc, the importance of the elevated elbow must be maximized. In the final transfer of forces, the girls should be instructed to lead with the elbow, bringing it through high above the throwing shoulder. This eliminates the snap throw and permits a final flail so essential to great distance.

TEACHING THE SOFTBALL THROW

For most girls, learning to throw correctly first involves the elimination of faulty habit patterns. This is followed by concentrated practice on the proper throwing technique.

At the outset, little attention should be given to such refinements as fingertip control, point of aim, distance, or accuracy. The attainment of the general configuration of the throwing pattern should be the initial emphasis of the teacher. She should help the learner to develop a sense of feel for the gross essentials of the act; to shift her weight to the rear foot and extend her arm rearward and then to step forward into the throw. The step and the push are particularly important for girls because they help to compensate for girls' typically weak shoulder girdle muscles. The push also helps the learner to overcome her inertia. It teaches her to stride before throwing, thus adding this force to the force of the arm.

One practice situation that has been used successfully in teaching girls to throw is a drill in which a girl stands sideward to her target, reaches rearward as far as she can, and then pulls the ball upward and forward to a point of delivery well above the right shoulder. This drill seeks to give emphasis to the great range of motion through which the human is capable of moving. Moreover, it encourages the learner to expend her energy both upward and forward and nullifies the tendency which most girls have to throw through a short, flat arc.

While working with beginners, the teacher must emphasize the fact that the axis of rotation in the throw is the shoulder, followed by an extension of the arm at the elbow joint. This latter point is of fundamental importance because many girls have a tendency to throw with a fixed elbow, thus attaining only a minimum of force from the inward rotators of the upper arm.

When teaching, it is doubtful if much verbal attention should be given to the follow-through. This is particularly true with such complicated events as the shot, discus, and the javelin; in these events too much attention to the follow-through frequently results in a premature release of the implement. When this is the case, the forces of motion are dissipated into the body and not the object being thrown. For the girl who is learning to throw, however, the follow-through is important, not because it adds distance or direction to the throw, but because it permits the learner to relax and to coordinate her efforts more efficiently.

Careful observation of the movement patterns of girls who are learning to throw will reveal that many of them tend to recoil into themselves when they release the ball. These learners are stiff; they keep their weight over the rear foot and thus cannot impart sufficient force to the ball to send it more than a short distance. On the other hand, when the girl gets the picture of pushing, stepping, and following through, she tends to compensate for her physical weakness and her initial reluctance to let herself go into the throw.

Throwing can be fun, and it is a skill of great importance. Teachers should work patiently and persistently with girls so that they can learn to throw well, for the development of this skill will pay dividends in their subsequent performance of most sports.

Chapter 13

Discus

Careful study of track and field records during the past fifty years reveals that the greatest changes have occurred in the field events. Perhaps nowhere is this more obvious than with the discus where the current record of 205 feet 2 inches is more than 200 percent better than the championship throw of 69 feet 2¼ inches recorded in 1920. As in other events, however, this change has been gradual, with moderate improvement being made year after year.

During the 1940s Francis Gorn-Kaszubski was the top U.S. performer in the discus. A member of the 1948 Olympic team, Mrs. Kaszubski was stricken with pneumonia the day of her preliminary competition in London, England. Erlene Brown attained international stature in this event following her introduction to the discus just prior to the 1956 Olympic Games. Mrs. Brown's best throw of 176 feet 10½ inches, made in 1960, still stands as an American record.

Only two other American performers have "thrown" the discus over 170 feet. One of these is Olga Fikotova-Connolly who competed as a member of the 1956 Olympic team representing Czechoslovakia. Following the Olympic Games, Miss Fikotova married Hal Connolly, an American hammer thrower. After coming to the United States, Mrs. Connolly won the national discus title in the years 1957, 1960, 1962, 1964, and 1967. Because of her marriage to an American citizen, she also has been able to represent the United States in Olympic competition.

The other American female athlete to exceed 170 feet in the discus is Nebraska schoolteacher Carol Moseke Frost. While Mrs. Frost is an outstanding performer for her size, she is no match for the more powerful European discus throwers. Indeed, both Nina Ponomaryeva and Tamara Press, former world record holders from the U.S.S.R., are tall, powerful women. Liesel Westermann, of West Germany, the current world discus record holder, as well as Anita Hentschel, Karin Illgen, and Christine Spielberg, of East Germany, are other top performers who manifest the relationship between size and excellence in this event.

PERFORMANCE TECHNIQUE

The discus throw might well be described as a twist and whip. The event is a twisting one, the body turning through an eight-foot circle, hips and legs driving to a position of balance and power from which the whip of the discus can be effected.

Perhaps no event is more difficult to master than the discus. The performer must have considerable speed, a high degree of motor coordination, good balance and strength. Size is an asset in this event, though the participant need not be an amazon. The essential prerequisite is the ability to develop maximum twisting momentum during the spin across the ring. Since momentum is determined by the body mass times its speed, the smaller girl can compensate for her lesser mass by learning to spin with increased speed.

The 1 3/4 Spin

The exact size of the discus ring is 8 feet 2½ inches in diameter. To produce the greatest possible centrifugal force the participant begins her spin from the extreme back portion of this circle. Facing the rear of the circle, feet approximately shoulder width, the right foot is planted on an imaginary line bisecting the circle into a right and a left half. The discus is held loosely in the hand, the body relaxed though poised for action. The spin is preceded by two or three preliminary swings of the discus forward and backward across the body. A rhythm established, the discus back, and the weight over the right foot, the performer suddenly begins to unwind. The action is initiated by the legs and hips as the weight is shifted to the left and the body is thrown out of balance toward the center of the ring. The upper body is completely relaxed, the right arm being pulled along behind with the discus at shoulder height. During this portion of the spin it is essential that the feet remain in contact with the ground as long as possible.

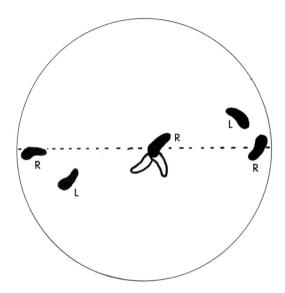

Figure 13.1. Footwork for the discus throw

Displacement of the body weight forces the performer to establish a new base of support in the direction of the spin. This is accomplished by pivoting on the left foot, lifting the right foot and driving it forward to a support position near the center of the circle. With every effort being made to accelerate the spin, the performer now pivots around the right foot, extending the left leg to its final placement near the front of the ring and several inches to the left of the center line. This key throwing stance must place the performer in a balanced position, permitting her to transfer centrifugal force and muscular power to the discus.

Whip and Delivery

In the powerful delivery position the legs are bent, the weight is over the rear foot, the body is rotated far to the right, and the arm is extended, continuing to carry the discus at shoulder height. This stance is wide and open so that the drive of the rear leg and hip is up and forward into the throw. The throw must be effected through a long range of motion, delivering the discus at an angle of about thirty degrees and spinning in a clockwise manner. This is the critical phase in discus throwing and demands hours of patient practice.

Figure 13.2. The preliminary windup prior to the spin. Note the grip of the discus and the balanced position of the performer.

Figure 13.3. Completing the first half turn. Note that the discus is trailed behind the body as the performer drives around the left pivot foot to establish a balanced and powerful throwing position at the center of the circle.

Figure 13.4. The release position. All possible forces have been transferred to the discus, namely, turning speed and muscular power.

THINGS TO REMEMBER WHEN TEACHING THE DISCUS

1. The learner should be made to recognize that the forces which impart distance to the throw are produced by the unwinding action of the body. The performer must first wind up, then unwind during the spin across the ring. The spin must terminate in a balanced and powerful throwing position which permits the discus to be delivered in a relaxed and graceful manner.
2. The learner should be made to recognize that although the critical force is imparted to the discus by the spin, ultimate expenditure of this force is dependent upon balance at the instant of delivery. She should also be made aware that the final action sequence includes a powerful extension of the ankle, knee, and hip, rotation

of the trunk, an outward and downward thrust of the left arm, followed by the whip action of the throwing arm.

3. Strength is profoundly important to ultimate success. The serious performer will therefore engage herself in some type of resistance training for the purpose of developing the specific strengths essential to this event. (See chapter 16 on conditioning exercises.)

4. Since torquing force is basic to the discus throw, the trend in this event is toward greater and greater range of turning motion. The transition thus has been from 1½ turns to 1¾ turns and more. While as yet no one has been highly successful with two full turns, this undoubtedly will constitute the form of the future. The serious performer therefore commits herself to a style which permits a long, fast, and powerful turn. Some tips to facilitate the attainment of such a goal are as follows:

   a. Rotate the whole body farther clockwise in the preliminary position, *i.e.*, place the left foot on the center line of the circle rather than the right foot as is typical of current technique.

   b. Following the preliminary swings with the discus, quickly shift all of the body weight over the left foot and sprint around this pivotal point, driving the right foot forward to a new and balanced base of support.

   c. Try to move the mass of the hips well ahead of the trunk and trailing discus. Do so by literally "picking up" the right heel from its preliminary position at the rear of the circle and placing it in the appropriate position at the center of the circle. Concentrate on a quickening action where foot placement is concerned.

   d. Keep the discus close to the body during the turn to minimize rotational inertia (the resistance to turning). Take a long preliminary swing to attain the greatest possible range of motion, then permit the discus to settle behind the body and downward over the left hip. Retain this position until the last possible instant, when the discus is lifted upward to again utilize the long, fast-moving lever for maximum release velocity.

TEACHING THE DISCUS THROW

A logical series of steps to be followed when teaching beginners to throw the discus is listed below:

1. Teach the grip.
2. Teach the swing and release.

3. Teach the pivot step and throw to develop a sense of timing and to cause the learner to get the feel of driving up through the body from the ground.

4. Early in the learning experience the learner should be introduced to the 1¾ spin. The spin should be explored with an attitude of relaxed abandon. The learner should be encouraged to let go, to spin with performance-level speed, to search until the balanced throwing position is found. (Speed will compound the errors at first, though in the final analysis skillful performance will be more readily attained, for a skill learned at one rate of speed is a different skill than when learned at another rate of speed.)

1. *Grip*

Assuming that an ordinary dinner plate were the discus, the grip would be taught as follows.

Place the plate face down. Lay your hand on the plate with fingers spread, the tips of the fingers extended over the edge of the plate. The thumb is pointing away from the fingers and is lying comfortably on top of the plate. The wrist is cocked slightly toward the little finger. When the plate (or discus) is lifted, it is held in the hand by centrifugal force as the arm is swung backward and forward across the body. (The learner must avoid flexing her wrist. This is a common error and frequently causes a girl to lift the front of the discus at the instant of delivery, creating a resistance which destroys the desired sail effect.)

Figure 13.5. The discus handhold.

2. *Swing and Release*

The beginner should concentrate on learning how to deliver the discus properly. This can be accomplished by assuming the throwing stance behind a line, the left side toward the direction of flight, right arm extended rearward, and weight over the back foot as described. The discus is swung back and forth across the body several times to establish a sense of timing. Its path is a line extended from a point well to the rear, and several inches below the height of the shoulder, to the forward delivery point which is about shoulder height. The discus is carried with the palm down, the force of the swing keeping it securely in the hand.

After several exploratory swings, attention is shifted to the delivery. In the discus event the point of delivery is sideward, with the index finger imparting the final force and clockwise spin to the implement. Mastery of these skills demands careful concentration and hours of practice. The learning throws should not exceed thirty feet, though the performer should try again and again to deliver the discus smoothly and with no sign of wobble.

3. *Step and Throw*

Learning to control the flight of the implement is essential to successful performance, thus considerable time and attention should be expended on the swing and release. Once this phase of the skill is mastered, the competitor should be encouraged to proceed toward a moving delivery. Perhaps this can best be accomplished by teaching the girl to step and throw—a prelude to the spin.

To perform the step and throw properly, the girl stands in the center of the circle, facing forward. Her feet are shoulder width and her body relaxed, the discus held loosely at her side. Following a preliminary leftward swing, the discus is carried back across the body, and the weight is shifted momentarily to the right side. Without hesitation the body follows the discus in its clockwise path, winding up for the powerful whipping action to follow. Immediately the weight pivots back over the right toe, the left leg is extended forward to establish a wide, solid base, and the discus is whipped forward again into its trajectory. (This motion actually is a right pivot on the right foot—a step forward onto the left foot and a transfer of the body mass from the right foot onto the left foot—with a long, coordinated whip or throw.) The step and throw should receive extensive practice, both as an aid to learning the whip and delivery and as an adjunct to the development of a powerful hip drive.

4. *The 1 3/4 Spin*

Even the experts do not agree as to the best way to teach the complete spin. Some advocate the part-whole approach, with a gradual increase in speed. It is the writers' belief, however, that it is best to introduce the spin as a total, coordinated action in which both speed and balance are essential. When guided by this point of view, the teacher instructs the learner to take her preliminary stance at the back of the circle, to wind up, and then to just let herself go. In this way she will not become encumbered with such factors as exact foot placement, body position, and the like, but will perceive the central purpose of the spin, which is the development of controlled speed. By taping a discus to the hand and practicing the spin with the proper weight and speed, the performer avoids undue fatigue and attains a maximum of purposeful activity.

Adapting the Discus to the Gym Class

Perhaps the best approach to mass instruction for the discus event is to begin with the basketball throw. This can be done in the gymnasium, using the eight-foot circle and the spin. The throwing technique is almost identical to the whip motion used to deliver the discus. The ball is controlled by centrifugal force and delivered by the same force, which is developed by the windup and the unwinding motion of the spin.

There also are soft rubber discs which are available for practice purposes. These can be used successfully in the gymnasium because they possess accurate flight characteristics and are not likely to injure students or facilities.

TRAINING SCHEDULE FOR THE BEGINNING DISCUS THROWER

The training schedule for the discus thrower would be almost identical to that used by the shot-putter, the discus being substituted for the shot. The practice session should be preceded by a jog of 440 yards and fifteen minutes of conditioning exercises.

M. Stride 100 yards at three-quarter speed, rest, and repeat. Drill on the 1¾ spin for twenty minutes without the discus.

Take ten to fifteen throws from a stand at the front of the ring. Train down with relaxed striding for ten minutes.

Weight training.

T.   Stride 220 yards at three-quarter speed.

Take several starts with the sprinters.

Sprint 75 yards, rest, and repeat three times.

Go to the shot-put area and work on putting form for fifteen minutes.

W.   Warm up well, with emphasis on stretching the shoulders, hips, and lower back.

Take several practice throws from a stand. Rest and throw six times for distance.

Train down with relaxed striding on the grass.

Weight training.

Th. Stride 220 yards.

Sprint 75 yards, rest, and repeat three times.

Practice 1¾ spin for twenty minutes without the discus. Go to the shot-put area and put several times from a stand.

F.   Take several starts, sprinting fifteen to twenty yards each time.

Take several practice throws from a stand. Then throw ten times for distance. Stay relaxed.

Weight training.

TRAINING SCHEDULE FOR THE SKILLED PERFORMER

It is advocated that some type of resistance training be pursued throughout most of the year. Thus the reader will note that this kind of activity is continued on a twice-weekly basis even during the competitive season.

Early Season

M.   Two laps of jogging, followed by fifteen minutes of exercise and stretching for warm-up.

5 x 50 sprint with walk-back recovery.

Five minutes of recovery shuffle.

Standing throws for ten minutes to loosen arm and shoulder muscles.

Several minutes of "shadow turns" without discus.

Fifteen to twenty full-turn throws for form. Concentrate on grooving the total skill.

Weight training: bench press, two arm curls, butterfly pulls, leg press, low back exercise. (See chapter 16)

T. Warm up as indicated.

3 x 150 fast stride with 220 walk recovery.

Twenty minutes' work, both half and full circle with shot-put.

Ten to fifteen standing throws for power pull and hip-lift emphasis.

10 x 10-yard single leg drives in shot-put position. (Alternate legs each time.)

Finish with five minutes of recovery shuffle.

W. Warm up as indicated.

Five to ten standing throws to loosen arm and shoulder girdle.

Twenty-five to thirty-five throws with full turn. Continue to concentrate on balance and power. (Preferably use two discuses so that feedback information can be incorporated into an immediate second throw.)

Complete workout with several short sprints.

Th. Warm up as indicated.

10 x 50 sprints (with near full recovery between sprints).

Twenty minutes' work with shot.

Weight training.

F. Warm up as indicated.

If possible, train someplace other than on the "home track."

Explore the effects of trajectory, angle of attack, wind directions, and the like.

Twenty-five to thirty-five throws with emphasis on torquing speed. (Sprint around the pivot foot.)

Finish with several short sprints.

S. Twenty minutes of easy striding and stretching.

Weight training.

Competitive Season

M. Five minutes of jogging followed by fifteen minutes of stretching and calisthenic activity.

Five to ten standing throws using five-pound barbell plate. Emphasize total body involvement in lift-whipping action.

5 x 50 sprint with walk-back recovery.

Twenty to thirty throws for distance with emphasis again on the total body involvement.

T. Warm up as indicated.

5 x 75 sprints with walk-back recovery.

Thirty minutes of work with shot if also involved with this event. For the discus specialist, fifteen minutes of "shadow turns" followed by ten to fifteen coordination throws.

Weight training.

W. Warm up as if this were a day of competition.

Take six throws with competitive time interval between each. Jog one lap and repeat. Thirty to thirty-six throws in all.

Complete workout with several short sprints.

Th. Warm up as indicated.

Five standing throws, followed by ten throws from full spin.

Concentrate on total body involvement, just abandoning oneself to the well-learned motor skill.

Complete workout with several short sprints.

F. Competition.

S. Fifteen minutes of jogging and stretching, followed by weight training.

NOTE: If competition is on Saturday, use Thursday for weight training and follow with Thursday's schedule for Friday.

PERFORMANCE TIPS FOR COMPETITOR AND COACH

1. The direction and force of the wind has a marked effect on the flight of the discus. Whenever possible, adjust your position in the circle so as to capitalize on a right-side wind. Too, when throwing into the wind, the angle of release should be less (twenty-five degrees) than when throwing with the wind (thirty-five degrees).

2. To avoid falling into the circle and a serious loss of balance and power, give initial emphasis to a shift of the body mass over the left pivotal foot. This action permits the performer to accelerate her turning motion by expending all available force through the center of the body mass.

3. Recognize that a vigorous preliminary swing tends to pull the performer out of balance, thus the length of this swing should be

determined by the skill and ability of the performer. For the beginner this swing is minimal; for the highly skilled performer it is markedly longer as she seeks to attain maximum range of motion.

4. It takes literally thousands of turns to become proficient in the discus event. When in doubt as to what she ought to be doing, the discus specialist should practice the turn.

5. While the discus event must be approached as a total skill, frequent attention should be given to part practice of this complicated motor pattern. Two part skills which should receive special attention are as follows:

  a. The initial shift left, with *sprint* to the balanced-power position at the center of the circle. Concentrate on letting the discus fall behind and downward over the left hip during this portion of the turn.

  b. The turning-lifting action which eventuates in the actual release of the discus. It is particularly important that female performers catch the significance of lifting the hip and chest ahead of the trailing arm. The actual release then becomes a summation of all possible turning and lifting forces. During practice, lift from a flexed right leg, which is the only way to attain maximum power.

6. Other Key concepts are the following:

  a. Sit—don't squat—when assuming a preliminary position at the rear of the circle.

  b. Drive or sprint—don't just pivot.

  c. Keep the feet down as long as possible. Let the torquing hips lift them from the throwing surface.

  d. Concentrate on continuity. Avoid a swing-swing sequence across the circle.

  e. Program yourself so that the right foot plant becomes the trigger for the actual throw.

  f. Recognize that release velocity stems from turning speed.

  g. Abandon yourself to the turn—neither too fast nor too slow—gambling on greatness.

  h. It takes thousands of turns to produce greatness.

  i. Keep the discus close to the body during the first three-quarter turn—away from the body during the final full turn.

Chapter 14

Shot-Put

By international standards American women are weak in the throwing events. This is particularly true in the shot and discus where an American athlete seldom is listed among the world's top ten performers. While the shot-put has been contested in women's track and field for more than half a century, this event was not introduced into the Olympic schedule until 1948.

During the period from 1956 to 1962, Erlene Brown, of Los Angeles, dominated the Shot-Put in the United States. Her American record of 54 feet 9 inches was set during a European tour on September 21, 1960. The 1963 national champion in this event was Sharon Sheppard, of Athens, Georgia, whose mark was 48 feet 3½ inches. Perhaps the performance of teen-agers Lynn Graham and Maron Seidler during recent years is indicative of a new trend in the shot-put in this country. Miss Seidler, who participated as a member of the U.S. Olympic team in Mexico City while still a high school girl, is only the second American to put the shot more than fifty feet (50 feet 3¾ inches).

Perhaps the most noted of all female field event performers was Tamara Press, of the U.S.S.R. Miss Press was the Olympic Champion in 1960 and 1964 as well as the world's top performer in this event from 1959 through 1967. She was the first woman to put the shot over sixty feet, exceeding this distance on many occasions. The current world record holder is Margitta Gummel, of East Germany, whose mark of 64 feet 4 inches was established during the 1968 Olympic Games.

PERFORMANCE TECHNIQUE

Shot-putting is an event involving a powerful driving action of the legs and hips, coupled with a thrusting action of the arm. In essence, the act of putting can be likened to a catapult; potential energy is produced by pulling the power arm back and downward and liberated by freeing this arm to explode upward and forward. The mobilization of energy by pulling an ordinary kitchen spatula back and down and the sudden release of this energy sending a marble into space is very similar to the mechanics of shot-putting.

More so than any other track and field event, the shot-put is looked upon with disdain by many women. This stems, in part at least, from the fact that some shot-putters are large, overweight girls. While body mass, strength, and speed are essential to high-level performance in the shot-put, these factors are not mandatory for success in the girls' physical education class. In fact, girls who possess only average body size but who are strong and quick can participate successfully in this event.

The women's shot-put is an iron ball weighing four kilo (8 pounds 14 ounces). As in the men's event, the shot is put from a ring seven feet in diameter. To produce the force which is essential to putting, the participant must utilize to the fullest extent those principles of mechanics which are favorable to this event. These include a low center of gravity and wide base for balance, flexion of the extensor joints for power, a shift of the body mass for speed, and a breaking of forward momentum for explosive delivery.

Although numerous techniques have been developed as a means of attaining the optimum effect from these mechanical adaptations, the so-called O'Brien style is used by most contemporary shot-putters. This style permits an effective blending of strength and speed with an extended application of force and can be learned by anyone who is willing to practice.

Shift

The initial stance is taken by the performer at the extreme rear of the circle, the right foot on a hypothetical center line, toe pointing out the back of the circle. The left foot, supporting little of the body weight, also is on the center line though comfortably forward of the right foot.

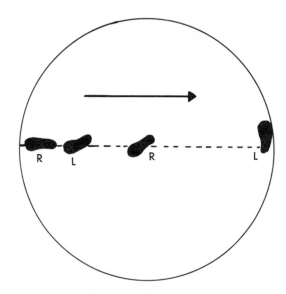

Figure 14.1. Footwork for the shot-put

The performer stands facing the rear of circle, body relaxed with the shot pressed against the neck and cheek. The left arm is extended up and back, and the eyes are focused on a spot some ten feet behind the shot-put ring. The shift is begun by a sudden and simultaneous flexion of the right leg and hip, coupled with the forward lift of the left leg. This is followed immediately by a powerful drive of the right leg. The drive is forward, not upward, shifting the body mass across the ring with as much speed as possible.

Drive and Thrust

Theoretically there is no distinction between one phase of the put and another. When properly performed, the shift, drive and thrust, and follow-through constitute a continuous, flowing movement which terminates in an explosive expenditure of all available energy. For purposes of analysis, however, the drive-thrust period is the most critical period in this event.

The shift covers about half the length of the circle, depending upon the size and speed of the participant. Following the shift, the right foot is again planted on the hypothetical line dividing the circle.

The left foot is planted immediately after the right, against the toe-board and several inches to the left of the center line. The right leg and hip are flexed well beyond forty-five degrees; the trunk, head, and free arm are extended toward the rear of the circle. The eyes continue to focus on the point ten feet outside the ring, an act which is essential if the body mass is to be properly retained over the source of driving power. When properly executed, the shift places the body in a controlled position, the powerful muscles of the legs and hips are on stretch, and the trunk is extended rearward. For optimum per-formance, the trunk is nearly parallel to the ground, permitting the shot to be carried to its lowest point prior to delivery. All available forces are mobilized for action. The thrust which follows is a violent letting go of all forces. The final action sequence is initiated by an extension of the ankles, knees, and hips, flexion and rotation of the trunk, and an extension of the putting arm. The thrust can best be described by the terms *up, out,* and *over,* as the shot is driven up, out, and over the extending forward leg.

Reverse

The reverse is actually a follow-through which comes somewhat naturally after the explosive expenditure of energy into the shot. Here too there are variations in technique. For some the reverse involves a half turn following the put, with the performer changing the po-sition of her feet as a means of controlling momentum. For others the reverse or exchange is not complete, as the girl merely turns forward into the put and lowers her center of gravity by bending her hips and knees. Whichever follow-through is used must come after the ex-penditure of force, and it must permit the participant to dissipate her forces within the shot-put circle.

THINGS TO REMEMBER WHEN TEACHING THE SHOT-PUT

1. Shot velocity is the first objective of the putter. For this reason, all efforts are directed toward imparting great speed to the shot at the time of delivery.
2. In part, the speed which the putter imparts to the shot will be determined by her own momentum. Since momentum is determined by the body mass times its velocity, girls with good speed can compete with girls who possess greater body mass.
3. About ninety percent of the distance of the put is attained from the application of forces during the final thrust. This force comes

Figure 14.2. The preliminary position before the dip and drive. Attention is focused on a spot several feet outside the circle.

Figure 14.3. The dip an instant before the explosive shift or drive across the circle. All of the body mass is balanced over the powerful driving leg. The shoulders are squared rearward, and the eyes are still focused outside the circle.

Figure 14.4. The balanced-power position just prior to the lift, or thrust. Note that the chest is over the lifting leg, the shoulders squared rearward, the eyes still focused outside the circle.

Figure 14.5. The shot has been released at the greatest possible height. Primary concern of the shot-putter is shot velocity. With the eyes now watching the line of flight of the shot, a follow-through occurs, resulting in a reversal of the feet.

195

primarily from muscular strength in the legs and hips and is most effective when applied through the maximum range of motion.

4. The performer should move in a straight line across the ring, increasing her speed through the balanced putting position, driving solidly up, out, and over the extended left leg. Shot-putting should be seen as a smoothly coordinated sequence of action, not a loosely connected chain of events.

5. The shot-putter should run, run, run—running is imperative for the development of speed and leg strength.

Steps in Teaching the Shot-Put

1. Holding the Shot

   The shot is held so that its weight is centralized at the juncture of the hand and the fingers. The fingers should be spread, the three middle fingers behind the shot, the thumb and little finger adding support to the sides. As the competitor gains strength, the shot can be elevated until it ultimately is supported by the uppermost joint of the middle fingers.

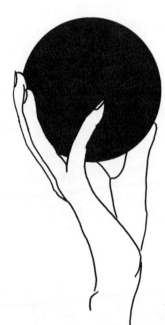

Figure 14.6. Handhold for the shot-put.

2. Putting from a Stand

The putting motion should be learned from a stand. The athlete assumes the strong putting or thrusting position, with the shot held against the cheek and neck (fig. 14.3). To initiate the thrusting action, the center of gravity is shifted back over the flexed right leg. There is a momentary gather, then the right leg drives the body up and forward, and the shot is put with a quick, thrusting stroke. The performer is especially careful to keep the elbow behind the hand and the hand directly behind the shot.

The standing put is extremely important to successful performance. For most shot-putters, the standing put produces ninety percent of the distance attained. Only ten percent is produced by the shift. It is imperative, therefore, that the learner as well as the highly skilled girl stand and put many, many times. It is this drill that teaches the performer to shift her weight over the power source and to explode into the shot. It also is this drill which produces much of the strength, balance, and control so essential to success.

3. Teaching the Shift

Since balance and control are important to shot-putting success, the serious competitor gives attention to the shift early in her training program. She is aware that putting from a stand is not identical to the coordinated driving-shifting motion, thus she incorporates both the shift and the thrust into a single practice situation.

There are two or three points of view about how to best teach the shift. The point of view which has proved to be most successful in the writers' experience is one which encourages a relaxed, natural approach. This point of view assumes that all individuals are different in their body structure and movement patterns, thus their adaptation to a skill must be individualistic. The learner is therefore shown the initial stance, the "teeterboard action" of dropping the shoulder and lifting the leg, and the powerful thrust forward into the shift. She is then asked to explore this sequence herself, striving primarily for a natural movement forward into the balanced and powerful putting position.

In subsequent practice sessions, the teacher provides continuous cues for the learner to follow. She encourages her to emphasize fundamentals, seeking always to attain speed and force without losing balance and power. The highly technical putting sequence is not easy to master, though it seems to come most quickly to those who stay relaxed and just do what comes naturally.

Modifications for the Gym Class

Perhaps the most popular modification for the gym class is the medicine ball put. Medicine balls are larger, they come in various weights, and they are less apt to inflict injury to the participants. For activity class practice the girls assume the thrusting position behind a line and, on the appropriate command, drive up into the ball, following through with a reverse. This drill teaches the girls to mobilize their forces and to expend them into the source of resistance. Moreover, it develops a feel for the reverse, or follow-through, which is essential to successful performance.

TRAINING SCHEDULE FOR THE
BEGINNING SHOT-PUTTER

Begin the workout session with a jog of 440 yards, followed by fifteen minutes of conditioning exercise.

M. Stride 100 yards at three-quarter speed, rest and repeat.
    Practice shift, lift and thrust for ten minutes (without the shot-put).
    Begin easily and put ten or fifteen times from the stand, emphasizing the leg drive and explosive thrust into the shot.
    Train down with relaxed striding for ten minutes.

T. Stride 220 yards at three-quarter speed.
    Go to the discus area and work on discus form for fifteen minutes.
    Weight training.

W. Warm up well with emphasis on stretching the muscles of the shoulders, legs, and lower back.
    Take several practice throws from a stand. Rest and put twenty to twenty-five times for distance, using the full circle.
    Complete workout with 10 x 10-yard single leg drives in putting position.

Th. Stride 220 yards.
    5 x 75 sprints with walk-back recovery.
    Ten to fifteen standing puts.

Pull the discus through from a stand ten to fifteen times.
Weight training.

F.   Take several starts, sprinting 15 to 20 yards each time.
Work on putting form without the shot for fifteen minutes.
Put six from a stand and twenty to thirty with the full approach.
Complete workout with 10 x 10-yard single leg drives.

S.   Fifteen to twenty minutes of striding and stretching.
Weight training.

TRAINING SCHEDULE FOR THE SKILLED PERFORMER

Perhaps the most noteworthy trend in the shot-put event in recent years is the emphasis on strength manifested by the serious performer. While strength and body size are not synonymous, and the writers do not advocate a heavy resistance training program aimed at the development of bulk, it is essential that the serious performer recognize the importance of strength for this event. It is to be noted that strength development exercises are included in the year-around training program for shot-putters.

Early Season

M.   Two laps of jogging, followed by fifteen minutes of stretching and calisthenic activity.
Five minutes of shadow-putting without shot. Concentrate on balance—on simultaneous placement of both feet at the front of the circle—on keeping the shoulders squared to the rear of circle during shift.
Ten puts from stand, followed by twenty-five to thirty-five puts for form. Use two shots when possible to capitalize on feedback information from first put.
Weight training.

T.   Warm up as indicated.
5 x 75-yard sprints.
Twenty minutes' work with discus.
10 x 15 yards of single leg drive in putting position.
Five minutes of easy shuffle for recovery.

W. Warm up as indicated.

Five to ten standing puts, followed by twenty-five to thirty-five puts for form. Give emphasis to explosive lift into the shot, watching the shot during the early portion of its flight.

Weight training.

Th. Warm up as indicated.

Ten by twenty-five-yard starts out of blocks for explosive speed.

Five minutes of recovery shuffle.

Ten minutes of form work without the shot.

Twenty minutes of work with the discus.

10 x 15 yards of single leg drive in putting position.

F. Warm up as indicated.

5 x 100 sprints with walking recovery.

Fifteen standing puts, each progressively longer than the one preceding, finishing with three at maximum effort.

Ten minutes of shuffle recovery.

Six puts for distance to complete workout.

S. Twenty minutes of striding and stretching.

Weight training.

Competitive Season

M. Warm up as indicated.

10 x 30-yard sprint buildups.

Ten standing puts, each progressively longer.

Five minutes of shadow putting, concentrating on speed and balance.

Twenty-five to thirty-five puts at near maximum effort.

Five minutes of easy shuffle to complete turnout.

T. Warm up as indicated.

10 x 25-yard starts out of blocks.

Five minutes of shadow putting, followed by ten full-circle puts.

Twenty minutes' work with discus.

Weight training.

W. Warm up as if this were a day of competition.

Put several from stand, followed by five to six sets of six from full circle. Jog lap between each set of six. At least twelve of these should be at full effort for distance.

Finish turnout with several short sprints.

Th. Warm up as indicated.

10 x 15 yards of single leg drives in putting position.

Put several times from full circle just for the "feel."

Five minutes of easy shuffle to complete turnout.

F. Competition.

S. Twenty minutes of recovery jogging and stretching.

Weight training.

PERFORMANCE TIPS FOR COMPETITOR AND COACH

1. The three key factors in shot-putting are (a) velocity of release, (b) angle of release, and (c) height of release. Thus the shot which is released at maximum velocity, at an angle of forty-five degrees, and at the greatest possible height will travel the longest possible distance. When a compromise in technique must be made to accommodate the human element, it is imperative that shot velocity be retained at the expense of either the height of release or the trajectory through which the shot travels. Release velocity is the most important factor in shot-putting.

2. During competition total concentration should be on an explosive expenditure of all available forces into the put.

3. To negate any pause in the shift-lift sequence, the right foot plant at the center of the circle should constitute the "trigger" which initiates the explosive putting action.

4. Establish performance habits during practice. Don't foul, don't get sloppy, don't put halfheartedly. Develop confidence which is essential to a recklessly explosive effort.

5. Stay under and behind the shot. The equal and opposite reaction to expending all available force directly into the shot produces a reverse, or follow-through, without fouling.

6. Attention should be given to the act of "snatching" the right leg and foot beneath the body mass after the shift across the circle.

The coach should stand alongside the performer and watch to see that this action is occurring. Maximum lifting force can only be expended when the flexed right leg is beneath the chest of the performer.

7. Following the shift, the left foot should be "slammed" against the toeboard to provide a firm base over which to apply subsequent forces. At the instant of release, both legs have extended, lifting the hips and driving the chest upward into the put.

Chapter 15

Javelin

Although Mildred Didrikson won the Javelin during the 1932 Olympic Games at Los Angeles, Russian athletes maintained supremacy in this event during the next three decades. This supremacy has been challenged, however, with outstanding performers of the sixties coming from Hungary, Romania, Austria, Poland, Yugoslavia, and the United States.

Karen Anderson, a member of the 1956 U.S. Olympic team, was the first American girl to throw the javelin over 150 feet. Her record of 159 feet 1 inch held until 1963 when Army Specialist Frances Davenport attained a distance of 166 feet 2½ inches. Like most other records, this one was soon broken when San Diego State College co-ed Ranae Bair lofted the javelin 173 feet 4½ inches. In 1967 Miss Bair showed remarkable improvement, throwing the javelin 196 feet 3 inches to rank among the world's leading performers. Indeed, her closest rival at that time was a virtually unknown high school girl from New Jersey, Barbara Friedrich, who on June 7, 1967, posted the year's best mark with a throw of 198 feet 8 inches.

Angela Nemeth, of Hungary, upset defending Olympic champion Mihaila Penes, of Romania, to win the gold medal at Mexico City in 1968. Miss Nemeth's winning throw of 198 feet was almost twelve feet farther than the first-place mark at Tokyo in 1964. The current world record of 204 feet 8½ inches was established by Yelena Gorchakova, of the U.S.S.R., in 1964. Elvira Ozolina, also of the U.S.S.R., is the only other woman in history to exceed 200 feet in this event.

Unlike the shot and discus, the future for American performers looks bright in the javelin event. This fact was made apparent at the 1969 N.A.A.U. meet where three of the top six were teen-aged performers. Surely the names Kathy Schmidt and Sherry Calvert will be found in the record books covering the 1970s.

PERFORMANCE TECHNIQUES

The javelin event can best be described as a modification of the overhand throw. The main difference is that the javelin is pulled through a longer range of motion, making it both a pull and a throw following a run.

The highly skilled javelin thrower is frequently an excellent all-around athlete because she must have good running speed, a high degree of motor coordination, excellent timing, and considerable strength. Although physical size is not an essential prerequisite to success, a girl in this event must possess the ability to impart force to the javelin in a final, explosive act. In the physical education class almost any girl who can throw and who is willing to practice can find enjoyment working with the javelin.

Approach and Carry

Because speed is absolutely essential to successful performance, the javelin thrower approaches the scratch line from a distance which permits her to attain as much speed as she can adequately control.

Figure 15.1. The Finnish javelin handhold.

For most athletes this distance is from 80 to 100 feet. The approach is relaxed, and the rate of acceleration is constant. The javelin is carried comfortably overhead. The extended arm is flexed at the elbow, and the tip of the javelin is tilted toward the ground. The javelin thrower usually has two check marks, one at the start of the run and a second at the point where she begins her gather for the throw.

Gather

To exert maximum force, the athlete must arrive at a position in which the left side is "facing" the intended flight of the javelin. This position puts the throwing muscles on stretch and provides for a maximum range of motion. Moreover, the side opposition stance permits a sudden breaking of the momentum by the forward leg and a transfer of this momentum to the javelin. Both the breaking action and the explosive transfer of momentum are imperative to the maximum javelin velocity. Numerous styles of footwork have been developed to put the athlete in this throwing position. These include the hop, the rear crossover, the glide, and the front crossover. All of these styles have something in their favor, and all have been used by successful javelin throwers. The front crossover seems to be used by most contemporary throwers, however, and this is the pattern which is discussed in detail below.

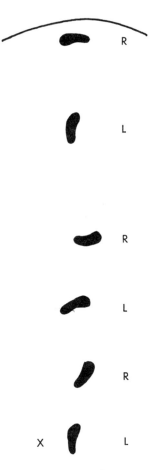

Crossover

The heart of the javelin throw is the final stage of the approach. For the front crossover, the critical period includes the last five steps. There is a period of relaxed acceleration between check marks one and two. As the left foot strikes the ground at check mark two, the javelin is permitted to drift back and down so that it is being pulled along behind the per-

Figure 15.2. Stride pattern for the five-step front cross-over approach.

former. During this time, the tip of the javelin is carried alongside the cheek, the head and eyes are forward, the hips are held in the forward running position, and the right shoulder is turned slightly toward the rear.

Figure 15.3 (above). Front crossover and delivery of the javelin. The approach is relaxed, the javelin carried comfortably overhead, with the body assuming a nearly vertical striding position.

Figure 15.4 (right). As the left foot strikes the check mark, the javelin is carried smoothly to the rear. The shoulder and arm rotate to the right, though the hips remain in alignment to attain maximum speed and range of motion.

Figure 15.5. The front cross-over has been completed. The arm and javelin are extended rearward as the body begins to assume the powerful throwing position.

Figure 15.6. The throwing stride is relatively long. The performer has turned into the throw and is pulling the javelin through with the elbow leading. All possible forces are captured at the instant of release—the speed of approach, rotary motion, and muscular power.

1. The second of the final five steps involves placement of the right foot, with the toe turned slightly outward away from the line of progress.
2. The third step involves placement of the left foot, with the toe turned slightly inward, or toward the right. (In neither instance is the stride modified with regard to length or tempo.)
3. The fourth, or crossover, step is taken by extending the right leg in front of the left so that the right foot is planted with the toe turned outward twenty to thirty degrees. (Throughout these three strides, the girl continues to look forward, though her throwing arm and the javelin are extended well behind her.)
4. The fourth stride is perhaps the most critical phase of the entire approach. It is at this point that the athlete must be under perfect control and in the most effective position for imparting explosive force to the javelin. Immediately after the weight of the body has been transferred to the right leg, the left knee is lifted slightly, and the left foreleg is thrust forward and downward to provide a wide, solid base of support. (This throwing stride is approximately the length of the body.) If properly executed, the crossover and the long stride put the body in a position with the hips forward and the arms and shoulders tilted backward (twenty to thirty degrees out of perpendicular). This bow position permits a subsequent "blast action" as the muscles of the abdomen contract forcefully.

It seems wise at this point to discuss the relative merits of the straight versus the bent forward leg. Traditionally most coaches have advocated the straight leg on the grounds that the long, straight lever produces a rotary force as a result of the hinged principle, that is, the breaking action at the lower end of the lever accelerates the upper end of the lever, thus providing additional force for the throw. While this logic is sound from a theoretical standpoint, it seldom, if ever, can be demonstrated in human performance.

Recently more and more coaches and athletes seem to be advocating the bent front leg. These individuals argue that the straight leg not only does not produce a hinged effect but that it actually negates linear velocity at a time when this is most essential to the javelin thrower. The bent front leg, they say, permits the performer to accelerate into the javelin and by straightening the leg just prior to delivery, truly adds another effective force to the throw. After carefully considering these two arguments and studying hundreds of feet of film, the writers tend to agree with the bent front leg concept. The reader is cautioned, however, that to teach the bent leg concept is dangerous—particularly so with girls and women whose legs tend to be weak. These individuals already have trouble initiating a final explosive lift, and when told to flex their front leg, they frequently just collapse.

The bent front leg should be recognized as a natural consequence of the running approach. Therefore, rather than discuss either a straight or a bent leg, the coach should emphasize the extension of both the right and the left legs at the instant of delivery.

5. The final step is merely a follow-through. If the athlete has gotten into the proper throwing position and has been able to impart her force to the javelin in a ballistic effort, this force will carry her body forward toward the scratch line. This body carry is known as the follow-through, and it is a natural part of the event. While the follow-through is important and essential to good performance, it should receive little actual coaching.

Mechanics of the Throw

Careful study reveals that javelin throwers tend to fall into two broadly defined groups. These are the larger, stronger girls who depend upon strength to attain their objective and the smaller, more graceful girls whose primary asset is speed and skill. The best javelin thrower will be the girl who can combine both strength and speed into a graceful, explosive act. Since most girls do not have great strength, nor do they necessarily want to work toward this end, it is the belief of the writers that the javelin should be presented as a beautiful, coordinated event. Though the importance of a powerful throwing arm must not be minimized, perhaps greatest emphasis should be given to the integrated totality of the event. The gather and delivery might be compared to a quick-moving, gay dance sequence. The girl should see herself as a "vehicle" whose purpose it is to carry the javelin to a point of release. She must be acutely aware of her responsibility to be relaxed and graceful. She must realize that it is the transfer of momentum to the javelin which she is seeking. Perhaps the best analogy for her to consider is the action of the flail. A pulling force is imparted to the handle, to be expended in a final explosive flail of the trailing arm. This is the javelin thrower at her best.

The final throwing sequence is particularly complicated. The instant the left foot makes contact in step 4, the right leg drives up into the hip; the hip is rotated leftward into the trunk; the abdominal muscles contract violently, pulling the shoulders forward while the left arm is thrust outward and downward to the side. All of these forces are now transferred to the right arm. The right arm is pulled through with the elbow leading, the radius first being shortened and then lengthened as the javelin is released high above the right shoulder. An instant before the javelin is released, the forward leg straightens to impart a final force to the throw. All available energy must be expended along the line of the javelin at an angle of thirty to thirty-five degrees. Any downward pull against the shaft results in "tail drag" and subsequent loss of distance.

THINGS TO REMEMBER WHEN TEACHING THE JAVELIN

1. The distance the javelin will travel is determined by its velocity and trajectory at the time of release.
2. The velocity which an individual is able to impart to the javelin is determined by the "captured speed of the approach," the muscular force which she is capable of producing, and the range of motion through which these forces are applied.
3. The javelin throw is appropriately called a pull, terminated with an explosive expenditure of energy. The elbow must lead during the final stages of the pull, with the point of release high above the right shoulder.
4. There must be no loss of speed during the gather and crossover. These last five strides permit the athlete to maintain her forward momentum while turning the body into the powerful throwing position.
5. The crossover step should place the body in a bowed position, the weight over the rear foot, the powerful throwing muscles on stretch. From this position muscular force is exerted sequentially from leg to hip to trunk to the throwing arm.
6. Balance is essential at the time of delivery. The body and the javelin must be under perfect control so that all available forces are expended along the line of flight.
7. The javelin should be looked upon as a beautiful and graceful event, with speed and coordination more important than great strength and power.

STEPS IN TEACHING THE JAVELIN THROW

Handhold

There are two commonly accepted techniques for gripping the javelin. The one which is advocated by the writers is noted in figure 15.6. In this grip the javelin is held in such a manner that the middle finger exerts the pulling force against the binding. The index finger lies along the shaft and provides some stability during the approach. The shaft itself lies diagonally across the hand, from a point on the soft pad just beneath the index finger to the soft pad at the juncture of the wrist and hand. Although there is latitude for choice with respect to the finger positions on the binding, the javelin *must* be held diagonally across the hand. Any deviation from this rule will result in a poor release and subsequent loss in distance.

Flight Control

Once the grip has been decided upon, the learner should begin immediately to develop control of the javelin itself. Perhaps this is best done by having the learner throw a distance of fifteen to twenty feet into a bank, into bales of hay, or at a target area on the ground. These throws should be relaxed and deliberate, with emphasis on control and accuracy. When the flight pattern can be controlled, the learner should move back a short distance and continue to throw. There should be no sense of pressure at this stage of learning, for the sole purpose of the activity is to develop a touch, a sense which often requires several days and hundreds of repetitions. (The writers have had considerable success in developing touch by having girls walk around the field throwing the javelin short distances at weeds, a drill which is referred to as "daisy picking.")

When a sense of control has been developed, the girl should begin to extend her throws to distances of thirty, forty, fifty, sixty, and perhaps seventy feet. These throws are made from a stand, although the base of support is extended to insure balance and to permit a greater range of motion. The trajectory of the throws should be near thirty-five degrees, with great care being given to flight characteristics. All of the energy must be expended into the javelin so that there is a minimum of javelin flutter.

Since throwing from a run and throwing from a stand are two distinctly different motor skills, it is the strong belief of the writers that girls should be introduced to the running throw as soon as they are able to control the flight of the javelin. Foot placement for the running approach was noted (fig. 15.2) and was discussed earlier in this chapter.

After studying the foot placement pattern, the learner should walk through her steps, javelin in hand, until she gets a feel for the turn and crossover. She should next jog through her steps, counting as she goes: 1, 2, 3, cross and pull. This drill helps to develop rhythm and should be continued until this phase of the approach is well learned. (The walking, jogging process should be of short duration, since the actual speed and tempo of performance must receive a large share of practice time.)

Approach and Crossover

Setting the check marks is imperative to mastery of the javelin technique. The performer must be able to make her approach and crossover without direct attention to the details and mechanics of the event. Though the approach doubtless will be extended at a later date, seven strides seem to be adequate for the learner. To determine where the check marks will be set, the athlete stands with her feet side by side, the javelin extended in the carrying position overhead. In her normal manner she steps forward onto the left foot, gradually accelerating until she has taken ten or more strides. The teacher determines the point at which the left foot struck the ground at stride seven and marks this spot. The athlete returns to her original position and repeats the procedure several times. The midpoint of these marks is checked at stride seven, and the distance between the starting point and stride seven is measured for future reference. This approach will be lengthened to ten or twelve strides after the learner develops a sense of control and timing.

Once the check marks have been established and the crossover steps learned, the participant is ready for serious practice. She must be made to realize that success is dependent upon speed and strength and their application from a position of balance. To attain these essential factors, thousands of approaches must be made. Though frustrating at the outset, the learner must be encouraged to move through the approach with considerable speed and to throw as best she can. Throwing from a trot is not the same as throwing from a run, and a skill developed at one rate of speed must be relearned at another rate of speed if greater success is to be attained.

Modifications for the Gym Class

In many areas, dangers associated with throwing the javelin have prevented its acceptance into the physical education program. The javelin is no more dangerous than the bow and arrow, however, and perhaps with the same restrictions would prove to be an exciting event for girls. Some teachers have experimented with a blunt-nosed javelin. Blunting the javelin can be accomplished by drilling and then gluing a solid rubber ball to the tip; or perhaps a javelin handle could be cut off and a rubber ball affixed to either end for balance purposes. Other teachers have placed bindings on sticks or lengths of rubber hose and found that these could be adapted for the learner. Each of these implements serves as a substitute javelin and can be used in restricted areas with little chance of injury.

TRAINING SCHEDULE FOR THE BEGINNING JAVELIN THROWER

M. Warm up with ten minutes of throwing, using either a football or participating in javelin Fartlek (jogging and sticking the javelin for fun).

Run through check marks several times to make certain that they are perfectly adjusted. Take eight or ten pop-up throws, emphasizing speed.

Take eight or ten full-approach throws with form the major concern. (Stay relaxed; lay back and pull from the ground.)

Weight training. (See chapter 16 for special exercises for javelin throwers.)

T. Jog 440—stretch well.

Work on crossover drill, trying to establish a feel for the instant when the throwing force must be applied.

Work with the hurdlers for twenty minutes to develop a consistent stride pattern. (A consistent stride pattern is most important to the javelin thrower.)

Finish with several 40- to 60-yard sprints.

W. Warm up well, with emphasis on the arms and shoulders, the legs, hips, and lower back.

Run through the check marks several times to make certain that they are perfectly adjusted.

Take six throws from a stand with two-thirds effort.
Take six pop-up throws at three-quarter effort. Rest.
Take ten to fifteen full-approach throws for distance.
Weight training.

Th. Stride 220—walk back and repeat.
Practice starts with the sprinters.
Join the long jumpers or high jumpers for twenty minutes of fun training.
Work on crossover sprints for ten or fifteen minutes.
Throw a weighted javelin or three-pound weight easily for ten minutes.

F. Sprint 100 yards—rest and repeat.
Run up and down the field for twenty minutes, throwing with a relaxed approach "as the spirit moves."
Run through the full approach and make necessary adjustments.
Take fifteen to twenty full-approach throws. Do not be concerned with distance. Concentrate on developing a "feel"—a rhythm which permits full expenditure of effort into the javelin.
Complete workout with several short sprints.

S. Twenty minutes of striding and stretching.
Weight training.

TYPICAL TRAINING SCHEDULE FOR THE SKILLED PERFORMER

The javelin approach and delivery is an extremely complicated skill. For this reason the serious performer should throw whenever and wherever possible. To avoid injury, the throwing need not be at full effort, yet it should be done consistently. Too, the javelin thrower must have strong, supple muscles. She should, therefore, participate in some type of stretching and strengthening activity during twelve months of the year.

Early Season

M. Jog 440 yards, followed by fifteen minutes of stretching and strengthening exercises.
Throw football for ten minutes.

Warm up with the javelin for ten minutes, throwing progressively farther and farther from a stand.

Set up check marks and run through several times to make necessary adjustments. Throw ten to fifteen times from short approach with emphasis on lay-back and long pull-through.

Take several throws from full approach at about three-quarter effort, followed by three throws for distance.

Train down with several sprints 50 to 75 yards in length.

T. Jog 440 yards, followed by fifteen minutes of exercises.

Several short warm-up sprints, followed by ten 30-yard drills using crossover steps. (This is a difficult, though tremendously important, drill for the javelin thrower.)

Starting practice with the sprinters for several minutes.

Concentrated work over four hurdles, emphasizing drive into hurdle and rapid action over the hurdle.

Run 220 in thirty seconds. Repeat after five minutes of rest.

Weight training.

W. Warm up well with usual jogging and stretching.

Take fifteen to twenty throws with increasing intensity, starting from a stand and working up to the five-step approach.

Set up check marks and run through full approach several times, letting the javelin go at about half effort. When completely warm, throw javelin forcefully into the ground (three or four times) from a stand to get mentally set.

Throw six times for distance.

Train down with relaxed jogging for ten minutes.

Th. 440 jog followed by extensive stretching.

5 x 75-yard sprints with javelin.

Work for fifteen minutes with three-pound weight, throwing from final five-step approach. Concentrate on total body action, particularly on "belly pull."

Take ten minutes of cross-step drill up an incline.

Weight training.

F. 440 jog followed by fifteen minutes of stretching.

Fifteen minutes of cross-step drill, releasing javelin progressively farther after each cross-step sequence.

Work on javelin control. Using short approach (7 to 9 strides) throw two times at 80 feet, two at 90 feet, two at 100 feet, and so on, until two maximum distance throws have been made. Emphasize accelerating away from the javelin, getting the hips forward while reaching back to pull the javelin from behind.

Complete workout with five minutes of easy shuffle.

S. Twenty minutes of striding and stretching.

Weight training.

Competitive Season

M. Two laps of jogging followed by fifteen minutes of stretching and calisthenics.

5 x 50-yard sprints with walk-back recovery.

Take ten to fifteen easy short-approach throws, loosening well.

Throw six to ten full-approach throws for distance.

Finish with five minutes of easy shuffle.

T. Warm up as indicated.

3 x 150-yard sprints with 440 walk-back recovery.

Ten minutes of zigzag drill down an incline. (This is done by running right, then cutting left—running left, then cutting right—continuing downhill. An excellent drill for quickening the reflexes and strengthening the extensor muscles in the legs.)

Ten minutes of progressive three-pound weight throwing.

Weight training.

W. Warm up as if this were a day of competition.

Take several pop-up throws for "feel."

Take three or four sets of six throws for distance. Space the throws as if competing, jogging 440 yards easily between sets of six.

Finish with five minutes of easy shuffle.

Th. Warm up particularly well—stretching, stretching, stretching.

Work over four hurdles several times, emphasizing push-off—push-off.

Set check marks and run through several times, just "letting" the javelin go.

Finish with several minutes of jogging and sticking the javelin.

F. Competition.

S. Twenty minutes of striding and stretching.

Weight training.

NOTE: If Saturday is the day of competition, reverse the Thursday-Saturday workout.

PERFORMANCE TIPS FOR COMPETITOR AND COACH

1. The javelin throw must be recognized as a straight-line event. The approach is made in a straight line; the javelin is carried, trailed, pulled through, and delivered along a straight line—all of which demands a remarkably strong and supple body.
2. Only that portion of the approach speed which actually is transferred to the javelin is of any consequence to the throw. For this reason the performer should concentrate on accelerating until the instant of delivery.
3. The crossover step actually occurs in the air. When properly executed, the heel of the right foot contacts the ground before the toe—and well ahead of the right shoulder. This action places the body in a lay-back or bowed position from which maximum force can be applied.
4. An instant before the left or forward foot contacts the ground, the right heel is rotated sharply outward, initiating the hip lift so essential to a good throw.
5. It is fundamental to success in the javelin event that the "work" be done behind the body. That is, the performer has the feeling of running up under, or away from, the javelin, then pulling ballistically through the shaft and into the throw. (Ineffective performers tend to pike away from the javelin, imparting most of their force above and in front of the body.)
6. Always select the appropriate distance-rated javelin. Nothing is more disheartening to the javelin thrower than to lose a good throw because the point failed to contact the ground ahead of the shaft.
7. When thrown into the wind, the javelin should be released at an angle of approximately twenty-five to thirty degrees, with an attack angle (point above the center of gravity) of not more than two to three degrees. When thrown with the wind, the javelin should be released at an angle of thirty-five to forty degrees, with an attack angle of three to four degrees.

Chapter 16

Conditioning Activities
for Track and Field

Girls frequently discover that a general lack of strength, flexibility, and endurance prohibits their happy, abandoned participation in track and field activities. They soon become stiff and sore and can control neither their bodies nor their implements. It is important, therefore, that every track and field session be preceded by a time of conditioning and that every serious attempt to develop a high level of skill in this area be accompanied by a long-term program of psychophysical preparation. It might also be wise to precede the track and field unit with a concentrated body development unit with emphasis on strength, flexibility, and endurance.

During recent years, girls and women have manifested an increased interest in conditioning activities. It is now common practice for better performers in all track and field events to utilize resistance exercises to improve their strength, endurance, and flexibility. Indeed, many coaches believe that the major difference between male and female athletes, in terms of their abilities to learn and perform, is a difference of relative strength.

Because interest is present and the need is very real, this chapter contains information concerning general conditioning activities, resistance exercise training, circuit training, and specific conditioning activities for each track and field event. In addition, principles of conditioning are provided as guidelines for the teacher and performer.

GENERAL CONDITIONING ACTIVITIES

It is important that the serious athlete train twelve months of the year; thus the training program is divided into cycles of activity which include time periods for competition, technique work, general conditioning, and development of strength, endurance, and flexibility. Usually the general conditioning program comes after the fall months of cross-country running. It may involve games unrelated to track and field or it may include a broadly conceived program of running, stretching, and strengthening exercises. Each approach has its particular advantages and should be utilized according to the motivation of the performers, conditions of weather, and availability of facilities.

Jogging and Running

There is no substitute for jogging and running in the training program of the track and field performer. Each practice session during all periods of the twelve-month program should be preceded by jogging five to ten minutes or longer.

Stretching

All stretching exercises should be performed slowly and through a full range of motion.

1. *Swing, stretch, and fall.* From a stride stand the girl bends forward, lets her arms hang loosely and swings them from right to left across her body. She swings, swings, swings, and then raises up, reaches high above her head, arches her back, and drops to the hanging posture again. This is repeated several times, easily and as relaxed as possible.

2. *Trunk twister.* From the stride stand, hands on the hips, the girl bends forward, twists in a circular motion from right to left, straightens her trunk and reverses the procedure from left to right. She repeats this exercise several times, twisting alternately to the right and then to the left.

3. *Cross-legged toe touching.* The girl stands, crosses one foot over the other, and with straight legs touches her toes, first the right foot and then the left, coming to a stand and alternating the position of her feet between each stretch. She repeats the exercise several times, alternating the position of the feet. (This exercise

is especially effective for stretching the flexor muscles on the backs of the legs.)

4. *The Pill Bug curl.* From a back lying posture, the girl pulls her knees to her chest, grasps them firmly with her arms so that she is in a tightly tucked position, and rolls backward and forward along the length of her spine.

5. *The Billig stretch.* The girl stands with her elbow elevated to the side (straight out from shoulder), her hand and arm pressed against a firm, vertical surface. The opposite hand, fingers pointing downward, is placed against the hip and pressure is applied, forcing the inside hip against the surface which is supporting the extended hand and arm. This exercise should be repeated several times on each side. It is especially effective for stretching the muscles and fascia surrounding the hip joint. (It is important to keep the body in vertical alignment when doing this exercise.)

6. *Hurdle stretch.* The performer assumes a long sitting position on the ground and then bends and turns one leg out and around so the heel of the foot is close to the buttock and the instep and knee are flat against the ground. The angle between the legs should be ninety degrees. The stretching action takes place as the performer bends her trunk down toward the extended leg several times and then to the other knee. The arms also stretch in the direction of the bend. Another part of this stretch occurs when the trunk is inclined rearward to a back lying position. The leg positions are reversed and the exercise is repeated.

7. *Inverted leg scissor.* A supine lying position should be assumed. The legs and hips are then raised overhead and the hips are supported by the hands. The legs are scissored up and down from the overhead extended position to the ground behind the head. This may be repeated twenty-five to thirty times.

8. *Supine arch-up.* From a supine lying position the performer places her hands by her shoulders, as if she were attempting a backward roll, and bends her knees so her feet are flat on the ground. The stretching action takes place when the performer arches up into a back bend. This may be done progressively, increasing the stretch as the hands and feet are brought closer to each other.

Strength-Building Exercises

The development of muscular strength is dependent upon three fundamental principles. Muscles must work against resistance, against increasingly greater amounts of resistance, and engage in this kind of activity consistently. It is the teacher's responsibility to convince girls that resistance exercises are beneficial and can be performed in a ladylike manner. Girls should be made to realize that they can increase their strength without developing bulging muscles.

1. *The modified push-up.* The push-up from the knees, with the body held perfectly straight, is an excellent exercise for strengthening the extensor muscles of the arms and shoulders and the powerful throwing muscles in the chest.
2. *Abdominal rocker.* This exercise is an excellent means of developing the muscles of the lower back. It is performed by lying on the stomach, placing the hands behind the head, arching the back and rocking backward and forward over the abdomen.
3. *The modified pull-up.* Any bar or other stable apparatus two or three feet from the floor which can be safely gripped by a girl can be used. The performer moves beneath the bar, takes a firm grip, and extends her body forward so that her weight is supported by the heels and the hands. With a straight back she pulls her chest to the bar, repeating the exercise several times.
4. *Hill zigzag running.* Aside from regular hill running, additional toughening of the ankles, knees, and hips can accrue from running up a hill and making sharp changes of direction in a zigzag fashion. The changes are like quick switchbacks from side to side. This may also be performed while running in a more controlled fashion down the hill.
5. *Leg and trunk ups.* From a supine lying position, the girl quickly lifts her legs to the vertical and raises her trunk upward so that her extended arms and hands can touch her toes directly over the hips. The girl is in a pike while momentarily balanced on her seat.

Cardiorespiratory Endurance

For the purposes of this discussion, endurance is defined as the ability to persist at or endure a particular kind of activity for a long period of time. While the topic of endurance tends to be controversial in terms of its exact components, most authorities agree that the general factor in question involves both muscular and cardiorespiratory changes. It is this general factor approach which is to be considered when developing the off-season endurance training program. Activities prescribed for general conditioning are therefore different than those pursued during the competitive season. (For a more detailed discussion of endurance training see chapter 8 on distance running.)

1. *Running in place.* While not as effective as running over the ground, this activity does produce cardiorespiratory overloading and subsequent changes in the heart-lung apparatus.
2. *Jumping jacks.* Also known as the side-straddle hop, this activity when continued over an extended period is an effective general endurance exercise.
3. *Rope jumping, continuous jumping on a trampoline.* All kinds of activities which involve more than half of the body working repetitively against minimal resistance tend to contribute significantly to the general endurance factor.

RESISTANCE EXERCISE TRAINING

The use of weights or other devices to provide resistance to movement has been practiced for more than 2,000 years. There is good evidence that Greek athletes carried weights in their hands as an aid to the development of power for the jumping events. Legend states that Milo, a Greek athlete from Crotona, lifted a young bull over his head each day until the creature was fully grown. The strength thus attained contributed to Milo's success in the Olympic Games for a period of four decades.

Despite this heritage, weight training for athletes in those events which require speed of movement and/or flexibility came under intense criticism during the first half of this century. For the most part, weight training was abandoned even by men because of the inflexibility which these activities allegedly produced. Times have changed, however, so that no serious athlete, male or female, would now embark on a training program without utilizing some form of resistance exercise.

Indeed, girls and women are recognizing the need to utilize resistance exercises if they are to attain their maximum potential. While this fact is well accepted by the more knowledgeable coaches and athletes, many female teachers and performers in schools and colleges tend to manifest rather naïve attitudes about the value and consequences of this activity.

Resistance Exercises

Resistance exercise constitutes a training program which seeks to produce gains in muscular strength and endurance through the systematic overloading of selected muscle groups. In its broadest sense this involves any type of resistance, though the particular emphasis of this discussion is the use of barbells, resistance-producing machines (such as the Universal Gym), wall pullies, and the like.

Contrary to what some people believe, resistance exercises do not produce a condition which is referred to as being "muscle-bound." Also, these kinds of exercises do not produce exaggerated muscle hypertrophy in female athletes. Mature women naturally possess nearly a third less muscle mass than do males. Too, the manner in which girls and women are affected by overloading of this kind is determined largely by their primary female hormone, estrogen; thus they could not modify their muscle masses even if they tried. Doctor Harmon Brown, hormone specialist and girls' track coach, recently affirmed this fact in a speech to several hundred coaches and performers assembled at San Mateo, California.

Principles of Progressive Resistance Activity

Strength, endurance, and flexibility are specific adaptive responses to particular kinds of external demands. Optimum development of these fitness factors is dependent upon the wise selection and the careful application of overload principles. Lockhart[1] has identified four overload principles or techniques whereby strength, endurance, and flexibility can be improved. These are (1) gradually increase the total load; (2) gradually increase the speed of performance in a progressive manner; (3) progressively increase the total time that a given position can be held; and (4) with constant resistance, progressively increase the total number of performance bouts. Exercise programs having significant value must utilize one or more of these four principles.

While there is some difference of opinion as to how these principles should be applied in a practical situation, most weight training or resistance exercise programs follow three steps. *First,* it is recognized that *resistance to movement is essential to the development of muscular strength.* Research has shown that strength gains occur when muscular tissue is called upon to resist force while lengthening as well as while shortening, or contracting. Thus eccentric activity can be utilized as well as concentric activity to produce the desired overload effect. This has important implications, for not only can an individual increase the workload in a given unit of time (by lifting up and resisting down),

---

1. Aileene Lockhart, unpublished lecture notes, Department of Physical Education, University of Southern California.

but she can produce the margin of strength necessary to control her own body weight when sufficient initial strength is lacking. (For example, the repeated resistance of gravity by lowering oneself from the extended arm to the chest resting position would eventually produce sufficient strength to perform the push-up from the resting to the extended position.) Or, by resisting a weight while lowering oneself into the "squat" position, one actually is contributing to the development of sufficient strength to extend the legs upward again against that weight.

The second essential feature of the successful weight-training program is that it must be *progressive in nature*. For continued gains in strength there must be a continued increase in the resistance applied. The rule usually followed in weight training is to increase the resistance against which one is working when a given exercise can be repeated more than twelve times. The practical rule is to start with a weight which can be moved through a particular range of motion (press, curl, etc.) eight times and to work repeatedly with such a weight until the exercise can be repeated twelve times. (Note here the principle of progression in the story of Milo and the bull.)

The *third* feature of the successful weight-training program is that it must be *consistent*. While there is no exact formula for attaining maximum results from an exercise program, the best evidence seems to indicate that an individual must train at least twice, and perhaps three times, each week for measurable gains to occur. It is probable that five bouts of activity each week are better than three, with alternate days of work varying in intensity and point of emphasis. The important idea here is that training must be consistent.

SELECTED RESISTANCE EXERCISES

There are many weight-training exercises from which the serious performer can choose. Those which are shown here represent activities aimed at strengthening the muscle groups most frequently utilized in track and field. The reader is reminded, however, that the wise use of these exercises is dependent upon an understanding of the physio-anatomical requirements of each track and field event. Strength is important. Strength development also is very specific, being determined by the quantity and quality of the demands imposed upon the body, with the greatest gains occurring at the site, or through the range of motion, where the stress is applied.

Arm and Shoulder Girdle

1. (figs. 16.1 and 16.2)

   Name: Bench Press

   Primary Areas: Chest, arm extensors, shoulders.

   Description: Starting position (fig. 16.1) shows the subject in a supine lying position on a bench, her feet on the floor for support. The barbell weight is supported on the hands at chest level and the weight is lifted by fully extending the arms in front of the chest to position in figure 16.2. The weight is then returned to the starting position.

FIGURE 16.1

FIGURE 16.2

2. (figs. 16.3 and 16.4)

   Name: Curls

   Primary Areas: Shoulders, arm flexors, wrists, grip.

   Description: Starting position (fig. 16.3) shows the subject in an upright standing posture with a barbell weight or weighted pulley grasped in both hands. The arms are flexed and the weight is lifted toward the chest (fig. 16.4) and then is lowered in a controlled manner.

FIGURE 16.3

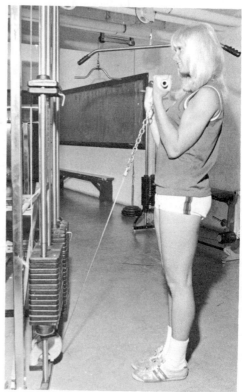

FIGURE 16.4

3. (figs. 16.5 and 16.6)   **FIGURE 16.5**

Name: French Curls

Primary Areas: Arm flexors, arm extensors, arm depressors, shoulders, and chest.

Description: Subject starts in position as in figure 16.5 in a back lying position on a bench. Both hands grasp a barbell weight or low pulley that is resting on the floor at the head of the bench. The weight is lifted with somewhat flexed arms and then extended fully in front of the face (fig. 16.6).

FIGURE 16.6

4. (figs. 16.7 and 16.8)

Name: Bent Rowing

Primary Areas: Upper back, shoulders, arm flexors.

Description: From a standing pike position (fig. 16.7) the weight is grasped with both hands and pulled upward to the chest. For best results the elbows should be lifted as high as possible to forcefully contract the adductors of the scapula. The back should be flat throughout this exercise and the feet spread for balance.

FIGURE 16.7

FIGURE 16.8

5. (figs. 16.9 and 16.10)

   Name: Snap Jerk

   Primary Areas: Arm extensors, shoulders, wrists.

   Description: The subject assumes a forward stride position for balance. The weight is lifted to the chest as seen in figure 16.9. The exercise involves a series of quick, thrusting lifts with the bar moving outward and upward at an angle of forty-five degrees. The quick, thrusting motion simulates the putting of a shot.

FIGURE 16.9

FIGURE 16.10

FIGURE 16.11

FIGURE 16.12

Chest, Abdomen, and Back

1. (figs. 16.11 and 16.12)

   Name: Straight Arm Depressors

   Primary Areas: Arm depressors and trunk flexors.

   Description: The subject grasps the overhead pulley as shown in starting position (fig. 16.11). Maintaining straight arms, she depresses the bar as far as possible and then returns it to the overhead starting position.

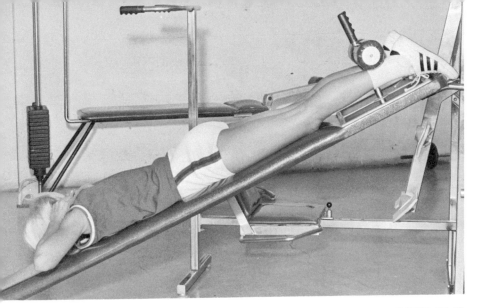

FIGURE 16.13

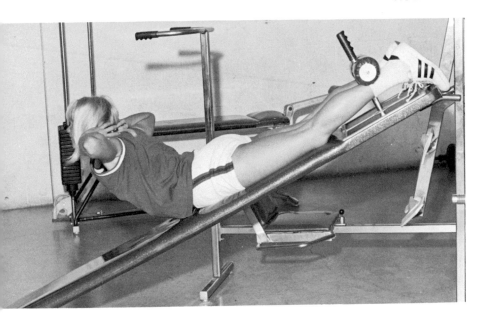

FIGURE 16.14

2. (figs. 16.13 and 16.14)

Name: Arch-up—Incline Board

Primary Areas: Upper and lower back.

Description: From a prone lying position on the incline board, with the heels hooked for support and a small weight grasped behind the neck, as shown in figure 16.13, the subject arches up as far as possible, figure 16.14. The arched position should be held for at least five counts.

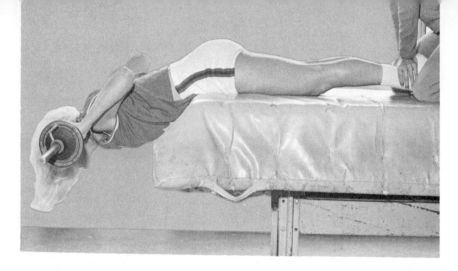

FIGURE 16.15

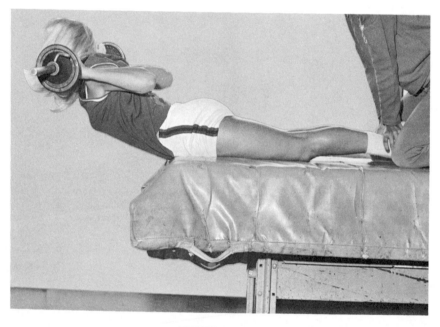

FIGURE 16.16

3. (figs. 16.15 and 16.16)

Name: Arch-up—Table Edge

Primary Areas: Upper and lower back.

Description: From a prone lying position on the edge of a padded table with the feet secured by another person as shown in figure 16.15, the subject grasps a barbell weight behind her neck and bends over the edge toward the floor. The subject then arches up as high as possible, holds the position briefly, and returns to the start.

FIGURE 16.17

FIGURE 16.18

FIGURE 16.19

4. (figs. 16.17, 16.18, and 16.19)
   Name: Hanging Leg Lifts
   Primary Areas: Trunk flexors, hip flexors, abdomen, arms and shoulders.
   Description: The performer grasps an overhead bar as shown in figure 16.17 and raises her legs as high as possible with either straight legs as shown in figure 16.18 or bent legs as shown in figure 16.19.

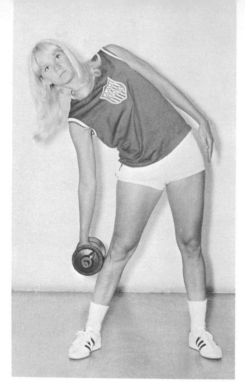

5. (figs. 16.20 and 16.21)

   Name: Lateral Lifts

   Primary Areas: Trunk extensors.

   Description: The performer holds a hand dumbbell or low pulley in her right hand, stands with her feet shoulder width apart, and reaches down toward the floor by her right foot (fig. 16.20). She then reaches down toward her left foot (fig. 16.21) and returns to the start.

FIGURE 16.20

FIGURE 16.21

6. (No figure)

   Name: Butterfly Lifts—Prone

   Primary Areas: Upper back and shoulders.

   Description: From a prone lying position on a bench, the subject grasps a small hand dumbbell in each hand. The arms are held straight and are lifted vertically as high as possible. The arms should be kept in alignment with the shoulders as they are raised and lowered throughout this exercise.

FIGURE 16.22

FIGURE 16.23

7. (figs. 16.22 and 16.23)
   Name: Butterfly Lifts—Supine
   Primary Areas: Chest and shoulders.
   Description: See description for Butterfly Lifts (Prone). This exercise is
   done while lying on a bench on the back.

FIGURE 16.24

FIGURE 16.25

8. (figs. 16.24 and 16.25)

   Name: Butterfly Pull—Modified

   Primary Areas: Chest and shoulders.

   Description: Lying on the floor on her side by the low pulley (or holding a single hand dumbbell), the subject grasps the pulley with one
   hand and braces herself by extending the other hand forward and
   one leg rearward. With a straight arm the pulley is pulled toward
   the front of the body and the extended arm (fig. 16.25). The arm and
   pulley are then carefully lowered to the starting point and the exercise
   is repeated.

Hips, Legs, and Ankles

1. (figs. 16.26 and 16.27)

   Name: Double Leg Press

   Primary Areas: Extensors of thigh, knee, and ankle.

   Description: Sitting on the chair, the performer assumes starting position (fig. 16.26) with her hands grasping the rails, and the balls of her feet firmly placed on the foot pedals.

2. (No figure)

   Name: Single Leg Press

   Primary Areas: Extensors of thigh, knee, and ankle.

   Description: See Double Leg Press (figs. 16.26-27).

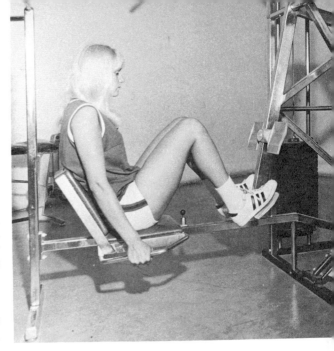

FIGURE 16.26

FIGURE 16.27

FIGURE 16.28

3. (figs. 16.28 and 16.29)

   Name: Squat Jumps

   Primary Areas: Extensors of thigh, knee, and ankles.

   Description: The starting position (fig. 16.28) is assumed with performer standing in a forward stride position, head erect, and barbell weight held firmly behind the neck. The performer squats easily to position in figure 16.29 and then jumps quickly and forcefully upward, switching leg positions in the air, and landing gently with easily flexed knees. She then lowers to a squat again and repeats the jump.

FIGURE 16.29

4. (fig. 16.30)

Name: Single Leg Press—Modified

Primary Areas: Extensors of thigh, knee, and ankle.

Description: Starting position shows performer bending over, with her hands and one shoulder on the supporting bar and one foot against the pedal of the leg press. This leg and foot fully and forcefully extend and then return to the start.

FIGURE 16.30

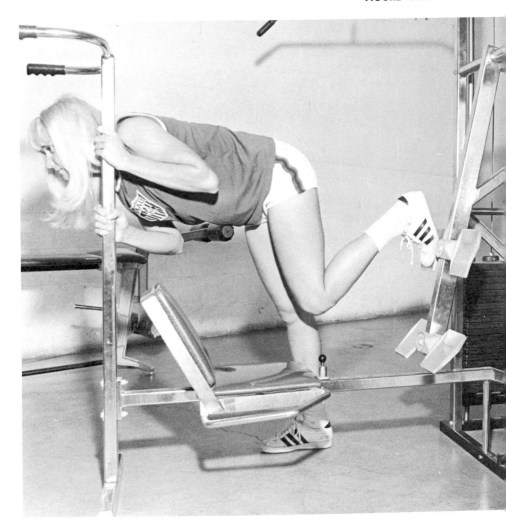

5. (figs. 16.31 and 16.32)

Name: Squat Stand

Primary Areas: Extensors of thigh, knee, and ankle.

Description: Subject assumes starting position (fig. 16.31) with her feet shoulder width apart and her heels elevated on a two-inch board. Her body and head are erect and a barbell weight is held firmly on the shoulders against the neck. The subject squats to a ninety-degree bend of the legs (fig. 16.32) and returns to the starting position. This is a controlled, fairly slow squatting motion.

FIGURE 16.31

FIGURE 16.32

FIGURE 16.33

FIGURE 16.34

6. (figs. 16.33 and 16.34)

Name: Squat Twist

Primary Areas: Extensors of thigh, knee, and ankles; trunk rotators.

Description: Starting position (fig. 16.33) is assumed with the feet shoulder width apart and in a forward stride position. The head and trunk are erect and rotated 100 degrees to the right. The legs are flexed about 90 degrees so the subject is in a half squat. A barbell weight is held firmly on the shoulders. From this position the subject simultaneously rotates the hips and trunk fully to the left and extends the legs fully (fig. 16.34). She then rotates and squats back to the starting position and repeats the exercise.

SPECIALIZED CONDITIONING ACTIVITIES

Sprints

While there is no assurance that special exercises will speed up or quicken motor performance, it is quite probable that greater strength, increased flexibility, and improved motor coordination would have a positive effect on running speed. The special sprinters' exercises, there-fore, involve the factors of strength, flexibility, and coordination.

1. Inverted bicycling with emphasis on full, fast leg movements.
2. The sprinter or leg-change exercise with both hands on the floor, arms straight. One leg is bent and the knee is close to the per-former's chest. The other leg is extended rearward. The performer jumps slightly and changes leg positions as quickly as possible.
3. High kicking helps to attain greater hip flexibility.
4. Resistance starts (see chapter 4).
5. Leg presses and single leg press modified for starting.
6. Hill sprints and freewheeling run.
7. Tandem push.
8. Hanging leg lifts.

Hurdles

Since hurdlers are sprinters with an added need for a special type of flexibility, they should perform the exercises outlined for the sprinters in addition to the following:

1. Hurdler's stretch.
2. Trail-leg action. A quick trail-leg motion which is repeated numerous times while standing at the side of the hurdle.
3. Stretching the lead leg and trail leg on the hurdle, as well as trunk bending.
4. Short-step drills (see chapter 6) with emphasis on quick leg clear-ance speed.
5. Trail-leg drill with exaggerated knee lift or punch (see chapter 6).
6. Lead-leg drill with exaggerated leg snap down.

Long Jump

The long jumper is a sprinter also. She combines lift and carry with as much speed as possible to successfully perform her event. She needs to improve her speed, leg power, and abdominal strength.

1. Squat jumps with emphasis on a ballistic spring into the air.
2. The "L" sit. Sit on the floor and extend the arms so that the entire body is supported by the hands. The legs are held upward as high as possible.
3. Hanging leg lifts with legs raised as near a vertical position as possible. Hold and repeat.
4. Consecutive double leg jumps over closely spaced barriers (eighteen to twenty-four inches high).
5. Straight arm depressors.
6. Arch-up on inclined board or table edge.

High Jump

The high jumper, in addition to possessing a high degree of natural spring, must have great strength and flexibility.

1. High kicking
2. Hanging leg lifts
3. Double and single leg presses
4. Single and double leg hopping over eighteen- to twenty-four-inch barriers
5. Toe raises and heel lowering on a step
6. Jump and reach for height
7. Straight arm depressors
8. Squat stand and squat jumps
9. Arching up on incline or table

Middle-Distance Races

Middle-distance runners find that exercises aimed at strengthening their arms and shoulders tend to minimize the extreme fatigue which often is experienced during the latter part of the race.

1. Bench press
2. Curls
3. Rowing
4. Chin-ups
5. Push-ups
6. Double leg press

Javelin

The javelin thrower must be strong and supple. Exercises which are aimed at the development of these qualities are essential to training and performance.

1. Trunk circling and rotating with a hand dumbbell held at arm's length overhead
2. Arch-ups
3. Javelin pulley (see fig. 16.35) or javelin resistance
4. Squat jumps
5. French curls and curls
6. Driving cross-steps
7. Bench press, parallel bar dips, and push-ups
8. Double leg press

FIGURE 16.35

Shot-put

The shot-putter must be very strong and quick. She must work continuously on weight-training activities which include all areas of the body. The following list is especially recommended:

1. Snap jerk
2. Bench press, parallel bar dips, and push-ups
3. Squats, squat jumps, and double leg press
4. Lateral lifts and squat twist
5. Arch-up, sit-up, and hanging leg lifts
6. Shot-putter's hop (see chapter 14)

Discus

The discus thrower also must be strong and supple.

1. Butterfly lifts, prone and supine
2. Bench press
3. Squat stand and squat jumps
4. Squat twist
5. Hanging leg lifts
6. Double leg press
7. French curls and double arm depressors

CIRCUIT TRAINING

Circuit training comes from England where the program was developed at the University of Leeds for students who did not have a required program of physical education. Since its introduction into the American educational systems around 1950, circuit training has been a very popular adjunct to physical education and athletic training programs. Although it has undergone many modifications, most programs of this kind seek to produce large gains in circulatory-respiratory endurance and muscular strength through the process of continued overloading.

Some of the values of circuit training include a variety of activity, little equipment and space needed, easily fitted to individual differences, continuous challenge, and well-defined aims.

Long periods of rest are not utilized in the circuit approach since the extended rest does not place demands on respiratory endurance. The exercises are so arranged in the circuit that demands on the various parts of the body are alternated. All areas of the body should receive attention in the program: arms and shoulders, back, trunk, abdomen, chest, and legs.

Two factors to consider when setting up the circuit sequence are (1) What is the intensity of effort required to perform each exercise? and (2) What part of the body is affected by each exercise? The sequence should be planned so as to allow recovery of some parts while other parts are being exercised. Additionally, the exercises for each area will vary depending on whether strength or endurance is the particular aim. Repetitions range from one, for maximum strength, to thirty, for endurance.

The work load or dose that an individual is to perform at each station may be established by several methods. Two are mentioned here:

Individual Method. The maximum number of repetitions a person can perform at each station with one-minute rest between the stations is considered her Maximum Load (ML). This ML is then reduced to two-thirds and is termed her Circuit Load (CL). The CL is established for each of the exercises to be used in the circuit and for each subject.

Example: Subject X has a Maximum Load (ML) of 30 for push-ups.

2/3 × 30 = 20. Circuit Load (CL) is 20 push-ups for Subject X.

Levels Method. The coach or teacher establishes for each of the exercises a circuit load that she feels is about two-thirds the maximum of her average performers. (This decision is usually the result of experimentation.) This exercise load is called Level II. Level I should be made slightly easier and Level III should be slightly harder. Both of these levels, I and III, are set up with the ability of the performers in mind.

The circuit may be made more or less difficult by several means: vary the required completion time; change the weight of the resistance; modify the number of repetitions.

Sample Circuit (Throwing Events)

1. Warm up—one-quarter-mile jog; five minutes of loosening exercises
2. Hanging leg lifts
3. Squat jumps
4. Curls
5. Straight arm depressors
6. Double leg press
7. Arch-ups
8. Bench press
9. Lateral lifts
10. French curls

SAMPLE CIRCUIT (Jumping Events)

1. Warm up—one-quarter-mile jog; five minutes of loosening exercises
2. Hanging leg lifts
3. Double leg press
4. Sprinter
5. Arch-ups
6. Squat jumps
7. Double arm depressors
8. Stair running
9. Lateral lifts
10. Chin-ups

Chapter 17

Planning and Conducting
the Track and Field Meet

Track and field meets are fun. The excitement of keen competition seems to be contagious when girls meet to test their various abilities in the running, the jumping, and the throwing events. There is a feeling about track and field meets that one seldom experiences in other athletic events—a feeling of anticipation, a sense of awe, a respect for the skill and dedication of an accomplished performance.

The successful track and field meet does not just happen, however; it represents hard work and cooperation on the part of many individuals other than the participants. Perhaps the director is most responsible for the success of a track and field meet, though all of the officials, maintenance personnel, recorders, equipment handlers, and, indeed, the spectators help to make a track meet a success. This chapter is an attempt to give the reader some idea of the work involved in organizing and conducting a track meet. It does not include a detailed accounting of every problem the meet director will face, but it does provide pertinent guidelines for her to follow in planning.

PROMOTING TRACK AND FIELD

Very probably a track and field meet will be little better than the publicity it receives. The finest of facilities and the best of performance records have little meaning without participants and spectators. Because this is so, the meet director should begin early to publicize the forthcoming event. She should contact all potential participants well in advance, giving them pertinent information about the date, time, and location of the event. She should publicize in the available news media, highlighting all of the teams as well as the outstanding individuals and their performance records.

While it is never wise to exploit an individual, it is sound planning to tell the interested public what the better girls have done, how they rank locally or nationally, and what they might be expected to do. People are interested in successful performance and are more likely to attend an event if they believe a record will be broken.

At the local level, promotion involves displaying pictures, posting names, and comparing times and distances. Short announcements in the school paper and skits in assembly also catch the eyes of potential participants and spectators.

PLANNING FOR THE TRACK AND FIELD MEET

In addition to public relations, there is considerable preplanning involved in organizing and conducting a track meet. This includes preparing and mailing entry forms, engaging officials, seeding performers, assigning heats and lanes, and preparing equipment and facilities.

Preparation and Mailing of the Official Entry Form

The entry form is a vital communication link between the meet director and the participating schools. It should include such essential information as the schedule of events, the exact time and location of the meet, and space for the names of all participating athletes. A sample entry form is to be found in the Appendix. It will be noted that this form has been developed specifically for a limited number of entrants to a large meet. It includes space for the names of the girls, their events and division of competition. With slight modification, this form could be used for entering an entire team in a dual meet.

The entry form should be mailed to prospective participants at least three weeks prior to the track and field meet. To insure adequate time for processing the entrants, seeding them, placing them in heats, and so forth, there should be a mandatory return deadline of several days.

Obtaining Officials for the Track and Field Meet

The officials for a track and field meet include the referee, clerk of the course, starter, judges at the finish line, field event judges, timekeepers, and inspectors. (For a detailed description of the duties of all officials read the DGWS Track and Field Guide or the Official NCAA or AAU Track and Field Rule Book.)

To conduct a dual meet approximately twenty officials would be required, with ten or fifteen additional officials necessary for a meet having several participating teams. Acquiring a group of officials this large is no simple task. All must be contacted well in advance of the meet to make certain they will be available.

Two or three days ahead of the meet the wise director would send postal cards to all officials, reminding them of their responsibilities. These cards should include the time, place, and date of the meet as well as a word about appropriate dress, the specific duties of the recipients, and the person to whom they should report.

Formation of Heats and Seeding of Participants

In a dual meet the number of participants in each event is usually agreed upon by the coaches beforehand. In the running events this number frequently is determined by the number of lanes available on the track. In meets where several teams are participating, the entrants may be unlimited or minimum standards can be fixed to restrict the entry list. Whenever there are more entrants than lanes, it is necessary to run trial heats.

Heats are formed after all entries have been received and classified. To avoid eliminating the better contestants prior to the finals, times are compared and the fastest girls are scattered throughout the necessary heats for each event. (These times should be required on the entry form.) The fastest girls are called heat leaders or seeded participants. When all heats have been completed in writing, the meet committee draws a number for each contestant to determine the lane in which she will run.

The following table can be used to determine the number of trial heats necessary when six lanes are available. (Similar tables can easily be constructed for seven, eight, nine, or more lanes.)

No. OF ENTRIES	No. TRIAL HEATS	No. QUALIFYING (FROM EA. HEAT)	No. SEMI-FINAL HEATS	No. QUALIFYING (FROM EA. HEAT)	No. IN FINAL
1 to 6	0	0	0	0	6
7 to 12	2	3	0	0	6
13 to 18	3	4	2	3	6
19 to 24	4	3	2	3	6

During the quarter finals, semifinals, and finals of the sprints and hurdle races, it is customary to place together in the center lanes the girls who have the fastest times. This practice gives the timers and finish judges a better opportunity to determine accurately the winner of each race. It also helps the fastest girls to keep track of each other throughout the race.

Equipment and Supplies

It is customary for the teams in a dual meet to supply their own shot-puts, discs, javelins, and the like. In large meets, however, these items frequently are provided by the host school or team so all contestants will have standard equipment. The host school also supplies starting blocks, hurdles, crossbars, and many other items, some of which are listed following:

THROWING EVENTS

Two to three each: discuses, shots,
  javelins, softballs
Clipboards and pencils
Event sheets
Numbered markers
Steel measuring tapes
Sector flags and markers

JUMPING EVENTS

Rake, broom, pitchfork
Standards and crossbars
Steel measuring tape
Clipboards and pencils
Event sheets

GENERAL

First-aid supplies
Official badges
Scorers' tables and chairs

Public-address system
Master score cards
Marking pens

RUNNING EVENTS

Starting blocks
Hammers
Hurdles
Finish yarn
Batons
Stop watches
Stand for finish judges

Two whistles
Starting pistol and blanks
Clipboards and pencils
Heat sheets and final sheets
Timers' report cards
Finish judges' report cards

Preparation of the Track

Preparing the facilities for a meet is a long and tedious job. It requires watering, rolling, marking the track and field, the transport of hurdles and standards, the setting of finish poles, and other similar jobs. All this work should be completed the day before the meet so that there is ample time to check facilities for accuracy. It is especially important that the starting and finish lines be established, the baton exchange zones identified, and the throwing sectors for the shot, discus, and javelin visibly marked. While the markings of the track itself are

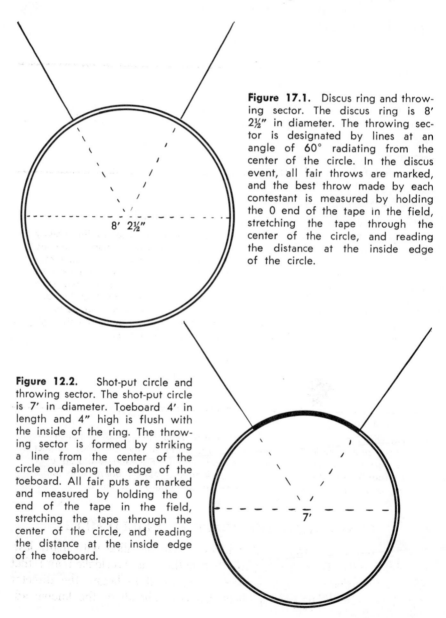

Figure 17.1. Discus ring and throwing sector. The discus ring is 8' 2½" in diameter. The throwing sector is designated by lines at an angle of 60° radiating from the center of the circle. In the discus event, all fair throws are marked, and the best throw made by each contestant is measured by holding the 0 end of the tape in the field, stretching the tape through the center of the circle, and reading the distance at the inside edge of the circle.

Figure 12.2. Shot-put circle and throwing sector. The shot-put circle is 7' in diameter. Toeboard 4' in length and 4" high is flush with the inside of the ring. The throwing sector is formed by striking a line from the center of the circle out along the edge of the toeboard. All fair puts are marked and measured by holding the 0 end of the tape in the field, stretching the tape through the center of the circle, and reading the distance at the inside edge of the toeboard.

determined by local conditions, markings for the three throwing events are fixed by the official rules governing track and field. These are shown here to guide the reader in the preparation of the track and to assist her in measuring accurately for each of these events.

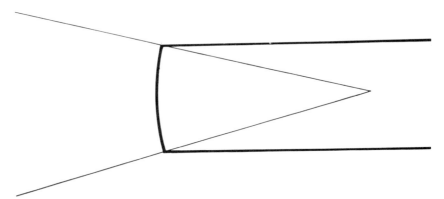

Figure 17.3. Javelin runway and throwing sector. The javelin runway is 13' 1½" wide and of indefinite length. The scratch mark is an arc 2¾" wide. This arc is of wood, metal, or white chalk. Each good throw is marked, and the best throw made by each contestant is measured by holding the 0 end of the tape in the field, stretching the tape through a point 26' 3" behind the scratch line, and reading the distance on the runway side of the scratch line. The throwing sector is established by extending lines from the measurement point out through the ends of the scratch mark for an indefinite length.

Figure 17.4. Measuring the long jump. After the jump, a pencil, or some similar object, is inserted in the sand at the point of contact nearest to the takeoff board. The loop end of the tape is placed over the pencil and the tape is drawn back to the takeoff board. The jumping distance is read at the pit side of the board.

CONDUCTING THE TRACK AND FIELD MEET

The day of the track and field meet will be filled with many last-minute details. To make certain that nothing is overlooked and that all is in readiness when the meet is supposed to begin, the director would be wise to prepare a check list covering all of the known administrative details. This list should include the names and phone numbers of all officials, maintenance personnel, and other individuals having duties which are essential to the success of the meet. It should list all of the necessary equipment and supplies, the locker room assignments, and the names of the visiting coaches or team managers. This check list should be both comprehensive and readily understandable, and it should be carefully reviewed before the meet has begun. (In two recent national meets embarrassing situations occurred which could have been averted had a premeet check list been available and appropriately used. In one of these meets the measuring tapes were completely overlooked and in the other the official entry forms were somehow left behind, making it impossible to run several trial heats when they were scheduled to go.)

A smoothly run track and field meet depends upon adequate preplanning and the coordinated efforts of many responsible persons. At least one-half hour before the first event the officials should assemble for their final briefing. They should be given clipboards and packets containing the names of the participants, a summary of the rules governing the events they will officiate, a diagram of the exact procedure for measuring if the events for which they are responsible involve height or distance, and other materials pertinent to their job. Following this general briefing, the head field judge and the head timer should meet their respective assistants to give whatever final instructions they wish. With all their questions answered and with their watches, clipboards, markers, and tape measures in hand, the officials go to their stations and the meet is ready to begin.

The referee should make a final inspection of the facilities and check with the judges and inspectors before she advises the clerk of the course to proceed. The clerk advises the announcer when to make the first, second, and final call for each event. The clerk then checks the participants off her master chart as they arrive at the starting line and places each girl in the lane to which she has been assigned. Although the clerk is responsible for the difficult task of keeping the meet moving and on schedule, she never permits her frustration to be reflected in her comments to the participants.

Two or three minutes before each race the starter takes charge of the situation. She directs the girls to stand behind their starting blocks, signals the timers that she is ready, and proceeds to give the starting commands. (Go to your marks—get set—bang.) Working together in this manner, the referee, clerk, starter, judges, and timers constitute an efficient team, adding greatly to the success of the meet.

Order of Events

Because many factors determine the events included in a track and field meet, it is not possible to state the exact order of participation. There are, on the other hand, certain guidelines which the meet director should follow.

1. The field events normally begin a half hour before the first running event. If there are four field events, it might be well to start and complete two of these before the second two are started. This procedure eliminates much of the confusion of running back and forth between events and permits two sets of officials to cover the four activities.
2. Because of the time involved in setting up the hurdles, it might be wise to run this race first, eliminating the problem of transporting, setting, and straightening the hurdles during the course of the meet.
3. The sprint races and the distance races should be well staggered so that a girl who wishes to participate in more than one race will have time to rest adequately between events.
4. Relay races are usually run last as a climax to the meet. The relay brings all of the teams together in face-to-face competition, giving the participants and the spectators a final exciting event to watch.

In meets where there are different divisions of competition, the shorter sprint and hurdle races for the younger girls probably should precede the longer races for the more mature participants. The time factor also would be extended accordingly. In no instance should a girl be required to run more than two sprint races in less than one-half hour's time. For longer distances, an hour of rest should be permitted between races.

Scoring the Track and Field Meet

Immediately after each event has been completed, the official entry forms should be taken to the scorer's table to be recorded on the master score sheet (see Appendix). Individual scores should be registered and a total score for each team posted. The revised total score should be readily available to the coaches and public-address announcer. By prompt and efficient reporting of scores, the place winners can be announced, helping to eliminate the time lapses so common in some track meets.

The scoring system for track and field meets varies with the number of participating teams as shown in the example following:

Place Winners to Be Counted	1st Place	2nd Place	3rd Place	4th Place	5th Place	6th Place
3	5	3	1			
4	5	3	2	1		
5	5	4	3	2	1	
6	10	8	6	4	2	1

In the event of a tie by two or more competitors for a place which receives a score, the combined score for the places involved is divided equally among the competitors included in the tie. For example, if two girls tie for second in a dual meet where three places receive scores, the points for second and third would be combined, with each competitor receiving half the total points. (In the illustration each of the competitors would receive two points.)

RESPONSIBILITIES FOLLOWING THE MEET

The meet director has at least two additional responsibilities after the meet is over. She should send a letter of appreciation to each of the officials for her willingness to serve without remuneration. She also should prepare a complete summary of the meet results, which includes the names of place winners, times, distances, and scores, and send it to all participating teams. These two courtesies will be rewarded by cooperation at future times and by an expanded interest in track and field for girls and women.

SOME GUIDES FOR ORGANIZING AND CONDUCTING A TRACK AND FIELD MEET

1. Begin early. Planning and conducting a track and field meet is a time-consuming job.
2. Publicize the meet well. Send preliminary information to all prospective participants well in advance of the meet date.
3. Set realistic deadlines and then hold to them.
4. Contact the officials early; keep them posted; provide a training session for them if need be.
5. Prepare a detailed check list (a tentative progress schedule) and follow it as carefully as possible.
6. Add "color" to the meet in every way possible. Announce each event; keep people posted on the progress of the participants where heights and distances are involved; present all awards with appropriate

ceremony; provide programs which list all of the participants and the records for each event; use flags, banners, and bands wherever possible.

7. Keep coaches and spectators off the field at all times.
8. Provide adequate seating for coaches and competitors.
9. Extend sincere appreciation to all of the people who assisted in planning the meet and helped to make it a success.

PROMOTING CROSS-COUNTRY

In some areas of the United States, cross-country running has become so popular that it is not uncommon to find more than a hundred girls participating in a weekend event. That such a situation exists is to the credit of the teachers and coaches who have given of their time and energy to promote this worthwhile sport. The methods used by these successful teachers and coaches provide guidelines for those who are interested in initiating cross-country programs in communities where they do not exist.

Perhaps the first prerequisite to success is the interest and enthusiasm of the teacher herself. Cross-country requires little equipment, and the physical demands are those which can be imposed on almost any girl who is willing to work. Providing a measure of fun and excitement is of utmost importance to the successful program. This can be developed in part through attractive posters and other kinds of creative publicity. Many coaches have found that the bulletin board, with pictures, quotes from noted athletes, performance records, and other materials, is an excellent adjunct to promotion.

By initiating the program with tolerable overload demands and by nurturing the natural competitive interests of the performers, the teacher can develop a delight in running. The wearing of special tee shirts and membership in the 100-mile club, 200-mile club, and so on, are also excellent motivators. It is always true that where the program is related to the needs and interests of the participants, with consistency and imagination, success is likely to follow.

PLANNING FOR THE CROSS-COUNTRY MEET

Selection of the Course

Currently there are three classifications for competition in cross-country. These include a three-quarter-mile course for girls eleven and under; a one-mile course for girls twelve to thirteen; and a two-mile course for girls fourteen and over. For best results the course should be relatively open, free from dangerous obstacles, with terrain which varies from 50 to 150 feet in elevation. Better courses provide at least one-quarter mile of level, open ground at the start so that participants can establish their preliminary order without confusion. Better courses also finish uphill to minimize the wild rush which often occurs when the chute is on the level.

Scoring the Meet

Perhaps the most tedious responsibility for the meet director is the compilation of information relative to scoring the meet. Numerous methods have been devised for this purpose, though one which currently is being used with success is the "chute and pen" method which utilizes some type of tag system to identify individual finishers. Tags are secured prior to the race, filled in by individual performers, and pinned to the shirt front.

The finish chute is a device constructed from rope stretched between stakes which have been driven into the ground over a distance of 75 to 100 feet. The end of the chute nearest the finish line is open like a funnel, narrowing to some thirty inches to avoid a shuffling of position after the finish line has been crossed. When this method is used, all runners are marshaled along the chute by "controllers" until their tags have been received by the official recorder. These tags are placed face down on a receiving spindle. When all runners have completed the course, the spindle is turned over, and the name and place of each performer are recorded on the official score sheet.

INDIVIDUAL SCORE TAG

Name ....

Team ....

Event ....

Time ....   Place ....

Following the recording of names, the official time for each participant is obtained from the master time sheet. Team scores are then figured by compiling the scores of the first five finishers from each team. In cross-country the team with the lowest score places first; the next lowest score, second; and so on. (For example, a team placing 2-3-4-7-9 for 25 total points would be victorious over a team placing 1-5-6-8-10 for 30 total points.)

Appendixes

RECORD OF DUAL TRACK MEET

Event_____ Date_____ Place_____

EVENT	TIME OR DIST.	FIRST	SECOND	THIRD	SCORE	SCORE
880-yd. run						
100-yd. dash						
100-m. hurdles						
220-yd. dash						
440-yd. dash						
1,500-m. run						
440-yd. relay						
Shot-put						
Discus						
Javelin						
High jump						
Long jump						

DUAL MEET EVENT SHEET

Field Event_____ Scheduled Time_____

Entries	Team	Height							
		4'0"	4'2"	4'4"	4'6"	4'7"	4'8"	4'9"
1								
2								
3								
4								
5								
6								

Scoring Key. Blank indicates that the jumper passed; x failure; ✓ cleared.

Order of Finish

	Name	Team	Height
First	_____	_____	_____
Second	_____	_____	_____
Third	_____	_____	_____

DUAL MEET EVENT SHEET

Field Event_____ Scheduled Time_____

Entries	Team	Trials			Finals			Best
		1	2	3	4	5	6	
1								
2								
3								
4								
5								
6								

Order of Finish

	Name	Team	Distance
First	_____	_____	_____
Second	_____	_____	_____
Third	_____	_____	_____

GUIDES FOR EVALUATING PERFORMANCE
IN TRACK AND FIELD EVENTS

Events	Physical Education Classes		Open Competition		
	Jr. H. S.	Sr. H. S.	Local	State	National
50 yards	7.2	7.0	6.5	6.2	6.0
75 yards	9.7	9.5	9.1	8.9	8.5
100 yards		12.5	11.8	11.5	11.0
220		33.0	28.0	26.5	24.8
440		69.0	63.5	59.0	57.0
880		2:42.5	2:35.0	2:20.0	2:12.0
1,500 meters			5:30	5:00	4:45
Mile			5:55	5:23.5	5:05
440 Relay		58.5	57.0	52.5	49.0
4 x 440 Relay			4:20	4:15	4:07.5
50-yard Hurdles	9.0	8.5	7.7	7.3	6.9
80-meter Hurdles		13.7			
100-meter Hurdles			16.0	15.5	14.8
200-meter Hurdles			33.5	30.0	28.5
High Jump	4'0"	4'5"	4'7"	5'2"	5'5"
Long Jump	11'6"	12'0"	15'3"	18'3"	19'0"
6-pound shot	28'				
8-pound shot		32'	35'	38'	
4 Kilo			35'	38'	43'
Discus			105'	125'	145'
Javelin		90'	110'	130'	150'

These marks would be considered very acceptable for each of the levels of competition indicated.

CHART SHOWING THE EFFECT OF PROGRESSIVE-INTENSIVE TRAINING ON SELECTED
WORLD RANKING WOMEN TRACK AND FIELD PERFORMERS

ATHLETE	EVENT	1954	1956	1958	1960	1962	1964	1966	1968	1969
Wilma Rudolph U.S.A.	100 M.		11.7	11.8	11.0	11.2				
	200 M.		24.2	24.4	22.9					
Dixie Willis Australia	400 M.			60.0	53.0	53.5	53.1			
	800 M.		2:28.2	2:18.4	2:05.9	2:01.2				
Iolanda Balas Rumania	High Jump	5'6"	5'8"	5'11⅝"		6'½"	6'3½"	6'½"		
Chi Cheng Taiwan	100 M.					12.7	12.1	11.7	11.2	10.3 (Yds.)
	80 MH					11.9	11.1	10.8	10.4	13.3 (100M)
	Long Jump					18'3½"	19'10¾"		20'5¾"	
Willie White U.S.A.	Long Jump		19'11"	20'2"	20'2"	21'1"	21'6"	20'8"	20'11"	
Elvira Ozolina U.S.S.R.	Javelin	116'5"	154'2"	169'1"	195'4"	191'4"	201'4"	193'1"		
Margitta Gummel E. Germany	Shot		35'1"	43'8"	50'5"	52'10"	57'6"	59'1"	64'4"	
Doris Brown U.S.A.	880-				2:15.3	2:17.3	2:15.1	2:05.8	2:02.2	
	mile							4:52.0	4:40.4	
	1,500 M.							4:20.2	4:16.8	
Liesel Westermann W. Germany	Discus				125'4"	149'5"	172'10"	188'3"	205'2"	209'10"
Maria Gommers Holland	400 M.					62.5	60.1	58.6		
	800 M.					2:32.0	2:15.8	2.12.9	2:02.6	
	1,500 M.								4:15.6	4:11.9
Kathy Hammond U.S.A.	220							25.1	24.2	23.6
	400 M.							55.0	53.4	52.1

TRACK AND FIELD
Entry Form

Event _____ Meet _____ Record _____

No.	NAME	TEAM	1	2	TRIAL 3	4	5	6	7	PLACE	MARK

Glossary

ANEROBIC. Performance in which oxygen demands are greater than the oxygen supply

ATTACK ANGLE. The difference between an implement's trajectory and the angle at which its forward edge is projected into space

BALLISTIC. A sudden or explosive movement

BATON. A round, light tube made of metal, wood, or plastic which is passed between members of a relay team

BILATERAL MOVEMENT. Two sides which are complementary to each other

BREAKING ACTION. Suddenly stopping forward progress

BUILD-UP. A gradual acceleration or increase in speed during a run

COUNTEROPPOSED. One limb swinging or working in opposition to the other

DISTANCE-RATED. A javelin which has been constructed to achieve its most efficient flight characteristics within a particular distance

FARTLEK. "Speed play." A Swedish term denoting a run for fun

FLAILING. A throwing action similar to "cracking the whip"

FLOAT. A period of relaxed striding when no attempt is being made to increase or decrease running speed

FLATTENED SPLIT. The exaggerated stride position assumed over the hurdle

FRONT RUNNER. A competitor who performs best when out ahead of her opponents

FOLLOWERS. Runners who prefer to "lay back," anticipating that they can win with their kick

HEATS. Preliminary rounds of a race to determine who runs in the finals

HITCH KICK. A style of long jumping in which the performer negotiates one or more running strides in the air prior to landing

IN-AND-OUT SPRINTS. Alternate periods of sprinting and striding

JOGGING. Slow, easy running

KICK. The "sprint" for the finish

LAP. One complete circuit of the track

LAY-OUT. The horizontal position assumed by a jumper when passing over the crossbar

LEAD LEG. The first leg over the hurdle

OVERLOAD. To impose greater than normal demands on the systems of the body

OVERSTRIDING. An uneconomical stride of exaggerated length

PACE. The rate of speed determined by the distance to be run and the ability of the performer

PARABOLA. A geometric figure constituting the trajectory of all airborne objects

PASSING ZONE. An area twenty meters in length, designated by two lines, inside which the baton must be exchanged

POLE POSITION. Running in the lane next to the inside curb of the track

POP-UP. A jump for distance following a short approach

PREFERRED FOOT. The foot for which a performer has the best "sense feel"—usually the kicking foot

PRIME MOVERS. The large muscles which act to overcome the inertia of the body

PSYCHOLOGICAL THRESHOLD. The self-imposed tolerance limits for enduring fatigue

RANGE OF MOTION. The full distance through which a muscle or group of muscles can work

RESISTANCE TRAINING. Working the muscles against resistance

SCRATCH. To commit a foul by stepping over the scratch line

SEEDING. Separating the better performers in the initial rounds of competition

SHORT-STEP DRILL. A drill for hurdlers in which the performer takes more than the usual number of strides between hurdles so as to give emphasis to the action over the hurdle

SHUFFLE. A very slow, relaxed recovery jog

STRIDE. Two half strides, or the distance from the right to the left to the right foot

TRAIL LEG. The second leg over the hurdle

TRAIN DOWN. To taper off after a race or practice session

UNDERSTRIDING. Stride which is too short for the performer

Selected References

CANHAM, DON, *Track and Field Instructor's Guide.* Chicago: The Athletic Institute, 1960.

COOPER, JOHN M.; LAVERY, JAMES; and PERRIN, WILLIAM. *Track and Field for Coach and Athlete.* 2nd ed. Englewood Cliffs, N. J.: Prentice-Hall, Inc., 1970.

CRETZMEYER, FRANCIS X.; ALLEY, LOUIS E.; and TIPTON, CHARLES M. *Track and Athletics.* 7th ed. St. Louis: The C. V. Mosby Co., 1969.

DOHERTY, J. KENNETH. *Modern Training for Running.* Englewood Cliffs, N. J.: Prentice-Hall, Inc., 1964.

————. *Modern Track and Field.* Englewood Cliffs, N. J.: Prentice-Hall, Inc., 1963.

DYSON, GEOFFERY H. G. *The Mechanics of Athletics.* 3rd ed. Warwick Square, London E. C. 4: University of London Press Ltd., 1964.

JACKSON, NELL C. *Teaching Track and Field for Girls and Women.* Minneapolis, Minn.: Burgess Publishing Co., 1968.

JORDAN, PAYTON, and SPENCER, BUD. *Champions in the Making.* Englewood Cliffs, N. J.: Prentice-Hall, Inc., 1968.

MILLER, KENNETH D. *Track and Field for Girls.* New York: The Ronald Press Company, 1964.

POWELL, JOHN T. *Track and Field Fundamentals for Teacher and Coach.* 2nd ed. Champaign, Ill.: Stipes Publishing Co., 1965.

QUERCETAINI, R. L. *Track and Field Athletics 1864-1964.* New York: London Oxford University Press, 1964.

STAMPFL, FRANZ. *Stampfl on Running.* New York: The Macmillan Company, 1956.

273

WAKEFIELD, FRANCIS; HARKINS, DOROTHY; and COOPER, JOHN M. *Track and Field Fundamentals for Girls and Women*. St. Louis: The C. V. Mosby Co., 1966.

WILT, FRED. *Run-Run-Run*. Los Altos, Calif.: Track and Field News Inc., 1965.

Index